COWPOKES, NESTERS, & SO FORTH

by

JUDGE ORLAND L. SIMS

1970 THE ENCINO PRESS Austin

To my father and mother, D. E. & ELLA SIMS
(affectionately denominated FATHER &
MOTHER SIMS *throughout our area during
their later years), typical of our better
pioneers who have changed a wilderness
into a pleasant land*

FIRST EDITION

© 1970 : THE ENCINO PRESS : 2003 SOUTH LAMAR : AUSTIN

FOREWORD

THE TITLE OF A BOOK can be misleading. Ordinary folk, you and I, browsing in a bookshop, may note a title, such as *Cowpokes*, glance at the jacket, and then drop the volume with disdain in the assumption that it is only another package of ramblings by some old has-been hoss-and-cow-waddy loafing in the shade.

But now and then a more tolerant explorer will turn to the Foreword to find out what the book really is about, as you are doing if you are still with this.

So be informed that this *Cowpokes, Nesters & So Forth* is a unique and sincere book about men, women, and events of West Texas when it was in the transition period from the vanishing frontier to the modern, written with significance against a background of prehistory when Homo sapiens were pursuing the shaggy wild ox, on down through Biblical times when *sheepherders* were becoming *shepherds* and cattle-tending youngsters were traveling through the centuries toward becoming the American Cowboy.

Which suggests that *Cowpokes* might be a boresome treatise in dullness. But from the first pages you will find that it is the factual and fabulous story of a segment of our West Texas told in Orland Sims' very own, individualistic, purely "Orlandish" lively and picturesque style.

So we find Orland Sims telling of folk he knows, knew, or heard about with an intimate insight into their courage, cussedness, stupidity, acuteness, extravagant wildness, their sins, their virtues, and their commendable worthwhileness. All told in a way that will inform, amuse, entertain, offend you, or maybe please you to the point of recommending the book to others.

I would be remiss if I did not tell you something about the author of *Cowpokes* and why I venture into doing this Foreword. Our acquaintance began on a rainy November Sunday afternoon in 1926 when my telephone rang, and a stranger told me that he had been reading my so-called Western fiction stories and would like to meet the man who could get such [improbabilities] into magazine print. His implied praise stampeded me out into the pouring rain to the little cow-country hotel where the stranger made himself known to me as Orland Sims.

The upshot was that in the ensuing year he and I, a more or less tenderfoot, drove in his red roadster all over this enticing land of Davis Mountains, deserts and cattle country. Besides listening with big ears to his fascinating accounts about the people and events in his corner of Texas, I perceived that he had the enviable gift of listening as well as talking.

I would see him meet total strangers and fall at once into conversation with such contagious friendliness that in no time at all they would become voluble about their own experiences and adventures. His empathy for fellow human beings doubtless was the magnet that drew them to him and so filled his hopper that it has overflowed into books.

Gradually I learned (he was no great hand to talk about himself) that Orland was a University of Texas graduate in civil engineering. He did not pursue that profession but chose rather to stick to his cattle ranching. Afterwards he branched out into other pursuits, one of which was to become a widely active member of the Masonic fraternity.

After a year in these parts, there came a telephone request that he come back to Paint Rock to be the county judge. Our meetings after that slimmed down to infrequencies. Yet it wasn't a great while before he returned for a visit, bringing his red-haired girl, Josephine, whom he later married, to show her off to the Scobees and other friends and brag about how lucky he was.

An instinct to return to familiar pastures has brought Orland back to Fort Davis in recent years on brief visits. Twice he proposed that we drive again, for old-time's sake, over a mountain road that we traveled in the red roadster. On these drives we would recall that bygone year of good fellowship with nostalgia—which is a habit of men in their culminating years. So I end this Foreword with appreciation to Orland Sims for inviting me to write it and with high good wishes to all readers.

BARRY SCOBEE

CONTENTS

PART II: NESTERS

PART III: & SO FORTH

GLOSSARY

PREFACE

SOME TWENTY-FIVE YEARS and several thousand gestating
"Cowboy Books" ago, my good friend, the late J. Frank Dobie, sourly remarked upon the birthing of a new cowboy
book, "My Gawd, not another one."

According to statistics, some 30,000 new books are pub-
lished each year in these United States, and I verily believe
that at least 20,000 of them contain references to the Cowboy.
So, a ham author must necessarily possess the gall of a government mule to foist any book on a bored public, let alone
one on Cowboys.

My excuse for, and in defense of this one, is that I have
just flat been 'suckered into' doing it: several years ago, in an
expansive moment, I casually remarked to a "news hawk"
that I might do a paper on Gun Slingers I have known for
the Tom Green County Historical Society, and he ran a story
about it in the next morning's paper. So much heat was put
on me that I sort of slung together "Gun-Toters I Have
Known," a copy of which found its way into the hands of the
Honorable Richard T. Fleming of the Special Collections Sec-

tion of the University of Texas Library, who showed it to Dr. Joe B. Frantz, Professor of History, and he put the bee on Bill Wittliff, of the Encino Press, who offered to print a limited edition of it. To my surprise, and I dare say to Bill's, the danged thing sold out in less than 90 days, and straightway he put the monkey on my back to do another one covering the entire spectrum of the frontier times and mores of West Texas. And, like Dr. Frantz's characterization of the old fashioned mother hubbard, it covers might nigh everything.

I have been privileged to have lived in sizable portions of the most significant centuries in world history to this date, literally spanning the interval from the ox-wagon to the jet plane. I have always been a pretty fair observer of and interested in might nigh everything; and, in addition, saddled with an 'omnivorous memory'—that is, for triviata.

I personally knew many of the characters, and witnessed the scenes and events herein. The rest were related to me, first hand, by my father or other old-timers whom I knew to be reliable. With a total lack of modesty, I present it to you as honest to God, authentic "Living History" that will be lost when the whistle blows on me.

This is my excuse and apology.

ORLAND L. SIMS

COWPOKES, NESTERS, & SO FORTH

PART I

COWPOKES

WE HAVE HAD 'EM ever since "Homo Sap" first tamed and domesticated the wild ox of prehistory. Someone would have to tend the critters, and it is only reasonable to assume that the job fell to the lads not yet of huntsman-warrior status, but old enough to pester the nubile girls and older womenfolk. They were the boys who looked after the cows—the cowboys, if you please, and that's about the way the dictionaries define them today, just as simple as that.

Prehistorians recorded the "profession" in pictographs yet extant on cave walls, notably those of the Sahara region of Africa. These herders were invariably shown afoot, and their descendents in those parts still take it the same way. The Sumerians and other ancients portrayed them in bas reliefs, on vases, pottery, and even in the cuneiform writings.

We even find them recorded in Holy Writ when Abraham made his great drive from old Ur of the Chaldees to Egypt via Haran, Canaan and points in between. This tremendous trek makes our own Texas drives seem sort of puny, even those to the Dakotas and Canada. It may well be assumed that he had cattle along, as reference is made to herdsmen. We do know that he had sheep and goats a-plenty whose tenders were called shepherds (sheep herders) thereby creating a distinction, reaching on through history to the present time, and putting them in their proper order as the cow people stoutly maintain. Howsomever, I don't think that there was too much difference then, as they took it afoot or rode jackasses. Later on we find the swineherd, rated well below the shepherd—if such a thing is possible!

We find 'em on down through the millenia to the lads who tended the kine in Yorkshire and Devonshire shortly after the Norman Conquest, beginning to be designated as "cattle lads." These were the prototypes of the Colonial product. The first reference that I have been able to find to the American "cowboy" was a term of obloquy applied to the Tory sympathizers who raided the cattle folds and byres of Revolutionary supporters.

However, it wasn't too long before the term "cowboy" was given to the mounted herdsmen of the Carolinas, and it carried no connotation of rustler, or cow thief. We find early mention of the mounted cattle herders with the immigrant trains that moved across the Cumberlands to Kentucky and frequent references to them in journals and diaries of members of the wagon trains of the Santa Fe and Oregon Trails. They were usually young men, even boys, likely under the supervision of an experienced "train man," who drove the spare stock—horses, mules, oxen, and even milk and breeding cattle—and were variously called "stock boys," "herders," "cattle drivers," and "cowboys." This latter appellation seemed to have come into pretty general use by the time of the Texas migration. Texas was a Cow Paradise: the herds flourished, and their tenders, perforce, developed the skills incident to their handling on the open range. The cowboy was here! He learned quickly, for he had an able exemplar of the art right on his doorstep—the Mexican vaquero who had a couple of hundred years' jump on him.

Shortly after the conquest, Cortez imported breeding cattle into Mexico, together with their handlers who had learned their trade from the Moors on the plains of Spain, themselves no mean horsemen. At first, only a few were mounted, but as the horse and cattle herds multiplied, their tenders became riders, and the vaquero (literally, cow-caretaker) developed. By the time the Anglos arrived on the scene, they found highly skilled professionals—real cowhands.

The newcomers were apt learners and were ready for business when the time was ripe. That time arrived right after the close of the Civil War. During the war, owing to the scarcity of able-bodied men, the untended cattle herds scattered and multiplied by the thousands, especially in the region south and west of San Antonio.

Drifting back home from the war, broke, jobless with lives disrupted, homes destroyed and kinsmen and neighbors scattered, Texans faced a bleak prospect indeed. After the tumult and the shouting of war, many were loath to settle down to the tame pursuits of farming and the likes. With hordes of unbranded, unmarked, half-wild cattle at their very doorsteps offering excitement, high adventure and even financial aggrandizement, it is only natural that many "took to the rope."

All a man needed was a little grub, a couple of blankets, a few horses, a long rope and a running iron. With the skills he already had, it was not much of a trick for a good, able-bodied man to start the nucleus of a cow herd. They had the cattle, but no market for them "excusin' " uncertain outlets for hides and taller at the ports of Indianola, Galveston and Brownsville. Although a good market developed in California by the middle 1850's, the hazards of the long drives over a hard, dry trail, the Indians, and finally the Civil War practically closed the outlet. Some of the more foresighted and energetic either threw in together or bought enough cheap cattle on credit to form a herd of sorts and lit out for New Orleans and other Southern markets. They disposed of the cattle at a profit, and, man being the copycat he is, others straightway followed suit. As a result, more cattle were trailed into those markets than they could absorb, so the search for a wider outlet began. They found that market when the railroads began to build into western Missouri and eastern Kansas; and here beginneth the saga of that romantic critter, the cowboy, with all its countless tomes of fact, fancy, myth and just pure, danged baloney. O Cowboy, O Cowboy, how many crimes have been committed in thy name!

Down through the years he acquired more monikers than Carter had oats: "cowboy," certainly the most generally accepted and popular one, "cowhand," "cowman," "drover," "traildriver," "cow waddy," "waddy," "cattleman," "cowpuncher," "cowpoke," and so on *ad infinitum* down or up to the precious one applied to him by the young schoolmarm from Wellesley—"Cow Person." He generally preferred the term cowhand, with cowpuncher as next choice. Me, I sorter like "cowpoke." The last two appellations found their way into the vernacular after the trail drive was well under way, as witness the following accounts.

One old hand told me that the term "cowpuncher" originated at a Kansas shipping point. This man's herd was late getting there, and he went to the shipping pens to check with the railroad agent about shipping arrangements. There he spied an old *compadre* from Texas sourly punching cattle up the chute with the loading crew. After exchange of greetings, he asked the woebegone laborer how come he was doing such degrading work, and the sheepish reply was "I sorter needed to eat." He had arrived with a herd a few weeks earlier, drawn his pay and gone on a "high lonesome." He awoke one morning flat broke, his saddle and gear in hock and his outfit on its way back to Texas. He just had to find a job, and the only one that he could get was with a loading crew. Another load started up the chute, and he vented his outraged feelings by savagely jabbing the cattle with his steel-shod prod pole, disgustedly remarking: "Hell, I ain't nothin' but a damned cowpuncher." The wry epithet caught on, and "cowpuncher" it remains. When my father sent his last herd up the trail, he caught up with it near Amarillo and sold his cattle there. They were short of loaders, and the hands pitched in to help. When they returned to Paint Rock, they were gleefully calling themselves cowpunchers.

Another old-timer told me this one: A proper Boston lady was visiting in San Angelo and was being shown the sights. It was shipping season, and herds were being held all around town waiting their turn to be loaded on the cars. With that many herds of restless cattle, naturally there was considerable mixing, causing a good deal of work. The lady was driven out to where the work was going on. She was entranced and intrigued with it all, much taken by the cowboys dashing about, calling them "centaurs" and demanding to see them at close range. Her host drove her to the shipping pens where the centaurs were working with the loading crews. Her dashing horsemen turned out to be a bunch of dirty, sweaty, unkempt laborers on foot, cussing and prodding the recalcitrant cattle up the chutes with long poles. The lady disgustedly asked her host: "Who are those filthy, uncouth oafs who are poking those poor beasts so cruelly with those wicked sticks?" Some of the boys overheard her and straightway gleefully denominated themselves "cowpokes." It caught on and still flourishes in the vernacular.

My first exposure to the cowpoke came when, as a tiny three-year old, I watched dozens of trail herds pass near our home in Paint Rock on their way to the ford across the Concho River, then a bold-running stream. The thousands of milling, bellering cattle, the dust, the yelling cowboys and the general excitement so etched themselves on the mind of one small urchin that they are very real and clear even today.

My real introduction came when my father sent his last herd up the trail, about when I was a-coming five. He wanted me to see the last herd to leave our country, as the railroad was building in. So he sent an old cousin to escort me to the holding ground some five miles away. I was picked up by the slack of my britches and set astride old "Fuzzy Top"—a gentle, broke-down cow horse named after Fuzzy Creek which, in turn, got its name from a dogie mustang yearling, possessed of tousled mane and tail, who "*used*" there. I was seated on a man's big saddle with my feet inserted in the sweat leathers for stirrups, with Cousin George leading my mount. They had pretty well cleaned up the herd preparatory to their start the next morning, but they still were cutting out an occasional stray, and thereby hangs a tale!

My father's remuda was composed of about 100 salty Spanish ponies from the country between San Antonio and Laredo. They were good cow horses, but plenty tough— pure D Españoles with intricate Spanish brands, usually down on the left leg, well below the hip. They were willing buckers ("pitchers," we called 'em), and they had to be broke every spring. The men had been assigned their mounts and were topping them off. I saw more pitching horses that morning than were ever seen in any rodeo, and there warn't no ten-second buzzer. A man had to ride him until he quit, and he had no hazer unless the horse was about to "turn the pack." There was no shoulder spurring or other fancy rodeo doin's. A man would have been fired if Mr. Bob Pierce had caught him doing any of that fancy stuff. He could tie his stirrups if he had a bad 'un, and it was no disgrace if he pulled leather. He was supposed to stay aboard so that another puncher would not have to chase his loose horse all over creation. One of the top peelers was a boy named Jimmy Gallagher who drew a little blaze-faced black, then unnamed. He was some *ladino*, and he threw Jimmy and was immediately christened Gallagher. When my father disposed of the remuda, he topped out the best ones, among them Gallagher who lived out his life on the ranch. He never quite reformed, and even after he had reached retirement age, he piled me a couple of times.

Cousin George wandered off leaving me astride Old Fuzzy who was hip-shot dozing in the warm sun. One of the men ran a steer past us, and Fuzzy, like an old firehorse, took after him. His scared rider dropped the reins, grabbed the horn and squalled in abject terror, which so excited Fuzzy that he "left for Cheyenne." One of the punchers roped him, and I was ignominiously banished to the chuck wagon and placed under the strict supervision of the cook.

I know only too well how exhaustively the subject of the Texas cowboy has been hashed and rehashed from Hell to Haw River by all manner of authorities: the researcher-historian, the pundit, wise in lore gathered from multitudinous bibliography, the somewhat watered-down, present-day practitioner of the "art"; the paper-back fellers; the western script writers; and finally, that *real authority*, the red-eyed, rocky-chair boy who has gained his expertise through countless hours before his TV set.

Although I know I am "breedin' scabs," I venture to categorize "Cow Personnel" thus:

THE BUTTON—the nuisance.

THE WRANGLER—the learner, the apprentice.

THE COWPOKE, PUNCHER, etc.—the journeyman, the fellow of the craft.

THE COWHAND—the master.

THE COWMAN—including the wagon boss, the trail boss—the grand master.

THE OWNER—the Cattleman, the Cattle Baron, the Tycoon.

THE COW BUYER—who might or might not fit into the above, but he was a knowledgeable cuss—he had to be. Also, he was right smart of a trader.

THE COOK—last, but certainly not least.

THE BUTTON

THE BUTTON was the kid, just barely dry behind the ears, a pestiferous teen-ager, usually the son or relative of the owner or one of the hands. He was frequently a smart aleck and always a star-spangled nuisance with a flair for getting in everybody's way and a penchant for getting into more mischief and trouble than a spotted-tailed ape. He was tolerated because of his sponsor and because he provided a convenient foil for pranks and jokes. The men sure poured it on him when the boss wasn't around, and being the owner's son in no way ameliorated the hazing.

THE WRANGLER

THE WRANGLER was usually a youngster (the "Little Joe" type of song and story), a learner, an apprentice, who had his eye set on becoming a cowhand. Now and then an old stove-up cowpoke who hated to give up took the job which certainly was no sinecure. He had charge of the horse herd (remuda), and it was a full-time job, especially if he was with a big outfit, if he had a mean bunch or if the range was short. After the cook, he was the first man up of a morning, and he straddled his mount and lit out before day to round up and bring in his charges by the time it got good daylight —no small job if they were scattered from hell to breakfast. I recall one occasion when he got back to the wagon well after sunup and was roundly "eaten out" by the boss. His defense was, "The danged hosses was all scattered out—only one or two in a place and some places they warn't any."

After the horses were safely penned in the rope "correll" (corruption of the Spanish corral), he had to keep a lookout for a sneaker-outer and get him back, which could take some doin'. However, this was not too often as the horses were trained to stay in the pen formed by a single rope stretched around stakes or trees, if available, or frequently held by the men themselves. If a horse broke out of the corral a time or two, he was four-footed and busted wide open. It didn't take many falls to teach him to stay put. The men roped out their mounts, which called for a good deal of skill, especially when one happened to be a wise old horse who kept his head well tucked down. They were snared by a small loop that was usually circled once around the roper's head counterclockwise. Normally, a right-handed man swung a fairly good-sized loop several times clockwise around his head.

After the catching up, old wrangler got a leftover breakfast that could be cold if the cook was a bit cantankerous that morning. He had to help cook, load the wagon and harness the team. He then rounded up his charges and followed the herd. If they had a noon stop, he was supposed to be with the wagon when the herd caught up. Fresh horses were roped out, and then he hadn't much to do except graze his horses along. When the cook stopped for the night about an hour before sundown, he had to help unharness, unpack and snake in a supply of firewood.

He always tried to find dry wood, for the green stuff not only made a miserable, smoky fire, it also riled the cook. Besides, you had to use an axe. If he could find a good-sized dead tree, he was in "high cotton." All he had to do was toss his rope over the limbs, and the horse would do the rest. After he had accumulated a good-sized pile of wood, by whatever means, and looped the free end of his rope over it, he mounted up and dragged it to camp. This could be ticklish business if he was riding a spooky or fidgety horse, hard to mount or "goosey" about the rope, as it was not much of a trick to get his tail over it—and then the little thing came off —most times it would be the rider. Such a dumping could be not only hard on old clothes, but most disgraceful, even disastrous. A spooked horse, dragging a pile of dry, rattling wood, could very well stampede even a sedate remuda, but it was almost certain to send any cow herd "skyhoodlin." Even if the horse took off in the other direction, somebody would have to do a lot of riding to get his rope on the runaway. In any case it was rough on the wood gatherer. If wood was very scarce, some of the other hands usually would pitch in and help scour the countryside; for "cow fuel" is a poor and malodorous substitute for dry wood.

Then, all that he had to do was have his charges at the catch-pen when the men came from work so that they could rope out their night horses, help hobble the others out if conditions warranted, and put the bunch out to graze. In my section, it was rarely necessary to night-guard the remuda.

"Little Joe" had himself a real job, and if he really worked at it, kept his nose clean, and got along well with the hands, they went out of their way to help him and teach him the facts of life appertaining to the cow business. If he caught on well, the day would come when the boss would give him a mount and tell him to throw in with the hands.

THE COWPOKE

THE COWPOKE-COWBOY-COWHAND (the Journeyman) knew his tough, demanding trade with all its hardships, even its dangers. As I knew him, the cowpoke of the period from the late eighties to the mid-nineteen hundreds was a real professional, experienced and knowledgeable in the ways of cattle and in their management. He worked hard and kept long hours, especially when he was on a long drive and had to do guard duty. As a rule, this took a couple of hours out of his sleep, but, if it was stormy and the cattle inclined to run, he might have to take it all night. What these men could stand still amazes me. They weren't inclined to gripe: "If you didn't want to work, what did you want to hire out for?" They were self-reliant and fiercely individualistic, although loyal to the outfit. Each man held up his end.

As a rule, the cowpoke wasn't loquacious, but he could say a mouthful when the occasion demanded. He was a right smart cusser, but he wasn't a patchin' to a bunch of roughnecks around an oil rig in these days. He never swore around ladies (even the words "damn" and "hell" being taboo). He used the four-letter, Anglo-Saxon words as a matter of course with no pinky-pants substitutes, but he wasn't smutty.

Of course, he possessed the skills of his trade. He was a pretty fair country rider—he had to be, for he never knew when a salty one would be put in his mount. And believe me, there were plenty of them carrying Mustang-Spanish blood. Though tough and tireless, most of them were good, dependable cow horses, but skittish and undependable at times. Just let something go wrong, like a snake rattling under foot or a scared jack rabbit bolting between his legs, and boy, a rider had to claw leather! If he "turned the pack" while out on the range, it could be downright disastrous. If the horse didn't hurt the poke and he was alone and well away from anywhere, he might have to walk miles, and I never saw a poke in all my life who cared for walking. Also, if the horse got away, it would necessitate considerable "galloping o'er the lea" to rope him, and if it was brushy country, he might tear the saddle up. These old horses never quite got over their penchant for swallering their heads, especially on cold mornings. I'll bet I have walked old gentle horses twenty miles all told to get the hump out of their backs, and, even then, one might take to the blue.

It wasn't especially disgraceful to get piled; that is, unless the rider was considered a "peeler" and thus had a reputation to maintain. I never saw a man thrown that the by-standers did not howl with glee even before they knew whether the victim was hurt. But they all took it in stride, allowing as to how "there never was a hoss that couldn't be rode, and there never was a rider that couldn't be throwed."

This bird could use a rope in more ways than a farmer can "whup" a mule. Of course he used it for catching his horse, roping cattle around the herd or out on the range, and it could be as handy as a monkey's tail or might' nigh anything that came up.

He was an ingenious improviser: give him a handful of horseshoe nails, a claw hammer and a pair of fence pliers ("pinchers" he called 'em), and some odds and ends of rope and plenty of rawhide, and he had it made. He might not tie the knots that a sailor or a Boy Scout can, but he could do all the working ones. The expert could fashion a "hacka-more" (Spanish *haquema*, for halter) out of a rope ravelings that was a joy to behold. Give him some cotton, or preferably mohair cord, and he could make a new "girt" (girth) for his saddle in a few minutes.

The general utility tool of the cowpoke was his pocket-knife, called a "Bilduky," "frog sticker," or more generally a "Barlow," after a popular name brand. The Barlow was a rather clumsy, two-bladed affair, but it didn't cost much. A smaller one-blader was the ultimate desire of every kid of my generation. There was also a three or four-blader of good Sheffield steel (called a "Shurffield") that was the real cow knife. It had a large pointed utility blade useful for digging gravel and thorns out of a horse's foot, skinning a carcass, slicing meat, cutting rawhide, opening tin cans, whittling repairs for a wagon wheel or most anything else around camp. There was a marking and a castrating blade and kind of a special blade that was always kept sharp for cutting leather or rawhide strings and any fine work. It was also useful as a whittler when trades or other matters of large import were under discussion.

Last, but not least, was the little blade which was kept sharp and pointed, as it served as his surgical and cosmetic tool. With it he could lance a boil, dig a mesquite thorn out of his knee, trim his finger and toenails, pick his teeth if there was no thorn or sliver of wood handy, and cut his chawin' terbacker.

Our cowpoke could really shine when it came to rawhide. It could double as most everything from a useable gate hinge to a hobble, a rope, a quirt—you just name it. Every headquarters had several dried cowhides hanging around, usually on the corral fences and instantly available. All the "artisan" had to do was to cut off a swath, give it a good wetting, and he was ready for business. They would remove the hair and do certain other mysterious things to it, including soaking it in water to soften it. One of the most interesting procedures was cutting strings from a prepared, circular patch, say from one foot to four feet in diameter, depending on how much string he needed. He would stick the point of a sharp knife in a board or log, twirl the circular piece of hide, and he had plenty of string. It was remarkable how uniform the width of the string turned out to be. If it started out half an inch wide, it was half an inch at the end. Of course, a much fancier job could be turned from a well-tanned hide, and this was the source of most of the material for riatas, quirts and similar gear. Strings no larger in diameter than an old-fashioned kitchen match could be plaited into veritable works of art.

Probably more hide was used for making hobbles than for any other single purpose. Ask a present-day practitioner of the art what hobbles are, and he would probably say that they had something to do with women's skirts. For his enlightenment, as well as the average layman's, a pair of hobbles was used to confine the wanderings of the equines by

tying their front legs together so that they could only progress by a three-legged, hoppity-hop gait. As the legs were
tethered only about two feet apart, their owner didn't get too
far from camp; that is, if he wasn't an "Old Alec." Such
shackles meant little to Old Alec, especially if he was only
a few days from the home ranch. He could travel every foot
of ten miles in one night even under short hobbles, and it
always took a man most of a morning to trail him down.
After one especially trying chase during which Alec skinned
his front legs raw, the puncher roped him and took off the
hobbles. Alec was reluctant to go back to the herd and sat
back on the rope. Finally, his exasperated captor turned him
loose and popped him on the tail with the doubled rope all
the way back to the herd. That sort of cured Alec of his wan-
derlust. Anyway, the hobble was a necessary piece of equipment in those days. Although made of any handy piece of
rope, rawhide was considered the better material, for, if
properly made, they could not be broken or lost and would
not skin a horse's legs.

It was interesting to watch an expert make hobbles. First,
he would prepare a couple of stakes, about the same diameter
as an average horse's forelegs, and drive them in the ground
the distance apart that he wanted the shackled legs to be,
say, about twenty-four inches. He would then take a well-
soaked cowhide, scrape off the hair and cut strips some four
inches wide and long enough for the hobbles and the button.
He would then double a strip, cut a slit in one end, and by
some sort of ledgerdemain that I could never get, would
stick the rolled end back through the slit, making a button
some 1½ inches long and about ¾ of an inch in diameter. A
slit in the other end made a perfect buttonhole. The center of
the thong would be placed around one stake, and the two
ends given some six or eight turns around each other and
buttoned to the other stake. Some eight or ten could be strung
on the same two stakes. All that was necessary was to let
them dry well, making sure that no prowling dog or coyote
got to the toothsome morsels. After they had become thoroughly dry and set, the twists remained and always fitted

into each other. They were then given a good application of taller, and a set of shackles was completed that would wear for years, getting better and more "soople" with periodic greasing until they acquired the beautiful gray-green patina that bespoke the finished product.

The poke would button a pair of hobbles around the neck of each horse in his mount and then pay them no mind until they were needed. I remember being on the streets of Paint Rock one morning long ago when a remuda was driven by. Every horse had a pair of rawhide hobbles around his neck. An old cowhand standing by me remarked: "Kid, there goes a pure D cow outfit."

Give that old improviser a horseshoe nail for an awl and a rawhide string, and he could repair nearly anything from his saddle to his wearing apparel. Such repairs were not so beautiful, but they served very well. Among many, many other uses to which rawhide was put, was the "possum belly," a whole hide stretched under the chuck wagon bed and used as a catchall. Up on the plains where wood was so short, it made a convenient means of carrying along a supply of dry wood needed as a fire starter for the stubborn, slow igniting *bois du vac.*

All in all, these old pros were a hard-bitten breed, a sort of race apart, and truly different. They looked different, they talked different, they rode different, and they even squatted different, preferring to sit on their heels rather than use a chair. How they could manage to squat comfortably in spite of their spurs—sometimes long-shanked and big-roweled— I'll never know, but they did. They walked different with a sort of a spraddle-legged, bow-legged gait, with short mincing steps like a modern gal toddling along on four-inch heels. You could tell one as far as you could see him. He was some punkins: in comparison, his modern counterpart is "as moonlight is to sunlight, and as water is to wine," as the feller says.

Nowadays, you can't tell a puncher from a soda jerk as far as dress and mannerisms are concerned. But I'll have to say that the modern does his work faster, easier, and probably more efficiently—he ought to, goodness knows, with all the labor-saving gadgets at his command.

While I rejoice in debunking malarky, I hate to disillusion the romanticists. The old cowpoke was just a workhand with a tough job to do, and he did it without the frills, furbelows and trappings of song and story. For instance, he was supposed to have had a gun, low-slung, on him; but, by the time I was big enough to ride with, I never saw a gun around cow camp unless it was on a lawman or in the cook's chuck box. I do recall a very few on men who were on "the dodge," but they were only stopping by for a meal or so. Most of the hands I knew were such indifferent marksmen that they couldn't hit a bull on the butt with a bass fiddle. However, before I was old enough to ride, I saw a good many guns, and I well remember celebrating pokes firing their guns as they left town on the run, but they were just having fun showing off. The sheriff disapproved of such activities, and he had no compunctions about throwing a toter in the pokey. The boss frowned on a toter on the works and made him stash his "iron" with the cook for the duration.

As for the other popular idea of him "a-totin' a git-tar"— just pure bunk. Just the other day, an old poke and I were reminiscing when he snickeringly asked me if I ever saw a git-tar in camp, and we broke into raucous laughter over the idea of one of these old punchers fondling a git-tar. However, I do recall a few jew's-harps around, but they didn't make much racket or provide any entertainment for anybody except the performer. I do remember an old kid who had a French harp, but he didn't have it long as an exasperated hand grabbed it away from him and threw it in the creek. On another occasion, when we were short-handed, a squirt brought along a fiddle. He was banished beyond the confines of the camp when he attempted to practice on it. One time, the boss had to ride into headquarters and was not expected back that night, so a devilish poke invited the kid to perform in camp. The boss appeared unexpectedly, gazed sourly at the culprit, then, without a word, grabbed the fiddle and busted it over the wagon tongue.

As for the "warblers"—well, except for the doleful solos of the night guards, I only recall a couple of songbirds. Once on a drive to the Pecos with a gentle herd of cows and calves, we didn't have enough work to keep us tired out and sought nightly entertainment by an old, snaggle-toothed puncher who mangled a whole bunch of sad-sounding ballads. The only one I remember was about poor Charlie who was killed by his horse falling on him, and I only remember two lines of it: "And I trust our Father greets him with a smile upon his face, and on his Right Hand seats him 'neath the shining Throne of Grace."

On another drive, we had a comical sort of a cuss along whose repertory ran to the humorous and the risqué. One song that we especially admired was about the motorman on a cable car in San Francisco who stole a passenger's piece of luggage:

> The grip man on the grip car spied the banker's little
> grip:
> He knew 'twas filled with gold and bonds galore—
> So the grip man of the grip car gripped the banker's little
> grip
> He gripped the grip and vanished through the door.

Then there was the ballad about Old Joe Clarke reputed to be 141 verses long with only one "fitten" to be printed, and it went something like this:

> I went to old Joe Clark's house and found him in the bed;
> I rammed my finger down his throat and found my
> chicken's head.

Another concerned a Peeping Tom who occupied a room next to that of a shapely young lady. There was a connecting door between the rooms with an open keyhole, and this gave old Tom an idea:

> Like Columbus, I determined new regions to explore,
> So I took a snug position by the keyhole in the door . . .

We were not so far behind the times—we had "pornog" in them days, but it was spoken or sung, never written.

I tried singing, like the feller who played in Sousa's band —once, but only once. This occurred when I was about a six-year-old. My daddy had a herd coming in from the south, and he drove out in his double-buggy to meet it, taking me along for my first night in cow camp. He always carried a bedroll along, as he never knew where night would catch him. My mama wouldn't let me drink coffee, so when I got the chance, I would really tank up, which I did that night at supper. As a result of the coffee, the excitement of it all, the hard ground, and my daddy's snoring, sleep just wouldn't come. It was a warm, bright moonlit night, so this small urchin slipped out of bed in his shirttail and climbed into the buggy. The herd was bedded down within earshot of camp. The cattle were restless, and the night guards were singing to them—the idea being that such vocalizing would soothe and settle them down.

That seemed like a good idea to me, so I burst forth with a treble rendition of "When the Roll is Called up Yonder." Of course, it awakened the whole camp; that is, all except my father who was about the soundest sleeper I ever knew. The men began to stir and snicker, so I obliged with an encore, "Bringing in the Sheaves." Finally, the grouchy old cook yelled: "Mr. Sims, for God's sake, make that damned kid shut up." You know what happened to that "damned kid." He got plucked out of that buggy, got his bottom paddled and was chucked back into bed with the stern parental admonition to keep his big mouth shut. For years a grinning puncher would greet me on the street in Paint Rock with a request for a nice religious song. Some twenty years later, when I thought I was right smart of a hand, I ran into a grizzled old puncher who snickeringly asked me if I was still singin'. It cost me several toddies to make him shut up. *Ay de mi!*

What did we do for entertainment in camp? Well, we didn't need any. After you had been in the saddle about sixteen hours and had just *et* a good, hearty supper, your bedroll was about all the entertainment you wanted. Occasionally, we would have a good storyteller along, but, unless he was a jim-dandy, he soon lost his yawning, sleepy audience. I do recall two or three of these men who were really outstanding storytellers, and I will repeat a few of the choice yarns later on.

"Diked out" in his working clothes, the old poke, as I knew him in those days, was about the most unromantic looking critter you can imagine. He wore might' nigh any kind of old clothes—hickory or denim shirts, duckin' britches and jacket. Some of the first ones I knew had on homespun, home-tailored, linsey-woolsey shirts and jeans pants. These "riding breeches" could be the funniest things you ever saw. I remember an old uncle who wore a hand-woven, home-tailored woolen suit of clothes. It was about the most grotesque raiment I ever saw. It fit most everywhere except in the right places, and his trousers were a joy to behold. The legs resembled stovepipes more than male wearing apparel. But, like the Dutchman's girl: "they might not be too good looking, but they sure were hell for stout." I surmise that he wore that one suit throughout most of his adult life, to his family's great embarrassment. Contrast those britches with the natty, permanently pressed Levis of today—*Ay de mi, otra ves*!

The poke's old hat was about as shabby as the rest of his attire—fairly low-crowned and generally floppy from slapping an unruly mount on the side of its head or waving it in the faces of running horses or cattle to turn them. It also doubled in brass as a convenient water pail or drinking cup for man or beast. It was also good for brushing back the scum or moss on a stagnant water hole so that the poke could belly down and drink out of a "clean" place. A few of the men wore the high-peaked Mexican hats of the vaquero, but they were kind of "bundlesome," especially in a high wind.

Another dream busted: the old puncher practically never owned a silk neckerchief and then rarely wore it around his neck. Practically all of them had large bandana "nose rags," which they usually carried in their hip pockets. If a man was

A typical West Texas cowpoke, 1890

with the "drags," and the dust was bad, or if he had "gizzard lips," he wore the thing tied over his nose and mouth. Constant exposure to the sun and wind was tough on the fair-skinned poke's lips. To some smart observer, these sore lips bore resemblance to the gizzard of a freshly dressed chicken, and "gizzard lips" they became with the unhappy owner inheriting the moniker "Ol' Gizzard Lip," or simply "Ol' Gizzard." I knew one man who went by that *nom de guerre* and answered to it most of his life. About the only emollient these sufferers had was "taller" of beef or mutton. Although the latter was supposed to be the more efficient, some of the old "hard shells" would not use it, averring that they didn't want nothin' to do with no damn sheep. If nothing else was available, wetted brown cigarette papers made a pretty fair "bandaid."

In our area, their outside clothes were inclined to be lightweight; so, when the weather turned bad, they put on all the pants, shirts and underthings they could get around in. One old toughie I knew boasted that he didn't even own a coat except his Sunday-go-to-meetin' one. One cold morning he showed up in his shirt-sleeves to the admiration of us younger fry whom he kidded as sissies. About the middle of the morning it turned hot, and old Tom began to shed clothes. By quitting time he had them hanging on bushes all over the place.

Speaking of undies, they wore heavy cotton undershirts and long-handle drawers, mostly handmade by their womenfolk. This lingerie would take no prize at a fashion show, but they were sure strong and warm as well as good sweat-soaker-uppers. In colder climes, these unmentionables were made of woolen fabric, usually red flannel and about as scratchy as the horsehair shirts worn by the *Penitentes*. These long-handles had a six or eight inch slit at the bottom of each leg. These slits had tape sewn to them which was wrapped around the ankles and tied. This kept the drawers legs from creeping up to your hocks. Later, the store-boughten kind came out with an elastic material called "Balbriggan" around wrists and ankles.

I think I introduced "shorts" to this area of West Texas. When I was a sophomore in the University of Texas I went out for track. We formed the habit of wearing shorts and singlets under our top clothes when we went to Clark Field to practice. They proved so comfortable in the hot Austin climate that we took to using them as our underwear. Other students followed suit, and before long the Co-op was swamped with calls for "track suits." When the supply ran out, we cut our Balbriggans off at the knees, leaving them sort of raggedy, but cool.

When I went home for summer vacation, I wore my shorties. One Sunday morning we boys went down to the river for a swim. Some nesters came down to run a trotline and sat around until we came out and got dressed. When I put on my shorts, there was goggling and snickers. Old man Gannon went home and told his wife: "I seen the funniest sight this morning. Orlin' put on gal drawers."

Longies are still extant hereabouts, for shorts can become mighty uncomfortable under heavy trousers during long hours on a horse. During my later years a-horseback, I wore khakis that were too light if I got caught out without my chaps. I got tired of coming in with torn pants and decided to buy some heavy, blue denim Levis. I neglected to put on my longies one morning when I donned a pair of new pants. I came in that night after a hard day's ride, skinned from hell to breakfast. I gave my Levis to one of the younger men, who grinned widely when I told him about my experience with them. He took them home and had them laundered twice before he wore them, making them soft and pliable. Well, one never gets too old to learn.

At first, the old poke's boots were clumsy, misshapen affairs that were prone to "run over" at the heels, making him still more onery looking, if possible. Here, I want to state that I spell the word "onery" instead of "ornery" as the lexicographers are wont to do. I spell it like the old-timers pronounced it—now make something out of it.

The clumsy appearance of these old boots was somewhat accentuated by the long and clumsy bootlegs which were devoid of any ornamentation and reached clear up to the knee, some being so long that the tops of the back of the legs were folded and wrinkled by the bending of the knees. They were always worn with the britches on the inside, which was achieved by wrapping them tightly around the ankles before wrastling the boots on. Some of them had long, flappy, leather pull-straps, making them all the more awkward-looking, but they sure protected the shanks.

San Angelo cowpokes, 1886

Along in the early nineties, bootmakers came to West Texas, and the boots became shaplier and better. "Shoemaker Ford," one of the first, settled in Paint Rock and remained there all his life. He was a master craftsman, and his boots became widely known all over cowboy land, as well as a number of foreign countries. Shoemaker was a real hand-craftsman of the old school, using a sewing machine only on the legs of the boots. He stitched on the designs and ornaments by hand. I spent many hours watching him wield awl and hammer. He used wooden pegs to fasten and support the high, arched insteps and hand-sewed the rest. He used only the best flax thread with hog bristles beeswaxed on to it for needles. It was quite a display of legerdemain to watch him prepare the thread for use. He would punch a hole in the leather with his awl, run a thread from each side of the hole and pull them tight. There wasn't any raveling seam in

JUDGE ORLAND L. SIMS

"Shoemaker's" boots, and these pegs held the arched instep as long as the boot lasted. Practically all his boots had high heels, not for looks, but for utilitarian reasons. He didn't want a foot slipping through a stirrup, which was about the worst thing that could happen to a rider. Also, they were useful for digging into the ground when a cowboy had a bronc or a big calf on the other end of his rope. I have seen Fogg Coffey dig in, drape his rope around a hip, kind of squat and throw a 1200 pound wild-one like it had been tied to a tree.

Shoemaker's work boot would almost outlast the wearer, and his dress boot, usually made of "French kid," was a thing of beauty and a joy forever to the dudish puncher. About all the criticism one could make about his boots was that he made 'em too tight. Most of the old punchers had small feet —their feet did not grow much if they grew up in a saddle —and they were as proud of their small, high-arched foot as any maiden. So, Shoemaker cut 'em close. This accounted in a large measure for the poke's mincing gait. It was a job to break in a pair of his boots, to pull 'em off and put 'em on. If you left them out from under the bedroll at night and they got damp, it took a lot of pulling, a lot of stomping and right smart cussing to get 'em on in the morning. The accepted accessory for breaking in boots was a dollop of whiskey poured down into the boot and shook around. One morning in Paint Rock I met an old pal who was crippling along like an old rooster that had got his feet frozen. I asked: "What's the matter, Jack, horse tromp on you or somethin'?" The sour reply was: "No, it's these danged new boots." I said: "If you will pour a gill of whiskey in each boot, they will set to your feet, and you will have no more trouble." The grinning reply was: "Humph, if I had two gills of whiskey, I'd play hell pouring them in my boots—they'd probably do more good in my stummick than on my feet."

Each town had a favorite bootmaker who kept his customers' measurements on file so he could turn out an order to any place in the world. Henry Rodermund of San Angelo was another of the old-time artisans. Boots were pretty much stylized, but innovations did creep in over the years. Now, the trend is to short tops luridly decorated in all sorts of designs and colors. They have flat heels and (God save the mark) rubber soles. With the improved stirrups, the squeeze chutes, and other gadgets, high heels are no longer needed like they once were. The flat heel certainly makes for easier walking, and thus, are a Godsend to the drugstore cowboy. It's got so it's impossible to tell a ribbon clerk from a real cowpoke anyway. That's why I quit wearing boots: it sorter disgusts me to see a guy, all rigged out in what he thinks the well-dressed cowpoke should wear, come strutting into a hotel lobby when I am well aware that he doesn't even know which side of a horse to get up on.

It takes right smart of doing to break your feet into shoes after you have worn boots a long time. Besides, boots are a lot more comfortable, especially if one's arches are weak.

In addition to my distaste for the exhibitionists, I had considerable help from the distaff side of my family. They 'low as how boots and tuxedos just don't go together well. Mamacita and I were in New York one time, quartered at the Waldorf. One morning I passed the assistant manager's desk, and he called to me and hesitantly asked me if I were a rancher. At my affirmative reply, another man sitting by him chucklingly asked for payment of their wager. I asked the manager why he bet that I was not a cowman, and he said: "I didn't know that cattlemen wore Bond Street tweed suits." I indignantly replied that we wore clothes in Texas; besides, it wasn't an English product but came from San Angelo. Another time, we were standing in the queue at a theater when a little girl standing behind me, in an awe-struck tone, asked her mother if that was Hopalong Cassidy standing in front of her. That did it—I broke in the shoes when I got back to San Angelo. I may not be as comfortable any more, but it sure doesn't appear so affected.

By the time I took to ridin', every poke in our country carried a yellow Fish Brand slicker (raincoat). It was tied to his saddle behind the cantle, and in this dry climate, it was broken out so seldom that it was usually "kinder dallapidated" when it was needed. The waterproofing gum that covered it had either melted and stuck together, or the saddle strings had cut holes in it. In either case, it didn't give much protection.

Earlier, I have been told, many of the men on the trail carried the long, heavy "soldier's" overcoats, which were relics of the Civil War. However, I saw very few overcoats in our area. About the time I thought I was a real cowpoke, a herd was started for the Pecos in the fall of the year. The day we left the ranch was warm and spring-like, and everybody was in his shirt-sleeves. When I picked up my bedroll at the ranch, I discovered that my foreseeing mother had added a heavy overcoat to it. I protested that I didn't need it, but she made me take it along. A blue norther came up about the second night out, and it was cold most of the trip. How I thanked my knowledgeable mother! When I would come off guard at night, I would give it to one of the men who would give it to his relief, and so on. That old coat and a thin, henskin affair that the boss had might' nigh saved our lives. I had to leave the drive before it reached its destination, and I left the coat with the men. When I got it back a month or so later, it was plumb wore out.

We had so little brush in our immediate area that few of the men had chaps (Spanish, *chapareros*), "leggins" we called 'em. They mostly were left at the wagon unless it was a cold or rainy day. However, they were useful as discipline enforcers. If somebody got smart and out of line, usually a button, he was laid across a bedroll or wagon tongue and popped on his posterior with the lower ends of the chaps. The men handled these seances—the boss conveniently absenting himself from the scene. It was all taken in good part by the culprit, and I never saw any trouble arise from the "layin' on of the leggins." It didn't take many applications for a man to learn his manners.

We sort of considered leggin'-wearers as sissies. That is, until we had to make a trip to the brush country. Then we found out what chaps were for. Owing to a misunderstanding, the cattle we came after had not been gathered, and the segundo, who was in charge during the boss's absence, sent us out on the roundup with the boys on the ranch. It was plenty brushy, and the first thing we did was to get our pants torn to pieces and our legs skinned something awful. It didn't take much busting through the brush to make us goosey about it. The upshot was that we lost more cattle than we brought in. The owner of the cattle delicately hinted to our segundo that it might be better for him to keep his men in camp, as "they might get skunt up." We were a humiliated lot, but we had our inning later. We were short-handed and hired a couple of the hands to accompany us on our trip home. They made it fine until we came to the open country; then, they "threw up their tails." They were so scared of the prairie dog holes they dassn't put their horses out of a trot, and they lit out for home as soon as we could spare them. It makes a big difference what kind of country you are used to.

Nowadays it's a lot different hereabouts, since the country has grown up in brush. Practically every rider now owns a pair of chaps and uses them everyday. They have sort of gone to seed in their use now: they even wear 'em in the sheep pen. As an illustration: an old kid came out from Louisiana and got a job on the ranch. About the first thing that he did was to get a pair of chaps, which he proudly wore about as much as he did his britches. Work got slack on the ranch, and he got a job with a neighbor. One day I met that old ranchman and asked him how the kid was getting along. He said that he was a good, willing boy, but that he was going to let him go, sourly remarking that he had to put them damned chaps on every time he left the house, even when he "went out the back way." Well, times do change!

The men did have some Sunday-go-to-meeting togs: if a man was affluent enough, he had a pair of pretty good boots and clothes to match. In the old days, a man was really "duded up" when he owned a pair of California pants, heavy wool affairs with big four-inch ivory and black plaids. But I haven't seen a pair in a coon's age. They have given way to the tight, white, permanently pressed monstrosities of the present day. As an example: not long ago when I was in the lobby of a swank Dallas hotel, a friend called my attention to an exhibitionist lolling in a chair and surrounded by bug-eyed Easterners. This bird had on those tight britches, pressed to a knife edge and stuck down into a pair of long, chartreuse colored boots with all kinds of fancy designs stitched on them; and of all things, he had on a pair of fancy, big roweled spurs—something a real poke never wears when he goes to town. To cap it all, he wore the spurs about four inches above the spur piece of his boots. My friend disgustedly remarked: "I'll bet that sonofabitch don't even know which side of a horse to get up on."

It might appear to most readers that this expression of derision, "not knowing which side of a horse to mount," is far-fetched, but I assure you that such is not the case. It is amazing to a West Texan how many people are so ignorant of the facts of life as they appertain to horses. The Indian mounted from the off, or right side of a horse, and even some of the old mountain men adopted the custom: notably Bill Williams, Bill Jackson, and even "Old Gabe" Bridger. The white man stuck normally to the near or left side. Horses were trained that-a-way, and it could be downright dangerous for a tyro to approach a horse on his right side. The tough ones had to have their heads pulled around as the rider prepared to get on him, and some even had to be blindfolded. Even a fairly gentle horse might shy and turn away if the rider was awkward. A horse can sense if a man is frightened or nervous, due, I think, to a glandular reaction which produces an odor. Anyway, if the rider is scared, the horse knows it just the same as a dog does. Also, he shies away from unorthodox or bungling mounting procedure.

In illustration of this esoteric sense, I recall the time some student pilots were sight-seeing on the ranch. During World War II, we had a training field only a few miles from the ranch. My good sister-in-law went all out to entertain the lonesome students and had a flock of them over for meals and sight-seeing. One day I was working cattle, and she brought a bunch of greenhorn boys from the East out to the works. They really had a bug-eyed ball watching real cowboys at work. We had to wait on some of the men who were bringing in another bunch of cattle, and the young men gathered around the punchers. They borrowed the foreman's chaps and hat, and every one of them had his picture taken in that riggin'. Sister suggested that I take some of them for a short horseback ride. We had a few gentle horses and helped the boys up on them. One young man was especially nervous, and I told him to get on my young son's pony, which was a very kind and gentle animal. He went over on the horse's right side, and "Old Jug" cocked an ear and shied away from him. I got the boy on the near side, held the reins, and showed him how to mount. He was shaking with nervousness, and the gentle old pony reacted. I got on my horse and led Old Jug for some distance before he settled down. During our short ride the frightened boy confided to me: "Sir, I was never around a horse before, and I am scared stiff. I am only a student pilot, but I would rather try to take off in a P-51 than to have gotten on this horse by myself."

On another occasion I was with a party going down the Bright Angel Trail at the Grand Canyon. There was a smart aleck from the East who was as green as my East Texan. The guide gave him a gentle little mule and, seeing that I was accustomed to riding, asked me to keep an eye on the tenderfoot. He put me in the rear of the party with "Smarty" just ahead of me. I had trouble with the kid until I got so disgusted that I quit fooling with him. We were about a third of the way down the steepest part of the trail when my charge insisted on dropping back behind me, then making his mule trot to regain the party. Since the mule was lazy, his rider had trouble kicking him into a trot, so he said he was going to stop to cut a switch. After a while, I decided to turn back and see what was happening. I heard the stirrups flapping on a running mount, and I met the mule head-on. I grabbed the reins, turned him around and started up the trail, expecting all kinds of tragedy. Before long I met old buckaroo limping down the trail and cussing like an old hand. I asked what had been keeping him so and was told that that blankety-blank-blank "pony" had kicked him and run off. I handed him the reins and told him to get back on and behave himself. Sure enough, he approached his mount from the right. The little mule cocked an eye at him and dropped his right ear, a sure sign that he was preparing to kick the daylights out of his rider. I yelled to the boy to get on the other side to mount and got the sour reply: "Hell, a damn mule hasn't got sense enough to know his right from his left." I managed to convince him and had no more trouble with him. When we topped out late that evening, a subdued, saddle-sore, terribly sunburned kid confided to me that it was remarkable how much sense his "pony" had.

I get a big kick out of watching the TV product getting on a horse. Most of them will grab the horn and the cantle and do a sort of hoppity dance step or two to get off the ground. Occasionally a real "expert" does a fancy sort of a jump up to the stirrup. One of our old cow ponies would have dumped such a rider behind the saddle or flat on the ground. If he did light behind the saddle, he was in for a tall ride and might even get his foot hung in the stirrup. Then he would be in real trouble!

Now you can sense the scorn behind the statement: "He doesn't even know which side of a horse to get up on!"

Another source of such stories centers around a few old-time pranksters still around. For instance, one of the best I ever heard was Cy _____'s caper. Cy, an old-time rancher from the Panhandle, swears that he has owned only one pair of shoes in all his life. He has always worn and still wears boots, although he has sold out his western holdings and retired to an East Texas farm. If you wear boots long enough, your feet and legs get set to them, and shoes are mighty uncomfortable. I even knew an eminent surgeon who wore boots, claiming that they gave needed support to his feet and legs during long hours at the operating table. Isn't that something?

But going back to Cy: His son was getting married in a city some hundred miles away, and it was to be a big, swanky, evening affair. Obstacles arose when Cy was told by his wife that he had to doll up for it. He did have a good tuxedo, but he stoutly maintained that he wouldn't don it unless he was permitted to wear boots with it. They finally had to compromise on his going that way or not at all. (He did have a pair of new, black dress boots.)

They were quartered in a swank motel in the town where the wedding was to take place. On the morning of his wedding day, the young bridegroom discovered that he had forgotten some necessary article of apparel and told his parents that he was going home for it. Now Cy is a great hunter, and one of his favorite guns had "gone Democrat" on him. So he told the boy to bring the gun back with him as there was an expert gunsmith in the town.

That afternoon Cy got himself all diked out well before the ceremony and got restless and decided that he just had to have a cup of coffee. His wife objected on the grounds that it was a good-sized walk around to the coffee shop and that Cy was sure to get dust on his trouser legs. So he stuffed his pants down in his boot legs, grabbed an old hat and took off. He happened to have two hats with him—a good Stetson and the old, dirty, bunged-up ranch hat—and of course, he grabbed the wrong hat. When he got around to the coffee shop, there sat the boy's car with Cy's gun in it, so he climbed into the car after it. Just as he came backing out— old soiled hat, swanky Tuxedo, pants stuffed in boots, shotgun and all—a large car bearing a Minnesota license drove up and parked. The important looking people in the car gazed bug-eyed at the strange sight. Finally, one of the men asked: "Going hunting, sir?" "Naw," dead-panned Cy, "I'M GOIN' TO A WEDDIN'." When he got inside the building, he stole a look back and saw the people laughing their heads off. Can't you just hear them telling and retelling about those crude Texans. That's the way these fool stories get started.

The real Texans are modest and never inclined to brag. So, if you hear a guy poppin' off, just scratch him a little, and you'll find he is lately come from Newark, Scranton or some other representative cow town.

In our section the weather was mild enough that we

never had tents out on the works, although further north they were a necessity. Our bedrolls were comparatively skimpy, consisting of a piece of canvas, usually a worn-out wagon sheet, a couple of blankets and two "soogans" (sometimes spelled "sougans"), which were heavy quilts made out of men's worn-out woolen clothes and well padded with cotton. Wool padding was a lot lighter and warmer, though it was hard to get well-scoured wool. The unscoured variety was too smelly and greasy. If a man had extra clothes along, he generally kept them in his bedroll. Usually two men "made down" together even if the weather was warm. That extra beddin' under them took a lot of the hard out of the ground, especially if they were in rocky or bunch grass country. If a man wanted a "piller" (pillow), he rolled up his coat if he had one or used his boots. Vide the baloney about using a saddle for a pillow—just try it! Besides, a cowboy had his saddle on his night horse if he was with a herd. The bed was rolled when he got up, tied with a piece of rope and heisted onto the wagon.

His sleeping gear was his clothes, and if the weather was bad, he even kept his britches on. If it rained, it was just too bad. Just try sitting up all night in a leaky slicker with no place to sit except on your heels or on the wagon tongue. The bedding and the grub took up all the space under the sheet in the wagon, and custom decreed that the cook got to sleep under the wagon. They tried to keep a fire going by setting the skillet lids on the fire, but that gave only slight cover from the rain so that the fire smoked so bad that it might' nigh put their eyes out. Did you ever try cooking a meal's vittles in a pouring rain? I recall one morning when it rained so hard that all we could manage was to boil a pot of coffee. We did have a few cold, soggy biscuits and a little fat bacon left over from supper of the night before. It wasn't much breakfast, but it helped a bunch of more-than-damp, shivering pokes. Seems to me that it rained more then than it does now.

The water-resisting tarp (tarpaulin) with its snaps and rings did not appear until much later. I still have a bedroll equipped with an elaborate tarp that really sheds water. A cowboy could borrow the cook's shovel, dig a ditch around the bed so that the water couldn't run under it, buckle up the tarp, crawl in bed and pull the flap up over his eyes, and he had it made. He slept dry even if the pent-in air did get sort of stale and musty before morning.

Toilet facilities were pretty sketchy to say the least. One did have the opportunity to get an occasional bath in a creek or water hole if the weather was not too cold. He could wash his face and hands of a morning; and if he were kind of particular, he could borrow the cook's dish-washing soap, usually a big, yellow bar with enough lye in it to cut the grease. It was plenty stout, but it sure cleansed. It made a mighty poor shaving lather that would leave a face sore for a week, so one didn't shave much. This soap also doubled well for laundering clothes; that is, if one ever had the time and the inclination to act as laundress.

If a poke was out with the wagon for several weeks, he became somewhat unkempt both as to clothes as well as beard and hair. One time we were out so long that our hair looked like the present-day rock and roll singers. We had a pair of sheep shears in the wagon, not for shearing sheep, you bet, but for clipping the long, unshed hair off a cow to identify a dim brand. A couple of our dandies decided to cut each other's hair with the shears. They got their hair off all right, even if it did leave their heads looking mighty splotchy.

When the outfit reached the shipping point, everybody took off for town in relays, and the barbershops did a land-office business. He bought some fresh clothes and had the shop porter fix him a good bath by toting buckets of hot water from off a stove. After scrubbing and donning fresh clothes, he really had the barber give him the works—haircut, shampoo and shave, and a big dousing of bay rum. If his beard was long and heavy, he sure looked pale after the shave but very genteel, and he certainly smelled sweet.

Then the poke went out on the town, stopping now and then to heist one, either a big mug of draft beer or a shot glass of "redeye" (sour mash, corn likker) downed in one

34

Four pokes of the Paint Rock area, 1890

gulp without benefit of a chaser. If he were an old tuffy, he might use a small beer for the chaser. However, such is not recommended unless one is well-conditioned to the "creature": it could make the drunk come mighty quick to the unwary.

He went to the restaurant and stowed away a big gorm of town vittles. He was then ready for a night on the town, including a whirl or two at three-card monte or poker and other forms of entertainment that I won't enlarge upon. If he was not too much under the weather or not in the pokey, his faithful horse got him back into camp—that is, if he got on the right hoss. He might smuggle a flat pint to the cook, but most bosses frowned upon liquor in camp, as it could foul things up mighty quick. He might have spent all his wages, but he had a mighty good time and was ready to go back to work.

I hate to bust another illusion—the old punchers didn't dig out a pack of tailor-made cigarettes amid wonderful mountain scenery to the accompaniment of resounding music, and light up a king-sized filter tip—he just gnawed off a chaw of "eatin' terbacker." Some of the older men smoked a pipe, usually at night after supper. It was intriguing to watch one prepare his smoke. He would take a thick plug of tobacco, slice off a pipeful, rub and crumble it in his hands, cram it into his pipe, fish a coal out of the fire, tamp it on the tobacco with his thumb and start puffing. It made a redolent but stout, satisfying smoke.

Cigarettes—"cigareets" as they called them—did not really come in vogue until I was a good-sized lad. They were frowned upon by all substantial folk as a sign of sissiness, dudishness and (privately) as a mark of degeneracy. They were the marijuana "pots" or even the LSD's of that day. Besides, if you smoked them, you got consumption or other dire ailments. But all the fulminations got no further than those of the A.M.A. and the Surgeon General's warnings of today.

Our first "cigareet" smokers were Mexicans who rolled their own from a vile smelling, fine-cut tobacco, black as tar and strong as "pizen," with corn shucks for papers. Later on, they used a North American fine-cut named "Little Joker"—they called it "Leetle Joke"—and brown papers. These old brown papers were cut rather long from brown material resembling the old-time butcher's paper: I still say they are the only kind of cigarette papers fittin' for a Christian to smoke. They do still have a pale imitation called "wheat straw," but they do not fill the bill as the old brownies did; which, by the way, cannot be found today. Anyway, they were not suspect as carrying arsenic or other deleterious substances as are the pretty white ones of today. And we didn't have any lung cancer—that is, if we did, we didn't know it.

The puncher really began to take to "cigareets" when Bull Durham came on the scene. A lot of present-day smokers don't even know what Bull Durham is and couldn't roll a cigarette if they had the makin's. This was a light-colored, granulated tobacco put up in white muslin cloth bags with the picture of a Durham (shorthorn) bull on the sack, which was closed by two yellow draw strings. One of these strings had a round tag on the end, a little larger than an old-fashioned two-bit piece, also carrying the picture of the same bull. Nearly every poke wore a vest, and the top left-hand pocket was the accepted place to carry his makin's. The tag hung down and was convenient for pulling the sack out.

A competing brand, also put up in a muslin sack, called "Duke's Mixture," was marketed after Durham went over so big. It was very similar to "Bull," but it never became too popular in our area, probably because it didn't have a tag on the string. It was popularly known as "Duke's Misery."

The old hands could roll a tidy smoke, lick the paper and put a twist in one end quicker than a cat can wink his eye. I have seen these men roll one atop a loping horse in a high wind and light it, too. But I never saw a man who could do it with one hand like those sleight-of-hand boys do in the movies. I could never roll one of those thin, beautiful articles like the old expert, but I managed to get the job done. However, most of them did shed sparks that were most destructive to clothes, carpet and furniture. I had to quit them after I had burned a big hole in the upholstery of Mamacita's new car and another in Mrs. Luckett's beautiful sofa. These embarrassing incidents, together with the talking-to that I got from my Josephine, put the kibosh on my roll-your-owners. I have fallen into line with the long, slim filter-tippers. I know only one man who still manages to roll his own despite the tobacco crumbs he scatters over the carpets and the incendiary marks he leaves on his clothes and on the furniture. I wonder how he gets away with it.

I'll have to say one thing for the movies—they haven't overdone the word "ma'am." The old puncher had a respect amounting to reverence for a "decent" woman, and he used that word "ma'am" frequently: "Yes, ma'am," "No ma'am," "I am pleasured to meetcha, ma'am," etc. Many men used it when answering their wives; in fact, I know a man in his mid-eighties who still says "Yes, ma'am" and "No, ma'am" when answering his wife. I am all for it. A number of men have been killed for a derogatory remark about some lady. I wonder what would have happened to some squirt who would have had the temerity to give the "wolf whistle" at a passing girl. As an illustration, I saw a drunk knocked over the hitchrack in front of a saloon in San Angelo when he snickered aloud as the wind raised a lady's skirt a few inches above her ankles. The victim, nursing his bunged-up jaw, sat up and whined: "Excuse me, suh, I didn't know that the lady was some of your folks." The other man snorted: "She's not, but you can see that she is a lady, and if you don't like it, stand up and I'll give you some more." Old smarty-pants got up all right, but he snuck off in a shambling run as fast as his wobbly legs could carry him. What would that old puncher think of the present-day "ladies" with their mini-skirts?

Of course, the horse was the cowpoke's principal tool: without him, there would have been no cowboy. So much has been written about him that I refer the reader to the extensive bibliography on the western horse, and I shall make only a few observations.

Many of the early horses I knew were not so outstanding due, no doubt, to the sprinkling of mustang or inbred Mexican blood. More than a few of them were ewe-necked, churn-headed, cat-hammed, flat-sloping pasterned broom-tails. And they ran to all colors: bays, browns, blacks, paints, skew-balds, buckskins with black stripe on legs and backs—likely atavars of the feral wild desert stock of Asia—cream duns (palominos), dappled-grays and whites, and so on. I never saw an appaloosa in the old days, but there were a few sabi-nos, more red than bay with many tiny white spots all over them, like as if somebody had used a squirt gun loaded with white paint on a red-bay animal. The grulla (gruyer, we called 'em), so denominated by the Mexicans, was the color of a sandhill crane. These latter were supposed to be about the toughest mounts in the remuda.

The cowpoke never rode a mare, and he shied away from sway-backs and "glass" or white-eyed horses, averring that he never saw a woman or a horse with a lot of white in their eyes "that wasn't mean." They didn't take too much to "paints," either, deeming them unreliable. But of whatever color or build, they were tough and made good cow horses. Most of them were "good-doers" who could subsist on grass and stand a lot of hardship. Most of them had good feet and, in our prairie country, rarely needed to be shod.

Of course, there were many outstanding individual horses. Every outfit had brag roping and cutting horses, and they *were good.* I wonder if they could compete with the finely trained stock of today's rodeo circuits. I don't think that many records would have been made by the ones that I knew.

The cutting horse was the real performer. I am sure the best one I ever worked with was a small, blood bay named Hyena, a rank misnomer as he was the nicest handling, kindest little horse I ever saw. Like a lot of his kind, he showed evidence of the Arabian Barb. Some of these horses would appear in nondescript manadas, mare herds, but they undoubtedly carried the genes of some distant Arabic for-bear.

Hyena was always ridden by the boss, and I carry in my mind's eye a picture of Mr. Bob Morris atop him. He was intelligent and alert. One only needed to let him know the animal to be cut out of the herd, and Hyena did the rest. If a cow proved to be recalcitrant, he would lay back his ears and give her a sound nip on her tail bone. Usually, the cut-out was handled so skillfully that it lit out for the "cuts" bunch. Then the working pair would return to the herd, and I don't know which was the prouder, Mr. Bob or Hyena. He had a short, mincing pace that reminded one of a pretty girl doing the dos-a-dos at a square dance. I know of no better description of him than that given the Abbot's horses in Canterbury Tales—he was "daintye." Mr. Bob never worked him without a bridle, although he stoutly maintained that he could have done so. He was an easy horse to ride for he turned on his hind legs. One that turned on his forelegs could jar teeth loose. All of them were so quick that they could turn out from under their rider if he didn't watch out.

An outstanding horse of later years was a white horse known as Snooks from the Hogsett people in Palo Pinto County, who had been ridden and trained by their foreman, Grady Blue. I only saw him work one time and that was in a cutting contest in Fort Worth. To finish off the show, his rider took off the bridle, and Snooks took out his yearling. He was sold at a high price to Jimmy Maddox of Sweetwater, and he won many trophies before being retired to a pampered old age.

I don't say that Hyena and Snooks were the best, but they were plenty good and could, I believe, hold their own in most any company today. Hyena lived his life out on the Sims Ranch, pampered and petted in his later years. I just cannot help getting sentimental about that horse, and I like to picture him as daintily stepping over the evergreen grass and asphodel of the celestial pastures. Anyway one took him, that horse was a honey!

Every old poke loves to think back on the good horses he knew, and one can get plenty of arguments out of him respecting the merits of those outstanding ones. However, I'll have to admit that the average run of horses today are superior in breeding, conformation, and maybe training to

those of yesteryear. One has to hand it to the younger generation of horse breeders who have developed the quarter horse
into the finished product of today. Sometime ago, I spent a
day going over the King Ranch in South Texas, and I saw
more good horses in that one day than I ever saw in all the
outfits of the early years put together. One now sees them
everywhere he goes in the ranch country—real horses!

These young fellers have also introduced many innovations in handling the day-to-day work on the ranch, taking
advantage of the gadgets and technology of our industrial
era. For instance, most of our local ranches were good-sized
spreads, all in one big pasture "excusing" a small bull pasture and a horse trap. So, when they started the works, a
wagon, a remuda and a whole bunch of hands had to be assembled. Now, they have the spread cut up into small pastures of a section or two with pens and loading chutes well
laid out for the fast, economical handling of the stock. Three
men can load their horses into a trailer, pile into the pickup
and be miles away from headquarters in almost a matter of
minutes. At their destination the horses are unloaded and the
stock is worked, whether cattle, sheep or goats (they run
them all in the same pasture now), quickly putting them in
the pens with a minimum of chousing. There the branding,
doctoring, etc., and even the loading of the shipping trucks
can be handled by these same three men. Stock can be drifted
into the pens, sorted, loaded and on the markets in a matter
of hours. It used to take us days, even weeks to accomplish
the same thing.

Take the work of branding, castrating, drenching, and doctoring: all is done in a chute without the backbreaking roping, bulldogging, man-killing work of yesteryear. Some of
these modern chutes can do everything except play Yankee
Doodle. The work is done so quickly and easily that the
punchers can turn the stock out, load their horses in the trailer and be back at headquarters for a hot lunch. They can do
a like job in the afternoon and still have time to drive fifteen
or twenty miles to the beer joint for a couple of beers before
supper. Then they can go to bed, and be rested and ready for

another day of toil on the morrow. No wonder we oldsters call them sissies.

However, with all its gadgets and corner-cutters, modern ranching is not all beer and skittles by any means, and the whole picture is changing faster than us old pokes can keep up with. The younger breed has to make full use of the inventions and innovations to stay in business. They just had to come to it. If a hand is needed and the rancher goes to the State Employment Agency, the first question the modern poke asks is "How much do you pay per hour?" and "I only work eight hours." Shades of the old hands who worked from can see to caint see for thirty dollars a month! As a result, the ranchman of today has to do most of the work himself. He may be fortunate enough to have a son or two, but the chances are that, after he goes to college, the son will take to writing, sports or getting a doctorate in nuclear physics.

After the horse, the cowhand's next most important tool was his saddle. Off hand, one would hardly think that there has been much change in this indispensable piece of gear, but there has. The old saddles, as I first knew them, were built on the outmoded A-tree with very little or no swell, and high, small horns and high, rolled cantles. These trees were much longer than those of the present day, some of them reaching twenty inches. Contrast this with the present-day, modern 14-incher. A saddler remarked to me the other day: "Why, two men could have comfortably fitted into one of those long old saddles." Practically all the old saddles sported saddle pockets which are never seen any more. It was surprising what could be carried in those old bags: from a six-shooter, Winchester ammunition, claw hammer, horseshoe nails, fence pinchers, worm medicine, a change of underwear . . . most anything. These large, heavily laden bags were sort of bundlesome when one was trying to saddle a snorty mount, and they could make plenty of racket when a horse shook himself. I was on guard one rainy night, when the boss's horse shook himself so hard and so rackety that the herd stampeded. One can carry all that junk nowadays behind the seat in the pickup.

These old saddles were hard on man and beast. They could get most uncomfortable after about sixteen hours of straddling them. I think this accounted for the sloppy stance of the old rider and for his shifting about sidewise with one leg up and the other stretched straight out, even sometimes hooking a leg over the horn if the work was light, such as the herd grazing. These poorly designed, heavy saddles, together with their skimpy wool-skin linings and makeshift saddle blankets, were plenty hard on the horses so that practically all of them developed sore backs: I have seen a dozen or so in one remuda. If a rider took extra good care of his horse, he wiped the sweat off his back and gave it a good washing when he unsaddled. If the horse was skinned up, he put some axle grease on the lesion after it had been washed. As a result, a good saddle horse was rarely seen that did not carry several spots of white hair indicating scar tissue. I even saw a horse trade busted one time because the horse had no saddle scars on his back. The prospective buyer refused to believe he was a well-broken animal even though the owner "guaranteed" that he was sound of wind and limb and was so easy handlin' that a woman could ride him same as a man.

There were a few Mexican saddles around, but they were never popular, mainly, I think, because of the saucer-sized, slanting, low horn and the different rigging.

But the old Texas saddles, frequently called "cacks," had plenty of strings so one could tie all kinds of stuff on them; however, only a few sported conches or much decorative stamping. They got hard wear and not overly good care, unless it was a Pueblo, Gallup and Frazier, or other expensive make. Later on Dunn Brothers, Andrews, and Alexander were well-known saddlers of San Angelo.

Dunn put out a saddle known as the Cattle Queen, probably so named because of the gal, *en dishabille*, stamped on the sweat leathers. She was fully twenty inches high and most scantily clothed in a short, short mini-skirt (shimmy) and sported elaborate garters. It was the chief ambition of my young heart to own a Cattle Queen, and as soon as I saved up the $40.00, I promptly bought one, to my parents' disgust: my father's because I had paid all that money for a mere saddle and my mother's because of what she called the bawdy stampings on it. One of the things that reconciled her to the big barn's burning down was the fact that the "nasty" saddle burned with it. That saddle was so heavy that it almost took a man and a boy to put it on a horse, and it was so long that it could have accommodated the fattest man in West Texas, a beer salesman who was a walking advertisement of the nutritious quality of his brew. Nevertheless, it was a proud young squirt who rode it. It sure did something to a youthful ego, even if it did accumulate sundry spur marks across the seat, indicative of the times its rider had been thrown.

They had all kinds of stirrups, ranging from the ponderous wooden monstrosities of the Mexicans to the small, round steel affairs, six inches or less in diameter. The idea behind this design was that the rider would not get his foot caught in a crushed stirrup if his horse fell with him. However, they didn't last long, as a few riders were killed when a foot poked its way through the stirrup during a fall. Then they came out with a stamped metal affair shaped a good deal like the good leather-covered ones of today. These, too, passed away. They were too danged cold, and they could be crushed under a fallen horse. We had lots of falls, either from getting pitched off or by a horse's falling. So much work was done in the herd that occasionally a horse would be thrown by a calf or yearling's running under him. This was considered the most dangerous thing that could happen to a rider: it was frequently fatal. Our whole country was infected by prairie dogs, and their burrows were a constant threat even to horses that were accustomed to them and expert at dodging them. If you busted your horse across a dog town, a slanting hole might cave in; then, boy, did you get dumped. Also, there were a lot of sinkholes in the swales of level country, and these were plenty dangerous, especially when they were covered with tall grass or darkness. We didn't pay too much attention to such falls and rarely got hurt much in them. Of course, such a fall would skin the palms and knees right smart. It was frightening all right, when one went sailing over his horse's head and knew that the horse was turning a summerset just behind him. The rider had to do some fast work on all fours to get out of his way.

I had a number of saddles as I grew older, but I could never find a comfortable one on account of my game leg. After three or four tries, Donaho of San Angelo and I finally came up with one that did the work. It was very narrow, had a very short tree, a good swell, a low cantle and, of all things, a padded seat. It is the sweetest little saddle I ever saw, and I am keeping it, although it has been years since I have been on a horse and Mamacita keeps urging its sale. She just can't understand how anyone could be attached to so prosaic a thing as a saddle. Before I got this saddle, I never came in at night until I was completely exhausted. But the little cack fitted me so well that I rarely got tired. Then my problem was finding a horse that fitted me. I did a lot of trading and got soundly cheated every time until I found "Old Paint." He was a black and white paint with a glass eye who carried all the foolishness and undependability usually associated with such eyes; but that horse sure could saddle! He had four good gaits: a running walk, an easy slow trot, a pace, and a fox trot that was out of this world. He would change those gaits himself, so all I had to do was sit up and ride him, which took some doings at times when something spooked him or when he got a contrary spell on him. Before I got him, I was usually the last one of the bunch when we strung out at night for home. But after I got him, things were entirely different: Old Paint and I led the pack. When the day's work was over and we headed for the ranch where the good feed of oats was awaiting him, Old Goofus really shone. His old ears would go to flopping, and he would really pick 'em up and lay 'em down, doing at least five miles an hour in a fox trot that was like riding in a rocking chair. After I got him I always led the men in, even if they broke into an occasional lope to keep up. He became so well known around the neighborhood that everybody wanted him. A horse jockey-trader was especially persistent. He kept raising his ante until one day he broke down and asked if I would take $750.00 for Paint. He only shut up when I told him that $1000.00 wouldn't touch him. That was big money for one onery old hoss in them days.

The old saddles, with their extra length and absence of swell, were a lot harder to stay with than those of today with their short, form-fitting trees and heavy swells. If an average rider knew he had to top a real salty one, he would frequently roll a blanket and tie it across his saddle next to the horn, making a "buckin' roll." I even knew one "nesterish" sort of a poke who used a soogan which made such a big roll that it kinda wedged him into his saddle. Also, he would hobble his stirrups by tying them together with a piece of rope. He might even wire his spur rowels so that they couldn't turn, but this was frowned on by the boss as it could cut a horse badly. Old fraidy-cat would get a hand to "ear his horse down," climb aboard, wrap his reins around his hand anchored to the saddle horn, and take a death grip on his rolled cantle with the other. With all these advantages, a poor rider could stay on provided his mount wasn't too rough. But it could be mighty embarrassing if he got throwed or if his horse refused to pitch. Of course, the bronc peelers never stooped to such unsportsmanlike practices—they rode 'em slick.

As stated earlier, the old pokes rode with a sloppy seat, due, I think, to their long, narrow saddles and their let-out stirrups. The vaqueros rode with such lengthened stirrup leathers that their feet barely touched the stirrups, and I think this influenced our riders. The present seat is easier both on the man and his mount. It is interesting to contrast the different "stances" or seats of horsemen in other countries, notably the Cossack and Gaucho of the Argentine. The Hauso of Chile ride with a seat more like our own punchers. The old mountain men affected short stirrups, and one chronicler of the time especially mentions the seat of old Bill Williams. That ex-parson rode all humped over with such short stirrups that his long legs stuck up so high that his knees were "level with his horse's back—just like an Indian squaw." This stirrup length could be overdone both ways!

Most of the Mexicans had *tapaderos* (toe fenders) on their stirrups, and these came in mighty handy in the brush and prickly pear country, although few riders in our area affected them, especially the large elaborate ones common in Mexico even today. I had a small pair on my last saddle, and I liked them. They not only protected one's feet from brush and thorns, but they kept them from running through the stirrups, and they afforded protection in cold or wet weather.

Next in order come the bridles and bits, which were about as varied as the riders—from the bosal—hackamore—halter to the wicked Spanish spade bit, a very heavy, cruel thing that could very well break a horse's jaw. The first bits that I remember were patterned somewhat after the spade, even to the roller on the tongue piece, but they were not near so heavy or punishing. Through the years, bits have become more improved and sensible so that you never see a horse with a torn mouth anymore. My last headstall was equipped with a sort of a bosal bit combination that was very easy on Old Paint, but could well handle him when he went haywire.

Most of our early bits were store-boughten, hand-me-downs from the hardware store and made of wrought or even cast iron. They were uncomfortable to the horse and easily broken. I used to see about as many sore mouths as I did sore backs. But the blacksmith came into his own and turned out handmade steel bits that were well designed, light, comfortable and plenty strong to handle anything except a cold-jawed horse.

A skilled German blacksmith, named Chris Hagelstein, settled in Paint Rock and soon became famous for his bits. He had a bright metal concho on the outer sides of the cross or tongue piece stamped "C. Hagelstein." This trademark became well known all over the cow country, even in Canada and South America. These old bits are now museum pieces. How I regret not keeping all those old-time accessories! But we didn't set much store on antiques in them days; besides, I was only a thoughtless, harum-scarum kid with a mind more on gals and good times than on museum pieces. Dad-gummit! I wish I'd had more sense.

The headstalls were about as varied as the bits, from the elaborately decorated Mexican variety (leather or horse-hair) to the plain leather strap with a slit for one of the horse's ears. The reins were also varied, from the elaborately braid-ed horse-hair, rawhide, plain or stamped leather, to pieces of worn-out rope. In those days, most of our Anglos kept their reins tied together, but there was no set pattern: "everybody to his own notion," the old woman said when she kissed the cow.

The old-time spur ranged from the heavy, ponderous Spanish variety with its thick shanks, large rowels, long-spiked and cruel, to the lowly, rusty iron "dinguses" off the hardware shelves. I guess the old "O K" was about the most numerous in our area. They were especially popular with the nesterish kind of cowboy, mainly because they were cheap. Now, my father was no hand to "put on side"; be-sides, a crippled leg kept him from doing much work on horseback. So his cowboy outfit was pretty sketchy and a source of much embarrassment to me: the crowning touch was the fact that he usually wore only *one* O K spur. I thought that a man of his standing should be togged out in the finest rig that money could buy.

So, you bet, when I got big enough to ride with the men and saved up the money, I threw away my O K's and bought me a shop-made pair. Chris Hagelstein made a good, strong spur, but it never took on too well, mainly, I think, because it was void of decorations. "Choctaw George" Hartsell, mas-ter mechanic of San Angelo, could do anything with metal and made the popular spurs of that time. He not only turned out a good, dependable, working model, but most of them were the fancy, made-to-order kind, any shape or size and lavishly decorated in silver and even gold. One particularly popular design had aces of hearts, spades, diamonds and clubs inlaid on the heel pieces and variously shaped shanks. Another one of my ambitions was to own a pair of "Choc" spurs. I finally managed to acquire a pair that were really "darbs" with silver inlaid heel pieces and shanks shaped like gals' legs complete with fancy garters, high-heeled slippers and all. This contributed further to my family's disapproval —a melding of the Scotch and the Puritan: my father was disgusted with a spendthrift son, and my good mother was sadly coming to the conclusion that her eldest was a low-brow, an opinion which, I fear, is even now concurred with by my long-suffering spouse.

Choctaw George's Bicycle Shop, 1896

I lost one of these spurs in a day run of the herd, to the relief and satisfaction of the distaff members of the family. The next pair, although well decorated, had shanks shaped like swans' necks, a concession to the "squares." They also went where the "woodbine twineth." After a long hiatus in public office, I acquired another and most conservative pair of light, short-shanked, undecorated alloy spurs. These lighter spurs with dull rowels do the job just as well and are much more humane than the old gig-gutters. I haven't seen a horse with bleeding flanks in many a year. The spur leathers were just about as varied as the other equipment.

Quite a few of the old, dyed-in-the-wool pokes boasted that they latched their spurs on to a new pair of boots and never took 'em off until the boots wore out. But no poke ever wore his spurs twice in my mother's house. If he didn't take them off before he came in, he was politely and firmly told that spurs were off limits in her house. He never offended the second time. These old long shanks could get in the way when the wearer was afoot. I have seen many a man trip over them, as a would-be pugilist found out when he matched a scrap with a young rooster who didn't wear spurs.

The best spur story I ever heard was the experience of old Billy Hamilton, who was one of those who never took 'em off. Now and again, Billy would partake too liberally of the "wild cow's milk." He was married to a very small, beautiful and high-tempered lady, known to her intimates as "Miss Duck." One night, he came in pretty well soused, and Miss Duck told him that if he ever did it again that she would give him a whipping. This tickled Billy so that he got on a real bender the next night. He came home tighter than a hoot owl, happy and carolling "Oh, bury me not," etc. Miss Duck heard the serenade and met him at the door with the broom. Billy laughingly side-stepped her swing, but tripped on his spurs and fell flat on the floor. The floor felt so good that he promptly decided to take a nap, which he just hadn't orter done. Miss Duck pulled a sheet off the bed, rolled him up in it and sewed it tight, making a very efficient strait jacket, so that all Billy could do was bat his eyes. She then went out to the barn and got the buggy whip which was a heavy rawhide affair, not one of those light rattan bodied things. Then she lit in on old Billy, who waked up in a hurry. He expostulated and howled and threatened, all to no avail. She would ask if he was ready to take the pledge and, upon his indignant refusal, go to work on him again. After she wore the whip down to a nubbin' and threatened to get a club, her old toper weakened and agreed to take the pledge. He did, and so far as I know, he kept it. They had a long, happy married life ever after. "How many lengthened sage advices the husband frae the wife despises!"

The rope, next to the cowboy's horse and saddle, was his prime tool: without it, he would have been practically helpless, especially in the open range days. While the emigrants brought in various kinds of cordage, the daddy of them all was *la riata* of the vaquero. As stated before, these "lassos" were plaited leather or rawhide (usually the latter), small, "soople" and strong. The vaquero used a longer rope, forty-five to fifty feet, than his Anglo counterpart, who limited his to forty feet or less. At first, the Anglo ropes were comparatively large in diameter and clumsier than the riata, but they did the work. Later, other materials such as maguey and other glamourous fibres, produced a smaller, stiffer and better-handling rope than the hempen varieties turned out by the ropewalks and shipfitters of the Eastern seaboard. Most rodeo fans are thoroughly familiar with the tight, twisted article of today.

The Anglo generally tied his rope to the horn of his saddle, but the Mexican usually wrapped it around the horn, locally called the "dally welte" or "dally," corruptions of the Spanish, *dar la vuelto* (literally, "wrap-around"). Each school argued that the other fellow's practice was the more dangerous. The vaquero wanted to be in position to turn his rope loose if the situation demanded, while the old poke was afraid of getting his fingers cut off between the rope and his metal horn. I knew several punchers who had lost fingers and one man who lost his whole hand in that manner. Both schools turned out efficient procedures that got the job done.

Some of these men were sort of specialists according to the kind of work to be done. There was the "fore-footer" or the "hind-legger" who specialized in snaring the legs of their victims. The hand who worked in the herd was usually an older and settled man who did his work quietly with little disturbance. He had to be pretty strong as well as efficient, for such work could be very exhausting on both man and horse. I was in one branding go-round when two men, spelling each other, gave out before the day was over. I was mighty glad when they had to stop and rest, as I was the button who was tending fire and toting irons to the branders. That was hot work and worrisome, especially if the cattle were stout and snifty. On the particular day mentioned, I got knocked down and tripped up several times by rambunctious cow brutes with scant sympathy from the pokes: my own father even laughed when I got butted through the fire by a big critter which got away from the bulldoggers, who were supposed to hold him on the ground after the rope was removed. That night was another that I didn't have to be rocked to sleep.

The fore-footer usually did his work on horses: the hind-legger was used on cattle. A man would rope the animal around the horns, and the legger would loop the hind legs. Together they threw and held the animal while it was branded or doctored. These men really developed an expertise that I rarely managed except by accident. Many outfits let their horses run wild until they were four-year-olds or more. It took some doing to get one of those wild, strong horses on the ground. They broke 'em rougher than now: they rode a horse until he quit pitching every time they saddled him, and then pronounced him "broke." Usually he wasn't, so some unfortunate poke had to do it over when he drew him in his mount. I recall one breaking that used the Sims' pens. The D and O H's had a whole bunch of the unbroken *ladinos*, and some of the local peelers contracted to break them for a few dollars per head. These were rough horses, and the breakers treated them rough. A bunch would be penned, and a fore-footer would dab his rope on a victim and bust him wide open. Another puncher would grab the fallen horse by the nose and ears and twist his head back of his shoulder while the roper and an assistant kept the rope tight. A hackamore attached to a good, stout rope was put over the horse's head. He was then let up on his feet; after some maneuvering, a man grabbed his ears and pulled his head down. This was called "earing him down." He was then saddled, and the rider crawled on while the rest of the gang got up on the fence and enjoyed the spectacle, especially the times when the horse "turned the pack." The thrown rider would crawl back on him and give him another whirl, if he wasn't too bunged up.

When the horse quit pitching, he was led out by a mounted rider and tied to a big rock or a heavy log if possible. They did not like to stake a bronc to a tree, as he was more likely to be injured than if he were tied to an object that would give to his lunges. The captive was watered regularly, but he had to rustle what grass he could within the length of his tether. If the grass was eaten down, he might be given an occasional block of hay. On the next saddling, he would be taken from the pen and allowed to do his stuff with a hazer along to help the rider keep him out of trees or other hazards. After a few days on the stake and the rough rides, the tired, bunged-up victim usually meekly submitted to being saddled and ridden without any more pitching. He was then pronounced broke. They do it earlier and much more humanely nowadays, and they produce fewer outlaws.

If you were a show-off or were afraid of snakes, you might even have a hair rope in your gear. These ropes were plaited out of horse hair almost entirely by Mexicans. By using different colors of hair, obtained from thinning out horses' tails or getting them from dead horses, real works of art were turned out. But these ropes were not very strong and were mostly for display purposes. I haven't seen one for many years. Strangely enough, I never had any yen to own one.

The other use for a hair rope was to make a "snake fence." Most punchers paid little attention to snakes, but a few did fear them. Some of these boys would loop a hair rope around their beds, as they were popularly reputed to turn back snakes who did not like the prickly hairs sticking out in all directions.

Mr. Tom Shaw, a local cow buyer, was deathly afraid of snakes and always carried a hair rope with his bedroll, which he took with him on his buying trips. He would drive out in his double buggy to a herd and usually spend the night at the wagon. On one such occasion, he carefully looped his hair rope around his bed. It was a hot, moonlit night, and Mr. Tom kicked his covers off. He was a very large, heavy man, and considerable abdomen was exposed when his shirt slipped above his drawers. A poke, sleeping nearby, waked up and spied that large, white bare area a-shining in the moonlight. He nudged his sleeping bedmate awake, and the two pranksters slipped over, gently removed the rope and dragged it across Mr. Tom's tummy. Squalling "Snakes, snakes," he was up in the wagon before he was wide awake. By the time quiet was restored, the two jokers were innocently asleep in their bed. Mr. Tom was so mad he got his gun and stormed around camp looking for the sonofabitch who played such a low-down trick on him. He could laugh about it later, but *much* later!

THE COWMAN

NEXT IN MY CHARACTERIZATION is the cowman, the apotheosis of the cowpoke. What the poke could do, the cowman could do better; besides, he had more experience and accumulated wisdom. The cowmen I knew were usually middle-aged, lean, grizzled, squint-eyed and weather-beaten. They knew cattle, horses, range, weather and men. They could do any job pertaining to their calling. They possessed all the skills from the roping and riding of the "rough string" to running the wagon, the drive, the ranch. If you don't believe this, I suggest that you read Ike Blassingame's *Dakota Cowboy*. While I never knew Ike personally, I am fully aware of his reputation among old Matador hands, and their opinions are good enough for me. Ike tells it all, matter-of-factly and modestly. He was a cowman in every respect.

I had the privilege of working with some of these wise old professionals, and they learned me a lot. They were knowledgeable, patient, understanding, salty, and tough tutors. They never failed to take me down when I got out of line or made an egregious error. This taking-down, whether by kind admonition, withering remark (and believe me, they could wither) or recourse to quirt or doubled rope, could truly make a Christian out of a squirt! They didn't make too good a cowman out of me, but I do say that they done a danged good job with the material they had!

THE BOSS

THE BOSS was the "ne plus ultra" cowman. In addition to the qualities of the cowman, he had the rare faculty of judging and handling men (like the colonel of a regiment) and keeping the respect and loyalty of tough, independent, individualistic, even turbulent, men. He didn't spare himself, his men, or his horses, but he sure did take care of his herd, and he got it to its destination in good order if it was humanly possible. Mr. Bob Pearce was my "beau ideal" of a trail boss. He was soft-spoken and had little to say, but one knew he meant that little. One hastened to comply with his orders, usually made as a suggestion, and he didn't make it but once. All the owner had to do was to furnish a herd and an outfit, turn them over to Mr. Bob, tell him where and when he wanted the herd delivered: that's all—Mr. Bob did the rest. He had the directional sense of an Indian. He never needed a compass: the sun and the North Star were sufficient for him. He had a map, all right, but he carried it in his head. He knew the best routes, the river crossings, water holes, and best grazing, and he always hit 'em on the nose. If he wasn't too rushed and got any breaks, his herd arrived on time at the delivery point in better shape than when he started. There were others like him, but not too many.

THE WAGON BOSS

THE WAGON BOSS was the stay-at-home counterpart of the trail boss. He had the skills, know-how and ability of his far ranging confrere, only it was applied on the local scene. He took the wagon out on the range, handled the roundups, the branding, sorting of the cattle and trailing them to the shipping points, sometimes quite a distance. He also brought in herds, settling them in the various pastures and just everything.

Mr. Bob Morris was my father's wagon boss when we were working at home or in our section of the state. He had the characteristics and ability of Mr. Pearce, but he was not as stern a disciplinarian. He couldn't very well be with the local boys, mostly neighbors whom he saw every day; besides, he was just too gentle and kind a man and possessed of great patience. If he had not been, he probably would have nailed my hide on the barn door, for I pestered him something scandalous.

We had the usual sprinkling of pranksters among the younger men, and they loved to aggravate him, provided they had someone to front for them. I provided that front for I was squirty and the owner's son. They would put me up to all kinds of foolishness, saying that the owner's son should do thus and so; me, I didn't have any more sense than to fall in with their urgings. But Mr. Bob, bless his heart, considered the source and usually resorted to fatherly admonitions, and he didn't tattle to my father. However, he could get plenty tough when the occasion demanded. I don't think anything riled a boss more than an unauthorized poke working in the herd. On one occasion that I never shall forget, they cozened me into the idea that I should be working in the herd the same as the boss. Mr. Bob ran me out two or three times, but I kept sneaking back until I committed an egregious mistake and really fouled things up. That did it, for Mr. Bob rode over to me and, bending that bleak look of his on me, said: "Kid, stay out of this herd or I'll take the double of my rope to you," and banished me to the ignominy of holding the cuts. Later in the day, I noted that the pranksters were rather a subdued lot. We all got the message, and I stayed out of the herd from then on. Finally, when I was about grown, and maybe a little wiser, the proud day arrived when he took me into the herd with him and set me to work.

I think he was one of the best men I ever knew. He was

my valued friend from the time I could ride until he made his last roundup. He did a lot for me, and I revere his memory.

On the smaller spreads, the ranch boss could double as wagon boss; but, on the larger ones, he might have several wagons under him and serve as ranch manager, responsible only to the owner. By the time I came along, the boss never allowed a gun or a bottle of whiskey on the works. Sometimes a buyer would show up with a bottle, but it was never tapped until all the details of the trade were worked out. If the buyer was in an expansive mood, he might be allowed to share his bottle with the hands to the extent of one drink to one man, and only then after the day's work was over. I was a button of about fifteen when we delivered two train-loads of cattle at Ballinger. We didn't get the second train loaded until long after dark, and a storm came up. We all got wet and cold, and the hands asked father to get them some whiskey. He refused, saying that he would take them to town where they could tank up after the work was finished. There was considerable grumbling, so the buyer sent a hanger-on to town for a few jugs. We were up at the chutes tallying out the cattle being loaded and knew nothing about the jugs being passed around in the dark pens. Some puncher got a snootful and left a gate open. Some two carloads of cattle got out, and we had to ride like drunk Injuns for a couple of hours in a violent storm rounding up the escapees. That learned me, and I always followed Father's example. Cows and booze just don't mix.

THE CATTLEMAN

THE CATTLEMAN, the owner and experienced cowman, was knowledgeable in the ways of cattle, values, markets, men, buyers and bankers. He had to be or he went broke. My father knew most of the cattle tycoons of his time, from Shanghi Pierce to Marion Sansom, one of the last of the old breed. Father was a member of the Texas Cattle Raisers' Association almost from the start, and there has been a Sims on the list through the years. Father never missed a convention for many years, and he took me along a few times. I remember the awe of a button when introduced to one of these great men, and I treasure the recollection of their kind and considerate attitude toward me. They always shook my hand cordially, 'lowed as how they were glad to meet me and reminded me that my Pa was a good man whose footsteps I would be wise to follow. Incidentally, I recall meeting Al McFaddin at a San Antonio convention and listening, bug-eyed, to his description of the oil well brought in on Spindle Top in Beaumont, which ran wild for weeks and flowed oil so heavily that it covered the prairie all around and ran down the creeks. I was especially intrigued at his mentioning that he rode around in the oil so much that the hair was slipping off his horse's legs. He wanted Father to come down and get his feet wet, but he said that he knew nothing about the black, stinking stuff that wasn't much good for anything except to swab on "tickey cattle." *Ay, de mi, otra ves*!

These men operated under a stern code: "The sorriest man in the world is the sonofabitch who would steal a sheep, and the next sorriest is the man who won't do what he says he will." My dad's stern admonition to me was, "Son, always stick by any trade or promise you make, even if it slips the hair." Those men were hard traders, but when they made a trade, they didn't need a contract. The terms of the trade were thoroughly thrashed out and confirmed with a handshake and the words: "It's a trade." I have seen many big trades made with no more fuss and feathers than that. Each man knew the other would do exactly what he promised. One of their sayings was: "I'd rather argue with you a week before a trade than a minute afterwards."

At first, many a deal was paid off in gold. Father told me of one trade he witnessed up in the Panhandle country. The cattle were tallied, and the two principals figured up the tot. A blanket was spread, and piles of gold coins placed on it. They each called one of their men, and they were set to counting. After a while, one of the men stopped and said:

"Aw, hell, Mr. L——, I can count cattle with any man, but all this money gets me mixed up." After the money was counted out, the boss called one of his men over, gave him the heavily laden saddlebags of gold, and said: "Take it to the bank." The bank happened to be 200 miles away, but the puncher took the bags without a word, mounted his horse and took off. Nobody seemed to think that this was in any way remarkable.

In those early times, everybody seemed to be chronically out of checkbooks, or even paper. Father gleefully told me a number of stories about these shortages. Pages out of the boss's time book (if he had one) a piece of paper sack from the chuck box, or even a piece of wood would serve the purpose. On at least two occasions, he saw checks written on wood: once on a piece of shingle that happened to be in the wagon, and once on a piece of 1x4 white pine window casing. A nester was building a house a couple of miles away from where the outfit was camped, and a hand was sent over to borrow a piece of paper. The nester had no paper, and his shingles hadn't been hauled out from the town, a good many miles away. So, he sawed off a piece of window casing about eight inches long. This block of wood and a lead pencil did the trick, and a neat check for some thousands of dollars was turned out. The banks accepted such checks without comment. Wonder what would happen today if a computer got hold of a check written on 1x4 lumber.

THE COOK

LAST, BUT BY NO MEANS LEAST in this categorization comes the cook. Upon old cook, cookie, coosie (Spanish: *cusinero*) largely depended the morale of the camp. A poor, sloppy, filthy, grouchy one could bust it higher'n a kite, while a good, clean, pleasant coosie made for a happy, smooth-running outfit, no matter how bad the weather or how tough the work. Such a one was more precious than rubies! Mmm, mmm what he could do with what he had was something to savor. Hot fried steak off the hindquarter cooked in deep hog fat with some beef taller added, baked short ribs or slumgullion stew, fried spuds with onions, a simmering pot of frijoles, big, light sourdough or baking powder biscuits just out of the Dutch oven, and even a "pore man's puddin" concocted out of cold, crumbled biscuits and well-sweetened canned tomaters, followed by good Arbuckle's coffee, strong enough to float a pistol—my mouth is even now a-watering in remembrance. Fried side meat ("sow bosom" in the vernacular) and black molasses laced with the bacon drippings and sopped up by hot buscuits made a breakfast that would stick to your ribs until suppertime.

Occasionally, he would dish out a batch of stewed, dried fruit, and he might make a puddin' or even pies out of it. We had one cook who was hipped on dried apples, which got pretty tiresome. After we began to pass them up, he took to making fried pies out of them. Now, a fried pie made out of old-time dried apples can become mighty innocuous if you have them every day, so a "poet" in the outfit came up with a song: "Tromp on my corns and tell me lies, but don't pass me no apple pies." This so miffed cookie that we got no more stewed fruit of any kind on that trip. For a number of years I have been an habitué of the banquet circuit, and almost invariably, they serve soggy apple pie, bringing that old ditty to mind.

It was a cryin' shame what a poor cook could do to good groceries and to morale. I remember one old coot who was known as the fastest and the nastiest in all of Texas and half of the Chickasaw Nation. The pokes were not much hands to gripe at the cooking, as they were afraid that the cook might quit, and nobody, but nobody, wanted the job. This is reflected in a story extant all over the cow country, and I am sure that it happened a good many times. A cook quit and the boss talked a reluctant puncher into taking the job with the understanding that the first man who criticized the cooking had to take over the job. This feller was such a poor chef that he figured somebody would forget the proviso and go to kicking. But nobody did. After a number of days, old substitute biscuit-shooter got so tired of his job that he purposely fouled up the food until it was simply terrible. One morning at breakfast, one of his boarders picked up a big old soggy biscuit, burnt to a crisp on the outside and raw on the inside, and remarked "sotto voce" to the man next to him: "This is the worst piece of bread I ever saw in my whole life!" The cook, all primed for just such a remark, jerked off his flour sack apron, threw it at the complainer, and jubilantly yelled: "That does it, you kicked at my cookin' so the job is yourn." Old critic grinned broadly and said: "But, hell, that's just the way I like it!!"

"Coosie" and his outfit, 1891

Coosie was usually middle-aged or even older. A lot of them were ex-pokes, too old or too bunged-up to make a hand anymore, who just couldn't give up being with a cow outfit. He usually needed a shave, had tobacco drippin's on his chin and a smudge of flour on his face. He certainly bore little resemblance to the modern chef. Instead of the chef's cap, he wore an old flop hat, greasy and blackened from the smoke of many campfires. Instead of a crisp white uniform, he wore an old shirt and duckin' britches stuffed into worn, scuffed boots, all floury and spotted. He did wear an apron of sorts made out of an empty flour sack which was usually pretty grimy.

His tools were an array of pots and pans, skillets, Dutch ovens, a big black coffeepot; a butcher's knife or two; a long fork; a couple of dishpans, one of which doubled as a bread pan; a shovel for handling coals; and an iron rod with a crook on one end, usually an old branding iron, for handling the hot skillets and lids.

The eating utensils were usually battered tin cups, spoons, plates, and black-handled iron forks and case knives. The camp was his domain, and he lorded it over the hands. He could get mighty riled at the wrangler's failure to provide him with an adequate supply of cookin' wood or at a puncher who tampered with his fire, got in his way or attempted to sneak a bit of food before the meal was ready, but he rarely objected to anyone pouring himself a cup of coffee, as the coffee was always the first thing prepared after the fire got to burning. He could be downright irascible, but the hands humored him, especially if he was a good provider.

They generally had plenty of fresh meat with the wagon, especially if they were on the home range. On a drive away from home, beef was not always available, as there might not be any suitable animals in the herd, in which case, you had to make do with sow bosom or a goat you might buy from a nester. I recall one time when we ran out of beef and frijoles, and the bacon ran so low that it had to be reserved for seasoning the black-eyed peas, which happened to be in good supply. We didn't think much of these one-eyed beans (as we called them), and we got mighty tired of goat meat. Everyone took it in stride except one sloppy, nesterish puncher. Old June got downright offensive with me, the owner's teenage son, because my "Pa was too tight to furnish decent grub to his hands," and furthermore, he didn't like the way it was cooked. I was getting ready to pop him over the head with the cook's branding iron when a grizzled old puncher witheringly remarked: "You know, I always noticed that the ones who have the least to eat at home are the ones who do the most bellyachin' about the grub in camp." Everybody roared, as we all knew that this was true in June's case. I had no further trouble with him.

When working the home range, the boss would pick out a suitable animal, have a hand put his rope on it and work it slowly as possible to the wagon, where the cook would knock it in the head with his axe. They would fit a gamblin' stick to the hind legs, fasten a rope to it and have the horse pull it up in a tree or to the propped up wagon tongue. It was then butchered, and the quarters hung up. Strange to say, little of the meat spoiled. Flies didn't bother us to speak of, and the pure, dry air quickly put a glaze on it. It just got better and better the longer it lasted. You just don't get meat like that any more even if it is blue-blooded and grain-fattened.

Occasionally, they would prepare a "sonofagun" composed of pieces of the animal's innards—the brains, tongue, sweetbreads, liver, heart, etc. If the animal was a calf, his marrow gut added flavor to the concoction, which was easily the most savory of all stews when properly prepared. Man! Man! You ain't rightly lived lessen you have flopped your lip over a "sonofagun" prepared by an expert. He would dump it all into a big iron pot, add cold water and put it on the fire, letting it simmer for hours. Nothing was added but salt, black pepper and, maybe, some Chile Pequin. It didn't need nothin' else. The last sonofagun I tasted was prepared by an amateur who put all kinds of condiments and vegetables in it. Another old-timer sourly remarked to me that it was more like rabbit stew than sonofagun. Incidentally, no self-respecting cowpoke would ever eat rabbit unless he was starving. They were considered nester grub, and they had a saying that "anybody that would eat rabbit would talk to hisself, and anybody who talks to hisself tells lies." My wife says that it ain't so, that rabbit is one of her favorite foods, as folks in Parker County like rabbit. That makes her a nester!

A lot of the early settlers in Coke County were nesters and were reputed to live on rabbits and mesquite beans during a drought. Coke County residents were called Rabbit Twisters by the high and mighty cowpokes, and I have seen several pretty fair fisticators when the epithet was applied to a Coke Countian. Well, it takes all kinds.

Way back yonder, it was not considered reprehensible to eat stray beef, even if it was branded. The neighboring outfits did it to you, and you did it to them: it was a joke that nobody ever ate his own beef. And thereby hangs another tale.

Some years ago, I visited Mr. John Bustin, an old-time West Texas ranchman and former partner of my father. Mr. B. sold out his Texas holdings and moved to the San Fernando Valley in California. One night after supper, we got to gassing about old times, and he gleefully told me the following story: he was working cattle in the hill country between Eden and Brady and told one of the hands to pick out a fat heifer and help the cook butcher her. When they got to camp that night, the black-and-white-spotted hide bore Will Currie's brand. When Mr. B. got after the man, he innocently replied: "You never said for me to kill one of yourn." But they couldn't waste all that good beef.

The next day at noon, who should ride into camp but Mr. Currie. Naturally he was invited to get down and feed his face, which he proceeded to do. While they were eating, one of the hands surreptitiously rolled up the black-and-white hide and stuck it in a prairie dog hole. Mr. C. was hungry and thoroughly enjoyed the good fresh beef. When he got ready to leave, Mr. B. had the cook sack up a hind-quarter and presented it to Mr. C. to take home with him. He thanked Mr. B. saying: "John, I believe that is the best beef I ever ate." Mr. B. replied: "Will, you never ate any beef like that before in all your life—it's your own!" The men howled, and Mr. C. rode off grinning.

When I got home, I got Will in a crowd and told it on him,

to their huge enjoyment. Mr. C., a substantial citizen and a proper and dignified churchman, grinned an embarrassed grin and said: "John Bustin must have gotten me mixed up with somebody else." However, this carried no stigma as such doin's were "custombre" in those early times.

Although old wagon coosie did double as a bunkhouse chef, his heart was not altogether in it. I think he rather looked down on the job, considering it sort of sissified and nesterish. He just preferred the wide open spaces with all the hard work, the rain, blowing dust, etc., to being cooped up within the four walls of a kitchen.

Old bunkie did have it all over old wagon stiff. He was sheltered from the weather and had many conveniences. He had a wood stove to cook on and a big woodpile, even if he did have to chop the firewood. He had plenty of water from a well or a barrel skidded up from the creek. He had plenty of shelf room, a handy table and even chairs to sit on, and he didn't have to sleep on the hard ground. He had more groceries and utensils to do with and more leisure. He might have to use more side meat and less beef, as they did not kill as much beef at home as they did out on the works, but he could keep a cow and have milk if he wanted to go to the trouble. He could also have plenty of fresh "aigs" if he was energetic enough and the varmints weren't too bad.

My favorite bunkhouse cook was Ol (Oliver) Strong. Ol wasn't the best cook in the world, but he was sure good company. He had been everywhere, seen everything and done everything, even to serving as "head hostler" for a horse and wagon circus. He was a rare raconteur with a great sense of humor, and you can well imagine the yarns he could spin about his travels, his fights, amours and escapades. I "learnt about wimmen" and a lot of other things from Old Ol. If my good mother had had the least inkling of the kind of bunkhouse education her eldest was absorbing, he would have been yanked back to town instanter.

However, Ol wasn't a bad guy, and, really, he wasn't dirty. He had a store of homespun wisdom and the ability to impart wholesome ideas and practical advice to his bug-eyed disciple. Believe it or not, he had a good influence on me, and I could have done with a lot more of his education. I was most disconsolate when his feet got to itching.

Coosie generally was the pharmacist of the outfit, and his stock of medicines usually consisted of a can of Black Draught, a nauseous enough potion to cure most anything —the worse the medicine tasted, the surer the cure. He generally had a bottle of turpentine, good for might' nigh anything on the outsides and even a specific for certain ills of the insides. If there was no turpentine, kerosene from the lantern would do. Sometimes, there was a bottle of horse liniment around, and it was hell for stout, so much so that the sufferer felt the liniment more than he did his hurt.

We had many, many stories about Old Cusinero, too many to relate herein, but a few so stand out in my memory that I pass them on to you. We had one culinary artist, and he was an artist, who went by the *nom de guerre* of "Cooper"—why, no one ever knew, as that was not his real name. Coop had been out on the work for several months, and when the herd came into the shipping pens at San Angelo, the whole bunch took off. Coop had a wad coming to him, and he really went to town—new clothes, all the works at the barbershop and a big night on the town. During the night a norther blew in, and it was freezing cold the next morning. Two of the younger and better-behaved punchers spied Coop standing in front of a saloon, shivering in his shirt sleeves. When asked what he was doing without his coat, Old Shiverer replied: "Well, I woke up this morning without a cent in my pockets, and I never wanted a drink so bad in my life. I tried to get the barkeep to credit me, but he wouldn't, and I swapped him my coat for a couple of drinks." One of the young men said: "Ain't you ashamed, spending all your wages in one night?" Cooper reflected a moment and said: "Well, I don't know as I am—you see, I had a mighty good time!"

One of my favorites was old George, a small colored man, who is still a legend in my county. George was a kind of a Will Rogers character—funnier than a clown! He was very fond of his likker and was an expert in cadging drinks. He

66 JUDGE ORLAND L. SIMS

would sidle into the back of the saloon, take off his hat and stand wistfully at the end of the bar. Invariably someone took pity on him and set 'em up. One Christmas Eve, George was at his spot, looking so woebegone that several celebrators sympathetically inquired what was troubling him. George, close to tears, replied: "Things is just terrible. Here it is almost Christmas and not a drop of likker or a dime to my name. And the little pickaninnies are all sick." George had a sizeable family, and the sympathizers crowded around wanting to know what ailed the children. George, looking all the more forlorn, answered: "I don't rightly know, but it looks to me like they's got the black leg." A shout went up, and George got several quarts to take home for Christmas. (Blackleg was a virulent and deadly disease of calves that caused many losses until a vaccine was discovered.)

On another occasion, George got kind of tanked up, and remarked to his barroom audience that he had seen two men butchering one of Mr. Sims' calves. The word got around, and George was summoned before the grand jury of which my father was foreman. He was an experienced cross-examiner, and he lit into George. After the preliminaries, in which he was duly sworn, George was reminded of the heavy penalty of false swearing. When asked if he knew of any law violations within the last six months, George scratched his head, cogitated profoundly, looked my father straight in the eye, and said: "No, Mr. Sims, I just don't rightly remember none." Upon being asked how he could reconcile the statement with that made in the saloon, George imperturbably replied: "Well, Mr. Sims, I was talkin' then, but I'se swearing now." They hammered him good but could get no other reply out of him. So, the rustlers went free.

Another famous cook was "Crow," one of the blackest men I ever saw. In addition to being a *cordon bleu*, he was as cute and funny as George ever was. He was in great demand as a cook on the hunting and fishing trips of the San Angelo sports, and his *pièce de resistance* was soft-shelled turtle stew. On one occasion, a bunch went fishing up on the North Concho River and took Crow along. They set out some lines and caught a magnificent soft-shell turtle, almost as big around as a washtub. Looking forward to a great stew for dinner the next day, they staked him out in the river. They were camped on a high bank of the river, and the cattle had worn down a deep path to the water. They had a visitor from the East who was a ventriloquist, and he hid near the path when Crow went down to the river to get his turtle. Crow got his prize and started up the path, humming to himself. It's a fact that when you carried one of these turtles by a hind leg that he invariably stuck his neck out and gazed up at you. The ventriloquist, in a thin, reedy voice, said, "Crow, Crow, what you goin' to do with me?" Crow looked down at the turtle staring him in the eye and tremblingly said: "Suh?" The turtle replied: "Crow, what you a-goin' to do with me?" And Crow shouted: "I'se a-goin' to drop you right now, Suh." And he did. Somebody caught the turtle before he got back in the river, but Crow absolutely refused to have anything further to do with it. By their prank they killed the goose that laid the golden eggs—Crow never cooked another turtle!

And so on, ad infinitum!

HIATUS

BY THE EARLY 70's visions of the free and unlimited grazing of the open range west of the 98th meridian beckoned the more adventurous cowman ever westward, right on the heels of the retreating buffalo and Indian. Of necessity, these outfits had to be large enough to cope with the raids of the Indian remnants. By the time that the army cleaned up an area, more and more grazers poured in, to the unhappiness, and even resentment of the first-comers who felt that they had vested interests in the free range by virtue of having opened it up.

These newcomers were usually smaller and less adventurous operators: the little people were of a different breed. They were the boys who came west to settle down and make permanent homes of their own. The land was ridiculously cheap, and they began to buy up the choicest locations on permanent water. They spread out from these bases to the open range all around them. The filling up of the range, the mixing of the herds and all the other complications impelled the pioneers to look for more fresh range, and the exodus of the larger herds began to far West Texas, on to New Mexico and finally Arizona.

However, the stayers also had their problems. More and more small settlers arrived, and to complicate the situation, some of the Johnnies come lately trailed in flocks of sheep, my own father among them. Things became so sticky that something had to be done, and that something was the wire fence. These first fences were pretty sorry affairs, as the smooth wire was not very effective in turning the stock, especially around the water. But trust Yankee ingenuity to come up with a solution—wire with barbs on it. The manufacturers came up with all kinds of designs until there were more varieties than there are fiddlers in hell. Some of these were weird contraptions, ranging from bunglesome flat ribbons with sharp points stamped or cut into long, wicked, stock-mangling stickers to two strands twisted together with shorter, more humane barbs. This design stuck, and "bob" (barb, barbed) wire came into universal use. A new era had arrived.

This wire was hard on stock totally unaccustomed to fences, and many variations were tried, from posts and stays close together to the use of something plainly visible attached to the wire. We had a variety of this concept that I never heard of anywhere else. When the Loomis-Ostrander Company from New York State fenced their holdings, they used a new patent, wire with small, thin wooden blocks inserted in the twists. This design didn't take on and was discontinued. This outfit was way ahead of its time and introduced many innovations, most of which didn't jell.

They experienced so much trouble with gates being left open that they installed an electrical warning system powered by large, wet cell telegraph batteries with current carried on the top wire of the fences. Each gate was equipped with iron plates that separated when the gate was opened, thereby breaking the current and causing a drop to show in the office at headquarters. These drops were on a board resembling the switchboard in small telephone central offices of not too distant days. After a suitable interval, the drop was replaced on its hook, which carried the number of the gate. If the drop didn't stay put, a rider was dispatched to close the gate. It worked fine until some enterprising prankster discovered that the current could be broken by sticking a piece of wood between the iron plates. Result: many fruitless miles were ridden by the hapless poke on duty. They finally staked out a frequently used gate and spotted the trouble. They put up signs at each gate, threatening dire consequences to anyone who left a gate open or separated the plates. But that only added spice for the jokers. It wasn't long before every kid learned the trick and made life a misery for the guardians of the gates. My father once took me along in his buggy to open gates for him. As I closed a gate, I slyly stuck a chunk between the plates, only to have it detected by a canny Daddy. What he did to me was a plenty, so I lost all further interest in that prank.

They did file on a few offenders who called for a jury when the case was tried, and the snickering jurors always brought in a verdict of "not guilty." So them highfalutin' Yankees had to discontinue the project.

After the fencing was well under way, a new variety of malefactor appeared on the scene—the fence-cutter. Some of the old die-hard open range advocates and small homesteaders took to cutting fences about as fast as they were put up. My old friend, Mr. Ashby Tillery, a longtime treasurer of our county, had been in that war when he was a boy. His father had a contract to build miles of fence for one of the big outfits and had Ashby along with the crew. One morning, they went out to the job and found that fence-cutters had cut three miles of fence that had just been completed the day before. Every wire had been cut at every post and some of the posts burned. So they had to do the whole job over. Things got so bad that many gunfights ensued.

JUDGE ORLAND L. SIMS

An old-timer in San Angelo recently told me of a ludicrous twist to a fence-cutting. Late one very dark night, a puncher, returning from work with another outfit, was driving his mount of horses on ahead of him. He arrived at the new fence about midnight and stopped to rest his horses. All of a sudden, a wire was cut nearby, and the "zing" of the cut strands so frightened the loose horses that they took off down the fence. The man pulled his gun and grabbed his horse with spurs to follow. His horse spooked and went to pitching. The exasperated rider finally jerked him up and slapped him on the side of his head with the gun. The gun discharged, and a frightened voice yowled: "My Gawd, them damn' Harrises are down on us with all their gunmen and they'll kill us all." The cutters never learned what had happened, and the Harrises were troubled no more.

The situation got so bad that the governor called a special session of the legislature. A law making it a felony to cut fences was passed, and it produced results. In one area where conditions were especially rough, the ranch owners imported some detectives. These men, experienced rangemen, dressed in disreputable, nesterish clothes, rode into the country singly or in pairs, ostensibly riding grub lines, and soon made themselves solid with the cutters by loudly and profanely expressing their dislike for wire fences. So it wasn't long before they were invited to participate in the pleasant pastime of cutting fences of "them damn' rich land hogs." So the cutters were caught with their britches down and went off to serve a long term in the pen. It did not take many convictions to stop the depredators. Fence-cutting became a rare thing by the time my father got his country fenced, and he had only two cuts. This was done by thieves to facilitate getting the stolen stock away. Incidentally, both cuttings were found the next mornings, and the thieves were easily apprehended.

By the mid-80's practically all of our country was under fence, and another era set in. A good many of these fenced areas included many surveys belonging to the state as well as absentee owners, and little attention was paid to rentals unless the owners set up a howl. As a result many ranchmen still had a lot of free grazing. This idyllic condition continued for some years until the country really began to settle up. A small owner would fence in his land, and this led to further complications and frustrations of the big boys. However, they learned to get along, not always without bickerings and even gunfights.

With the coming of the fenced ranges, life became somewhat easier for the festive cowpoke. He did not have to spend so much time out with the wagon, and the problems of straying stock and outside work were pretty well resolved. He had a house to live in, better grub cooked on a real stove, a real bed instead of the hard ground and usually plenty of water. He could now take a bath whenever the spirit moved him. All he had to do was to take the tin washtub off its nail on the outside of the bunkhouse, take it into the kitchen, heat up water on the stove and luxuriate. He even had a mirror to shave by and a place to hang his Sunday-go-to-meetin' clothes. But he did have to do menial tasks such as building and repairing fences and replacing washed-out water gaps, which he didn't cotton to so much. One cannot blame him too much. If you ever had to dig post holes in rocky ground with only a crowbar and half a "termater can" to dip out the dirt, or sweated or frozen in water and hock-deep mud replacing water gaps after the creek got up, you know what I mean.

Since there were more folks around, he had more opportunity for entertainment and relaxation with barbecues, square dances and even camp meetings. It gave him the opportunity to spark neighboring gals, so that he might even team up with his intended, get the owner to build him a house on the range, and experience the luxury of wimmen doin's. So, it looked like the festive cowpoke finally had it made. But there was a creeping menace just over the horizon—*the nester.*

PART II

NESTERS

WEBSTER DEFINES NESTER as: "(Western) a settler, home-
steader, small ranchman, or even a squatter without legal
rights." But that was not how the cowpoke defined him—
better leave it unsaid. In his lexicon, a nester was a farmer,
any farmer, and farming was a dirty word. Perhaps this disdain stemmed from the age-old supercilious attitude of the
mounted man towards the humble man afoot. Also, his subconscious may have realized that the coming change, whereby the man with the plow would take over the sea of grass
and danged nigh everything else, was right at hand.

The first time I experienced this dislike and disdain was
the time my father sent me (a very small button) along with
the outfit over to the Coleman country to pick up a herd he
had bought. Riding down the road behind the remuda in the
salubrious spring weather with knee-high grass and oodles of
pretty wild flowers, spirits ran high. Then we passed a nester
shack with a sad looking nester dejectedly (or so he seemed
to me) walking behind a team of broom-tailed mares pulling
a turning plough. With one accord, the punchers burst into
raucous laughter and ribald song that went:

73

> Pore old nesters got no socks,
> And they got no money for the missionary box.

Also, another:

> They was a old nester, and he had a wooden leg,
> And he always chawed terbacker, if terbacker he could beg.
> He was chinchy with his money and never wore no socks;
> But he always had terbacker in his old terbacker box.

The ranch owner shared the poke's feelings, but for other reasons. Their presence fouled up his operations, especially if the nester had fenced off his pre-emption in the middle of the ranchman's spread. His fences were not much count, so that the rancher's stock broke into the nester's crops, creating damaging complications.

A few of these nesters were in fact squatters, drifters with families, always plenty of dogs and a few old rough milk cows and hogs—all pestiferous to the range cattle. Such nesters were generally accused of varying their diet of pork and rabbits by knocking off a fat yearling now and then. This stigma applied to the whole tribe—the good with the bad—and the nester usually returned the dislike with interest. Things could get pretty sticky when the nesters came pouring into an area. However, many of the nesters had pretty daughters, and marrying into a nester family could bring drastic change to the high and mighty cowpoke's attitude.

My best example of this was the saga of John Brown, a pure D cowman who had been up the trail and all over until he became my father's ranch foreman, and he was a dandy. He was one of the kindest and most considerate men I ever knew, and he had a special knack of getting along with kids. He would let us eat his canned peaches and tomatoes when we were near the bunkhouse fishing, and sometimes might even go with us. He would even saddle up a couple of gentle ponies and take my brother and me out in the pasture with him. As a result, we adored him.

When he quit his job, two small boys almost went into decline. It all came about when my father decided to put in a small field to raise grain for the saddle horses. He had the land grubbed and ordered a Cassidy riding plough to break the sod. He was resting the ranch that summer, and John had very little to do except to entertain us kids, always underfoot in the summertime. So father told John to round up the remuda and break six or eight of the larger horses to work in harness. That was all right with John until he casually asked who was going to do the ploughing. When told that he had been elected, the gentle John blew his top. "Me, plough— me, a nester—No, sir, Mr. Sims, I like you and I'd like to work for you as long as I can, but, Mr. Sims, I'll just be damned if I'll become a nester!!" So, John loaded his belongings on a packhorse and took off for the high plains where there was nothing but ranches, and a cowhand could keep his self-respect.

Years later, when I was a grown man, we had a big cotton crop (Yes, sir, we had become nesters ourselves by then.) Our renters were doing their ginning all over the area, and I was putting in all my time just keeping up with things. One Saturday I was checking the gins in Miles Station (Miles, now), and the town was jumping with nesters, cotton buyers, and cotton-laden wagons everywhere you looked. I noted a typical-looking nester coming along the street with a wagon loaded with cotton bales. By his side on the spring seat was a woman with a baby in her lap and a couple of towheads standing at her back. Something was very familiar about the man, and I asked a bystander if he knew the man on the wagon. It transpired that his name was Brown. Something clicked loudly in my mind. I stopped the cotton-hauler and asked him if his name was John Brown. After looking me over, he grinned widely and said: "Ain't you old man Sims's boy?" After warm greetings were exchanged, he introduced me to his family. I said, "Well, John, it seems that you turned nester after all." His wife laughed aloud, and John managed a sort of hangdog smile and said: "Yep, I married a nester gal, and she soon convinced me that farming beats cow

punchin' all holler when it comes to providin' for a family."
The mills of the Gods may grind slowly," but they did an
exceedingly fine job on John.

I think old man Becton—any man 45 years or thereabouts
was called "old man" then—was the first real farmer in our
section. Others might farm a little on the side, but Mr. Becton farmed exclusively. He was a fine man and became a
leading citizen of our county, but even he bore the stigma
among the cow gentry. At first he was regarded as a misguided visionary who thought he could make a living farming in West Texas. My father met him shortly after he had
settled on his farm and took an immediate liking to him, remarking to me that he hated to see a good man so "tetched
in the head" that he thought he could grow cotton in Concho
County. But Mr. Becton showed the scoffers what a real
farmer could do. He made a good living for his family and
accumulated quite a stake. He became an influential and
respected citizen of our county, and his descendants have
played an important part in the development of the area. He
and a few more of his ilk kind of changed our attitude toward
nesters.

However, the nester's life wasn't all beer and skittles by
any means. He had to do his work the hard way and afoot.
He had to put up his land walking behind a turning plow,
muscling along the straightaway, dragging it out and lifting
it around at the turns by main strength and awkwardness.
It could be a real rib-buster when it hit a rock or a stump.
Then he harrowed it by dragging some weighted mesquite
trees over the land to smooth it for planting. He would piece
out his lines with a long rope so he could walk behind his
harrow, and nobody, but nobody, knows what real dust is
unless he has followed one of these makeshifts for twelve or
fourteen straight hours. If it was dry—which it generally
was most of the time, he could hardly see his team through
the fog of dust. It didn't take long to raise a sweat, thereby
creating a mud problem mighty hard on the eyes and the
complexion. When he came in at night, it was difficult to
determine his race or national origin.

After the land was prepared, he had to wait for a planting season in the ground. When the rain did come, and it always does come just before we go to hell in West Texas, old "Peers, the ploughman," really had to get busy with the planting. At first, an assistant, usually a kid, dropped the seed by hand in a furrow while the farmer covered it with his turning plow. Then some smart boy came up with a mechanical planter, a crude sort of a contraption mounted on one wheel and pulled by one horse, but it did the work. After the crop was up, our agriculturist hooked a horse onto the "Georgia Stock," equipped with a buzzard-wing sweep, to do the cultivating. This was also a walking job. Then he had to chop out the crop with a weedin' hoe. Just try slingin' a hoe from sunup to sundown and see how many aching muscles there can be in one human body.

If the hail or the drought or grasshoppers or a ranchman's stock didn't destroy the crop, the happy soil-tiller had to pitch in and gather it by hand. I sure would admire to see some of our gentlemen farmers of today pulling corn or picking cotton. Cotton-picking can be about the most backbreakin' job imaginable, and is it rough on the hands! My, my, about the only vacation a cotton farmer ever had was when he hauled his picked cotton to the gin. He never knew whether the gin would be overcrowded or broke down, so he always took a sack of horse feed and a snack of vittles along. If he had to stay overnight at the gin yard, his cotton made a fine bed, and he could do considerable visitin' with his neighbors. Then he had to match wits with the buyer, who held all the cards, as he was in constant touch with the market. The farmer just flat couldn't win for losing. Then he took the proceeds to the merchant who had "run him." By the time he had paid the amount of his account and the scandalously high interest, he didn't have much left. No wonder that "he didn't have no money for the missionary box." But he stuck it out, and a grandson could very well now be a Ph.D. out of Harvard or M.I.T.

Just compare the nester's lot with that of his counterpart today who doesn't have to set foot on the ground except to walk from his pickup to his tractor-drawn six- or eight-row planter or cultivator. But this fellow has many problems that the old nester did not have. I have always stoutly maintained that no man ever really knows the facts of life until he has run a country store, run for county office and raised two crops of cotton. Me, I orter know, I've done 'em all.

The Sims Ranch foreman in the milo patch, 1925

Our first exposure to the nester, en masse, came with the Eola land rush, somewhere in the middle 1890's. There were many thousands of acres of state-owned land all over our area. These lands were usually fenced in the pastures of the larger spreads, and the state got little income therefrom, as many of the ranchmen blandly ignored the ridiculously low rentals. A state law was enacted throwing a lot of this "vacant" land open to actual settlers. The land was classified into various grades, according to its potential, from good agricultural to arid grazing. The number of acres a man could file on depended on the classification, from a half section to four sections. These were designated homesteads, and the applicant had to improve his place and spend a certain length of time out of each year actually living on the land in order to "prove it up." The price was small, and the settler had up to forty years to pay it off at low interest rates.

The ranchmen in the arid grazing region were quick to sense the possibilities of acquiring a lot of cheap land. So a man would hire one of his hands to file on four sections and advance him the money to build a house and fence the land. The puncher would live on the place, usually batching it, and work for his boss on the ranch most of the time. When his time was up, the rancher paid him $1,000 for his claim and assumed the payments to the state. It was all done legal and above board. No mineral rights were reserved by the state, and many of these homesteads became the basis for substantial fortunes when oil was struck in West Texas. I wonder why I didn't have sense enough to go out West and do some filing myself.

There were a good many of these agricultural surveys in Concho County, principally in what is known as the Eola community. When this land became available, a small land rush ensued. I was a young button that summer, staying on the ranch with the foreman and his wife, and we knew nothing about the "opening up." One day, just after lunch, Mr. Tom left headquarters on his usual rounds. Night came and he didn't show up, so I did the milking and feeding chores. We waited supper on him for quite a spell and sat around waiting up for him. He had had some trouble with trespassers, even had to run them off with his gun. As the night wore on, his wife and I became uneasy, and about eleven o'clock, I decided to saddle the night horse and ride into town for help. Just then we heard horses crossing the rocky ford on the river. Two men showed up and told us what had happened. Mr. Tom had gone by town for something and learned that the rush was in progress, so he lit out for the scene. He found a vacant survey all staked off and attached the required notices on each corner stake. These two men had adjoining claims. It was all such a jumped-up affair that none of them had grub or bedding with them. A few disappointed late-comers, who might become claim-jumpers, were prowling around, so our men had to stay on their claims. Tom had his gun with him and volunteered to guard the claims while the two men went to the ranch for food and bedrolls. The lady hurriedly baked up a flour sack full of biscuits and stripped the kitchen of meat and canned goods. So, I importantly ran the spread for a few days until our boss returned. After his filing was completed, he decided that he was not cut out for a nester and sold his claim to a tardy arrival.

Incidentally, he did become a nester after all. When he left the ranch, he bought a small place of his own and branched out to become one of our largest and most successful farmers.

These actual settlers stayed on and developed that land into one of our most prosperous farming communities. They were good people and had a worthy impact on our later history.

My own first contact with the genus nester came when I was a teen-age cowpoke in the spring of 1902. I left headquarters early one chilly morning headed for the north side of the ranch. About sunup, I heard hammering and went over to see what it was all about, and there in the middle of the ranch was a crew of men building a house. I indignantly inquired what they meant by building a house on my daddy's land. A large, grizzled man truculently replied that he was building the house on *his land*. A puzzled and frightened teen-ager made immediate tracks back home to make an excited report. Father just grinned, told me to get in the buggy with him and left for the site of operations. After friendly greetings and amiable discussion, it developed that a real estate agent had located the man on the one small school survey on the ranch. Father, of course, was familiar with the survey lines, and he advised the man to halt operations until they could get a surveyor on the ground to make the exact location. Sure enough, the agent, who obtained his information from an old county map, had located the man on the wrong spot. The unfinished house was picked up and moved to the right location. Mr. Dave fenced his place and put in a farm on rather poor land. After two or three dry years, he threw up the sponge, sold his holdings to Father and moved to town and put in a wagon yard.

That fall a man from Bell County heard about the place and rented it for farming. He was an experienced farmer and got a nice cotton crop up to a good stand, only to have it wilt away in the drought. He came over to the ranch house on August 15th, downcast but game, and bantered my father to rent it to him for another year, as he just knew that it was good cotton country even if we did have a lot of dry weather. Father felt so sorry for him that he agreed to rent him the land and advance him $300.00 to make the crop on. That night it came a whopping big rain—further proof of the old saying that "just before we go to hell in West Texas it rains." Mr. Warren made one of the best crops ever raised on the ranch. After the crop had been gathered and sold, Uncle Bob (another Uncle Bob) came over to headquarters to settle up. Father remarked that it looked like he would not be called on to finance the next year's crop. Bob laughed outright and said: "Mr. Sims, that day in August when I came over to see you, it looked like I would make about a half a bale of cotton on the whole place, but I gathered might near a bale to the acre. I have more cash money than I ever had before in my life. Why, my old woman has bought some of every-thing in Sears-Roebuck's catalogue."

When it was all totted up, our rent came to $12.00 per acre, about twice what the land was worth, and that did it. We were going to get filthy rich renting land for cotton!

Father, never a man to do things by halves, really went to town. We never stopped until we had 4,000 acres in culti-vation. Clearing, grubbing, breaking, building the necessary six-room houses, sheds, pens and fencing the horse-cow traps took quite a wad of money, financed largely through the sale of 100 acres near what is now downtown San Antonio for $25,000. How crazy can we get?

Although we had plenty of mules that we had raised, the

harness, farming tools, seed and feed came to quite a penny. But things worked so well at first that we thought we really had it made. Renters came pouring in from Bell, Milam and other cotton-raising counties. We had no difficulty in renting the land for half the crops. We had several good years, and gradually quite a community with its own church and school grew up on the Sims Ranch. They were good people and had no difficulty in obtaining credit from the local merchants, and things rocked along fine.

But the droughts came, and things went haywire. The outlook was so bleak that the merchants withdrew credit, so we just had to take over and establish a commissary. Me, I was elected storekeeper. Once a month we would take their orders for supplies for the ensuing month. That way, we would not have to keep the store open but a couple of days a month—that's what we thought—and then came the "John Part" for me. I had to quit all my other work and become a danged storekeeper. Here again, I learned the facts of life. Something would have been overlooked on the grocery lists or underestimates made. The prime necessities usually underestimated were Brown's Mule Chewing Tobacco and Garrett's Snuff. So, the store had to be kept open even though the trade was mighty scattered. It was about as lonesome as being in jail, without any opportunity of savoring the finer things of life, notably *fishing*. Although I closed on Sunday, I couldn't go fishing, for my good Methodist mother sternly forbade any such desecration of the Sabbath. I sure got tired of my job; that is, until we made the big crop, and then I longed for the good old lazy days.

During the years, our people had accumulated enough to buy their own teams and tools and were farming on the third and fourth. But they were so heavily in debt to us that the outlook was mighty squally. There was so much more cotton than the renters could pick themselves that we had to import some hundreds of Negroes from East Texas and Mexicans from down San Antonio way. These people were housed in tents, army style, and were a happy lot. All was well—until. The gins got so far behind that we had piles of picked cotton

The Sims Store, 1886

on the ground in every field. Then it started raining, and it seemed to me that it rained every other day for weeks and weeks. That's one time in my life that I got too much rain. Trouble broke out among the idle men, and, to cap it all, smallpox broke out. We lined 'em up and vaccinated them like cattle, and the plague was controlled without a single fatality. (That's one record that I am really proud of.) When it did dry up, the cotton was such low grade that it took the proceeds of a bale to pay for the picking and ginning. Something just had to be done, and, like always, things worked out. I went to Galveston and made a trade with the Kempners who agreed to advance me $25 on every bale shipped to them for warehousing—the idea was to hold the cotton for a rise in the market. The market was so low that there wasn't any way but up. After a hair-raising experience with a hurricane which did small damage to the cotton stored in the concrete warehouses, the market began to climb. Finally, late the next summer, I cut loose when it reached 10½ cents. This was enough to pay everybody off with substantial balances coming to the nesters. I then became their fair-haired boy.

A good many decided to move on while the going was good, so we had to settle for a few who were not so good and dependable. The next year was just sort of so-so, and we became mighty tired of farming. By this time the renters had accumulated cows and work stock until the traps could no longer accommodate them. So the hungry stock simply broke out, largely over busted fences and conveniently opened gates. Result—they et us out of house and home, and we sold our own stock down to a nubbin. By that time, we had a belly full of nesters; besides, the make-up of our people had somewhat deteriorated, as the thriftier ones had bought places of their own.

Unpleasant incidents kept piling up, culminating in one of the renter's being caught in a neighbor's henhouse. That did it! We just didn't want no damn chicken thieves on our place. Along in the fall, my father hitched up his buggy and went over to fire old chicken-lifter. He did not return until after dark. I became uneasy and started out to look for him. Then I heard him coming, and he was singing "Amazing Grace," a sure sign that he was mighty well pleased about something. When I met him, he joyously yelped: "By gad, Orland, I have done it. I felt so good when I fired old chicken-stealer that I decided to get rid of another one of our pets who was something of a skunk. That felt so good that I just kept on until I had fired the whole smear, good, bad and indifferent. We now own the place again."

As mentioned above, the calibre of our renters diminished as the years went by. During the last year or so before Father "cleaned the plow," we had some pretty onery critters billeted on us. One bunch, consisting of several families and birds of a feather were especially no 'count. They were not very strong on work, but they were tops when it came to enjoying life. They thinned out the catfish and dealt misery to the coons, possums and squirrels. Every "Sattiday" night, a family would give a sociable, with dancin', drinkin' and a little fightin' thrown in.

Prohibition was in force, but these party-goers managed pretty well on patent medicines. These tonics were composed of laxative herbs laced lavishly with high voltage alcohol. One day I passed by an old geezer's place and saw him out at the barn. As I rode up, I noticed a hefty pile of "medicine" bottles back of the barn. I innocently (?) remarked that it appeared that he had a lot of illness in his family and expressed my sympathy. He sheepishly admitted that the contents of the bottles had served as refreshments rather than medicaments. I asked him if the medicine made good cocktails, and he replied that if you held your breath and drunk it straight out of the bottle, it went down tolerably smoothlike; and although it called for considerable trottin', it sure made the drunk come! We got rid of those celebrants as soon as their crops were marketed.

After all these people left, we had so many teams and tools on hand that we decided to farm it ourselves with hired hands. We got the crops up to a good stand, and things looked mighty rosy. Then the sky fell in on us—the grasshoppers swept across our lovely young cotton like a prairie fire—and that's all she wrote.

We gave a big barbecue and auctioned off our teams and tools, closed up the houses, opened the gates and went back to ranching. Now you know what I mean when I say that a cotton-grower should be entitled to at least a dollar a pound for all of that commodity he can raise.

A good many years later when tractors came into use, we did go back to some farming, raising only small grains and feed stuffs for our livestock. We did all right, and the farms still remain, but they are stock farms now. You bet, we never planted another stalk of cotton. So, in a way, we are still nesters like John Brown.

As I grow older and a mite wiser (I hope) the term "nester" no longer bears the connotation of the scorn of yesteryear. Don't get the idea that our old nesters were all crumbs, for, by and large, they were real, honest-to-God, down to earth, good people. I learned to love and respect them, and, in my heart, I cherish my memories of them. They really taught me a lot.

They were *sui generis* with a quaint, down-to-earth philosophy of their own. By and large, they were a happy-go-lucky crew, not too thrifty and not too ambitious, and not too overly concerned about the morrow which always had taken care of itself—and, anyway, what's the use of worryin'? With all their hard work, their rather primitive living conditions and their limited horizons, they made do with what they had and managed to get more out of life than I did, and I had a mighty good time!

With the laying by of their crops came their time for relaxing, loafing and entertaining. They were visiting, partying, catfishing, squirrel hunting and just frolicking around. They went picnicking on the river; my, my, what good eatin's they had—catfish fried in deep fat, squirrel stew, an occasional barbecued goat or calf that the boss furnished, luscious watermelons, mushmelons, roastin' ears, green "okry," big termaters, cucumbers, fresh black-eye peas, and the delicious cakes, puddin's and pies that their lady folks came up with. Late summer was also a time for barbecues and revival meetin's. Believe me, they enjoyed both—the eatin' and the "gettin' religion" again.

Most of them were honest, but sort of careless about paying their debts, and I had to stay on the job lest they spend the proceeds of their crops rather than paying me off in full. I recall one loveable happy-go-lucky old rooster who was especially careless about money matters. Uncle Ras (most of the older men were affectionately called "Uncle") was a very good farmer and always made a good crop if the weather gave him half a chance. One especially good year, he had some $5,000 clear after he had paid off all his obligations. He opened an account at the bank and purely adored writing checks. I realized that he would soon fritter his money away, and I looked around for a farm he could buy. I found a very desirable 320 acre tract of raw land nearby that could be bought for ten dollars an acre, 25 percent down and the balance payable in ten annual installments at reasonable interest. He could easily make the down payment, fence, clear and break the land, and build an acceptable house with the $5,000. He had good teams and tools and three strapping sons who could do the work. Very proud of myself, I hustled over to his house and told him about my find. He studied awhile and said: "Now, Orlin, I know you mean well, and I appreciate you thinking of me, but Fatha was a renta and Grandfatha was a renta, and what was good enough for them is good enough for me. I don't have to worry none about no land debts, interest, taxes and sich like, and besides, if I owned a farm, I would be tied down to it. Now, if I take a notion to move, all I have to do is to load my plunder on the wagons, help the old lady ketch the chickens, call the dogs and pull my freight."

His reaction made me so mad that I was fitten to bust, and I cussed him out but good! He just grinned and said: "That's the way my stick floats." (Incidentally, as I write this, I am madder at myself than I was at Uncle Ras. Why didn't I buy the damned land myself? It is now in cultivation and is well worth $90,000.) There you are! *Ay de mi!* After I had spent my ire on the old man, I told him that he would fool all his money away and be around to borrow from me before he got his next crop laid by. He laughed good-naturedly and 'lowed as how that much money would run him two or three years.

His old lady went to work on her Sears-Roebuck catalogue, and Ras did a land office business lending small sums to all and sundry. He loved his "toddy" and placed frequent orders with the Old Hayner distillery, a mail-order outfit widely patronized in our county which was dry. Seemed like every time I went by the depot a fresh case of twenty-four quarts of whiskey was waiting for Uncle Ras to pick up. One day I rode by his house and was greeted by a pack of fine-looking hounds. I asked Uncle where he got those good-looking dogs, and he replied that he had ordered them from an advertisement, admitting that they had cost him $40 apiece. That was big money in them days. I furiously told him that he needed a pack of hounds less than he needed a hole in his head. He rather lamely defended his purchase as being a good investment, as 'coons, 'possums and other varmints were getting all the old lady's chickens. On being reminded that $40 would replenish her stock of chickens several times, he sheepishly admitted that he just enjoyed having a pack of hounds around him. His enjoyment didn't last long, as his hounds ran off or got poisoned on nearby sheep pastures.

I proved to be a good prophet, only I gave him too much time to go broke. One morning early in June, with three cultivations and much chopping before the crop would be laid by, Uncle Ras gaily came into my office. He sat around for some time, chatting amiably about the weather—that it was gettin' a mite dry, but that his crops was lookin' mighty nice and so on. I rudely interrupted his monologue by asking him how much he needed. He sheepishly replied that he only needed a little grocery money as they were might nigh out of vittles at his house. By the time his cotton was marketed, his grocery money had become a sizeable sum, but this didn't bother him one bit. Oh, well, come easy, go easy!

Many of these people were real humorists, and one could have a peck of fun just sitting around listening to a bunch of them gassing. They were great jokers, and the pranks they would pull on one another were outlandishly ridiculous and comical. Every now and then I get a good laugh when I recall some of their capers.

One of my favorites was "Uncle Bob ———." Seems like I have mentioned an awful lot of uncle "Bobs," but they were really named Robert, Bob for short, stemming, no doubt, from the love and veneration that their parents had for General Robert E. Lee. In illustration of this veneration was an incident that occurred during the dirt road days when I was making an automobile trip to Austin. One of our passengers was a cultured, southern lady who was a torn down Daughter of the Confederacy. Another one was a crusty old Yankee from the state of Maine. There was no love lost between these two, and an occasional caustic remark did nothing to smooth their feathers. As we were passing the site of the old fort near Burnett, old curmudgeon casually remarked: "Did you know that old Bob Lee was once stationed there?" The lady fuzzed up like a mad cat and wanted to know whom he was talking about. The sour reply was: "Why, old Bob Lee, that old renegade, rebel general." Never, in all my life, have I seen such a shocked expression on anyone's face as on that good "Daughter's." This was nothing but sheer sacrilege to the good lady, who cast aside her well-bred manners and tore into Old Grumpy like a veritable fishwife. Boy, she really took the hide! He crustily retired into his shell, and we heard no more out of him for the rest of the trip. He did not make the return trip with us, preferring to pay his own way back home on the train rather than again face that outraged virtue.

But, getting back to our knittin', this particular "Uncle Bob" was a very small, very homely, very cocky redhead with all the combativeness of a cock sparrow, and he never failed to speak his mind, regardless. He was quite fond of the wild cow's milk, partaking rather copiously on occasion. When he reached the right stage of exhilaration, he was wont to wax oratorical regarding the merits and virtues of one Andy Jackson.

Miles Station was the railroad point for a large farming community, and 'most everybody foregathered there on Saturday afternoons, Uncle Bob usually among them. If conditions became propitious, he would loudly and vociferously proclaim the virtues of his hero. This propensity finally ran him afoul of the local law. Some of the local better element (especially the good ladies) complained to the authorities. On one especially busy Saturday afternoon, when our orator was making an impassioned address to the crowd on the bank corner, the law callously stepped in. Bob's cronies were admonished to get him off the streets if they didn't want him flung into the pokey. So they took him to the wagon yard and bedded him down in the hay barn, where he promptly went bye-bye.

Along about sundown, our hero awoke refreshed and in fine fettle but still a little high, and wandered from his *boudoir*. Just then a stranger and his wife, perched high on the spring seat of a wagon, drew up in front of old Robert, who stared unbelievingly up at the woman and loudly proclaimed to all and sundry: " 'Fore God, fellers, that's the ugliest woman ever I see!" The woman was *rather plain*, and her looks were in no wise enhanced by her garb (a slatted sunbonnet and a Mother Hubbard dress that could ruin the looks of a Dior model). The crowd tittered, and the huge scowling man clambered down from the wagon with a wicked-looking black snake whip in his hand. He thrust a menacing face down into that of his tormentor and growled: "Sir, I'll have you understand this lady is my wife."

> Ah, inspiring, bold John Barleycorn!
> What dangers Thou cans't make us scorn.
> With tuppeny ale, we hear nae evil;
> Dith usquebae we'll face the deevil.

Our fortified and unabashed hero ruffled up his feathers like a cock sparrow that I once saw eye-ball down a big Dominecker rooster in our chicken yard, and manfully returning scowl for scowl, bleated: "Sorry, friend, I hate to say it, but me and Andy Jackson never told a lie—that's the ugliest lady ever I see." The tittering crowd gathered around, and the large man lamely said: "Well, you must remember what the Good Book says: 'Beauty is only skin deep," Without hesitation, our old cock belted right back: "Well, by God, skin 'er, my friend, skin 'er!"

Alas, these lusty old characters have departed the scene, and their watered-down prototypes of today are scientific businessmen, knowledgeable but unpicturesque. To me, "nesterism" like "cowpokeese" has sort of lost its flavor.

PIONEERS

It was my good fortune to know personally, or through thoroughly reliable observers, a number of the original pioneers of our area, notably the Tankerslys and the Coffeys. They were brave, honest, God-fearing, kind, hospitable people, the kind that were the foundation stones of our nation. They opened up a new land for our inheritance, and their influence for good still lingers on. We keep their memories green. Although I am now related through marriage (a charming young descendant of theirs lately coming into the Sims family), I never knew the first Tankerslys personally, but my father did, and he held them in high respect and esteem.

One of the earliest dwellings in St. Angela, 1878

I did know Uncle Rich and Aunt Sally Coffey who settled on the Concho River "way back before the owls hooted the first time," as he put it. Mr. Coffey was a pleasant, genial man, endowed with a God-given sense of humor that enabled him to laugh even at himself, and he delighted to recount many tales on himself. He was one of the most entertaining men I ever knew, yet he was a thinker, a good man, and a dedicated Mason who never missed a meeting of his lodge if he was within riding distance of it.

There were plenty of Indians around when these people

first settled here, but they managed to get along with them by being hospitable and keeping their eyes peeled. The women fed the Indians (and you never saw one that wasn't hungry) and the men kept their hands on their guns.

Of the many yarns Uncle Rich loved to recount was the one about the time the Injuns caught him with his britches down. Relations had been good with the wandering bands, and they hadn't seen an Indian in months. Uncle Rich got kind of careless and failed to take his rifle along one morning when he went to plow a small field within some 300 yards of the house—a good substantial house made of logs that was a regular fort. On this particular morning, Uncle Rich was about midway across his field when he spied a bunch of Indians coming up on the far side. Discretion always being the better part of valor, Mr. Coffey really lit out for home. When he broke to run, the Indians, according to custom, began to screech and yell as they took out after him. Aunt Sally heard the yelpings and immediately knew what was up. She grabbed the rifle, stood in the door and yelled: "Run, Rich, run, Rich," keeping up her adjurations until he reached the house and fell, exhausted, on the floor. Aunt Sally slammed and bolted the door. As soon as he could catch his breath, Uncle Rich panted: "My God, Sally, did you think I was throwin' off on that race?" The Indians fooled around out of rifle range and rode off yelling and waving good-naturedly at the Coffeys. They acted kind of friendly like, but they would cheerfully have lifted Uncle Rich's hair if they could have caught up with him.

I had a tie in with an Uncle Rich incident many years later. We were rounding up and although I had the outside swing, I arrived at my appointed place well ahead of the drive. I was roosting on a high point east of Little Concho Creek and noticed a small half circle of good-sized rocks. My father drove up in his buggy, and I asked him if he had any idea what those rocks meant. He did, as it had been pointed out to him by one of his hands who was at Uncle Rich's home when the incident occurred.

A lone rider was jumped by a small band of Indians a

mile or two west of the site. During the chase, the Indians got close enough that a long arrow shot wounded his horse in a hip. The horse, weakened by loss of blood, made it to this point where he fell. Using the horse's body as a start, the man hastily rolled the rocks in place. He had a good rifle and stood off the Indians. Just after dark a heavy storm blew up, and the experienced plainsman, knowing that his foes would not attack during the storm, took his saddle, rifle and bridle off the horse's body and started out afoot for the Coffey place some fifteen miles away. The rain continued for most of the night, and the man made it to Uncle Rich's place early the next morning. Saddles and rifles were so scarce and hard to come by that the man risked his hair to salvage them.

I was poking around the rock pile and found an iron arrow point. I learned later that other points, both flint and iron, had been found there, and I have no doubt that it was from an arrow used in that fight. It looked like it had been made from a barrel hoop. The old barrels had heavy iron hoops, and the Indians gathered them in wherever they found a busted barrel. With the aid of a cold chisel and file bought from a trader, good points could be made. This was a well-made point, but you could discern the chisel or file marks on its sides. I treasured this artifact, but I made the mistake of showing it to an archeologist who swiped it from me. I did not discover the loss until he was long gone. Moral: Never show a good artifact to a dam' archeologist.

My parents arrived on the scene after things became a little more settled. This account of their experience is by no means an attempted biography, but rather it is a sketchy picture of later pioneer living. Their experiences were typical of those early arrivals and for that reason are recorded herein.

After the Indians were put on reservations, settlers really poured in. They ranged in class from the shiftless, ne'er-do-wells to the substantial people who wanted to put down their roots and establish homes in a new country. Of course, I place my parents in the latter class, the tops. They were natives of the State of Missouri and of thrifty and substantial parentage. Both had good educations according to the standards of their time and were truly the "salt of the earth."

Father, a young man who wanted wider horizons than Missouri, decided to try Texas along with three other young men. They went by train to Birdville (Fort Worth), arriving in the middle seventies. Buffalo hunting was in full swing and hides were stacked in huge piles all around the railroad yards. Our adventurers didn't cotton to hide hunting, preferring to go into ranching. So they bought saddle horses, a wagon, and supplies and set off to hunt for the land of their dreams. They "kind of sauntered along" to San Antonio viewing out the country. They stayed around San Antonio for some time, but three of them got so homesick that they returned to Missouri, where they eked out humdrum lives farming. So my father had to go it alone. He heard of the Concho, bought two flocks of poor quality Mexican sheep because they were cheap, a couple of wagons, ox teams, a few saddle horses, hired some hands, and set out for the "good land." He wound up on Brady Creek in McCulloch County, west of where the town of Brady now stands. He settled his outfit, tied some grub and a couple of blankets on his saddle, and rode toward the West. When he reached the prairie south of Paint Rock, he found "The Promised Land:" a sea of grass, stirrup high, rippling in the breeze; wild flowers everywhere; every draw a clear running brook full of fish; wild game all about; a herd of mustangs, snorting and circling him; but never a man or cow-brute anywhere in sight. He continued on over the Concho River, deep and clear-running with great groves of pecan trees lining the banks, and this was *Ultima Thule*. I can picture him taking off his hat and reverently intoning "Amazing Grace" as was his wont when well-pleased. He had found his home.

A drifting cow outfit had bought a few surveys of land on the north side of the river and had built a small, one-room picket house. He moved his stock there and bought out the cattlemen, who had their eyes on greener pastures farther West. This became the nucleus of his holdings whereon he lived out his life.

He had it mighty tough at first. The neighboring cow outfits didn't relish the idea of having sheep in their area, but he out-talked them and tended strictly to his own knitting. He didn't bother them, and they didn't bother him. His sheep were a light-shearing, coarse-wooled type, and he knew practically nothing about handling them. He learned the hard way. His nearest railroad point was Round Rock, some 200 miles away, and it took ten days or more for his ox wagons to get his wool to market and return with six months' supplies. For the first two or three years, these supplies were pretty skimpy—corn meal, a little flour, fat bacon, black molasses, salt, sugar, coffee and plenty of chewing tobacco. They could eke out their food with deer, antelope, wild turkeys, and even squirrels and (as a last resort) rabbits. But they had to get mighty hongry before they would stoop to eat rabbits. They used mutton taller to piece out the lard, which usually gave out before the half-year trek to market. Their clothes generally wore out, so they were pretty sketchy and covered with multicolored patches when they finally got to town. As he expressed it, he had to live like a coyote, domiciled in the 12x16 dirt-floored picket house, which served as parlor, dining room, bedroom and kitchen. They didn't have a bathroom—the bushes and the river provided those facilities.

After some three years, when he began to get the hang of things and to prosper, he was breeding up his sheep, picking up a few cows, and beginning to buy up more land (always "on time" whenever he got a few dollars ahead). By the time the T & P Railroad was built into Abilene only 90 miles away, he figured he had it made.

He helped organize Concho County and locate the county seat on the section where the town of Paint Rock now stands. They got the name, Paint Rock, from the Indian rock paintings nearby. This site was selected as it was near a good ford on the Concho River, pretty hard to find then as the river ran so boldly that you had to swim it at most places. Now, you can cross it dry-shod at most of the old fords—another example of our ignoring conservation, our lack of foresight, and our plain hoggishness. Nature was bountiful, and these pioneers could not visualize it any other way. The heavy sod and the frequent prairie fires kept down the brush and mesquites. If the range played out, you just moved farther on. Now, there ain't no more "farther on," and your range just keeps getting scantier and scantier.

Actual settlers began to pour in, and Paint Rock developed into quite a town with a store, a saloon, a boardin' house, barbershop and a courthouse of sorts. The town was first located on the wrong survey, and several houses had been erected before the mistake was discovered. So they just had to pick up the town and move it about a half-mile east. My father gleefully related that moving. One of the more important buildings was the saloon, and it took two let-out wagons to do the job. They just jacked it up, slid the lengthened running gear underneath and hitched some teams to them. The town drunk was a fiddler, and he clambered up on top of the building, playing "Turkey in the Straw." The teams were kind of wild and took fright at the music, so they ran away with old virtuoso sawing away and yelling accompaniment. They only dumped the building once, but they got it in place all right. The other less necessary buildings were moved with less fanfare, and the town was on its way.

A good many years later, when prohibition had arrived, Father bought that old saloon building and moved it out to the ranch for a barn and feed house for our milk cows. I'll bet that I have milked thousands of gallons of the lacteal fluid in and around that old barn. Some of that old lumber is still around—proof of the quality of our early lumber.

By this time, Father was well enough fixed to build a five-room house and go back to Missouri for his sweetheart. My mother, one of the handsomest and most attractive women I have ever known, was quite a belle in Kentucky and Missouri, and I could never figure how she could give up her glamorous life and move to a raw frontier. Ah, me, *amor vinces omnia*! They rode the train to Abilene where Father had left his buggy and team, loaded their furniture and household plunder on freight wagons and started the long tedious drive to their home. They got as far as Old Runnels, a few miles north of where Ballinger now stands, sometime after dark. Before they reached the hotel, Mother heard a lot of dogs barking and howling and was absolutely terrified when Father told her that they were "kioty wolves." During the night, Mother was awakened by something dripping on the bed, but Father assured her that it was nothing. When they got up the next morning, that nothing was a sizeable pool of blood. A man who had been shot occupied the room immediately over them, and during the night, his wound leaked through the bandages, through the cracks in the floor and on to their bed. The frightened, queasy bride was persuaded to try to eat some breakfast as she would get mighty hungry before they got to their destination that evening. The waiter, a roughly dressed cowpoke, unshaven and wearing a grimy, split flour sack apron, slouched in bearing their breakfast, consisting of some huge, soggy, sody biscuits and a dish of fried steak swimming in grease, with a grubby thumb stuck well down in the sauce. That did it! No breakfast for Mama.

They camped out in the newly built, unpainted house until their plunder finally arrived. They had a fireplace, a good wood cookstove, a couple of tin washtubs and a john out in the backyard. The town waterworks consisted of a water wagon pulled by two burros. The water was poured into two barrels by the side of the yard fence, and that was it. I have marveled through the years how a beautiful, cultured Southern lady ever put up with such doings. I wonder how a modern debutante would react under such circumstances. These old-time ladies, and I do mean ladies, truly had what it takes. No trees, no bluegrass, no fresh green vegetables or fruits, no bath facilities except the washtub, no church, no doctor, no companionship except for a few pore, wore out, pioneer women and rough, gun-toting men.

They made it all right, though. Father became well-to-do by the standards of the times, and she gave birth to and reared five sons. I'll say, they did their part.

The ranch was fenced, a good courthouse was built, and

waterworks of a sort were put into operation. The railroad built into Ballinger, and Mother could take her brood back to Missouri during the dry, hot summers.

Scattering preachers occasionally drifted in, and services were held in the courthouse, which also doubled in brass as the dance hall for the dances on the Fourth of July and Christmas. But Mother, a torn down Methodist, frowned upon such frivolities as the square dance and the shocking waltz. The whole community enjoyed the courthouse, what with the enormous tree on Christmas Eve, the ice cream and oyster suppers, parties and the revival meetings. The latter provided plenty of spiritual exaltation and rededication: but, I'll have to say that more than a few of the converts sort of backslid come the Christmas dances. They got themselves churched pronto, but were admitted back into the fold when the summer meetin's cranked them up again.

An adequate schoolhouse and a couple of churches were built by the mid-nineties, and an enterprising merchant even hauled ice by wagon from Ballinger. There were no iceboxes available, but an ingenious carpenter turned out a good substitute by making a large and a small box with sawdust in between. This innovation was much superior to the old milk cooler, a weird contraption turned out by the local tin smithy. It consisted of a number of metal trays superimposed on each other. The top tray was filled with water and the lower trays with milk, butter and other perishables. A large white cloth was spread over the whole thing and allowed to hang well into the water. The cloth soaked up the water, and it dripped down the sides—an evaporative cooler that kept things pretty cool. But it did not compare to the primitive icebox; besides, it didn't furnish ice for cold drinks and ice cream.

After a boy reached the mature age of seven, he was considered to have outgrown his little girl status, and his proud papa would sneak him to the barbershop and have his luxuriant curls shorn, to the urchin's joy and the distress of his weeping mother who had "lost her baby." He was now officially a male and was entitled to the habiliments thereunto appertaining. Accordingly, he was put into knee britches and long, black stockings held up by garters of "Injun rubber" or rag strings tied in place. His shoes were clumsy affairs with such straight lasts that they could be worn on either foot. For Sunday, or dress-up occasions, our proud urchin might sport a pair of brass-toed, red-topped boots, shaped something like a jockey's boots of today. The brass toes not only added a touch of eclat to the footgear, but they served the utilitarian purpose of protecting the boot toes against the wearer's propensity to kick every rock, tin can or other obstacle encountered in his path.

His undies were long-handled affairs like his daddy's and served to pad out and enhance the appearance of his spindly shanks. His winter gear was usually made of red flannel, nice and warm, but scratchy as all get out. On most kids these undies doubled as sleeping gear. They were not changed too frequently, so their wearer became somewhat fragrant, especially if he were wearing a small cheesecloth bag of asafetida around his neck which was supposed to immunize the wearer against the common cold.

Come spring, Little Lord Fauntleroy was emancipated from his flannels and footgear, and "Ye gods and little fishes," how Tommy did cavort over the landscape! No fat little colt was friskier than a barefoot boy, newly liberated from clumsy footgear and heavy, itchy flannels, and he felt like he could outrun ary jack rabbit. Of course, his feet were pretty tender at first, but after a few stone bruises and stumped toes, he could knock fire out of the rocks.

I recall one family of boys who were our envied heroes. They didn't have to wear shoes in the winter unless it was bitter cold or there was snow on the ground. They paid little attention to frosty mornings, although their feet became a mite blue before they got to the stove in the schoolhouse. In addition, they rarely had to go to Sunday School in the wintertime as "um's feet were so cracked and sore that um couldn't wear shoes," as they expressed it. It was a rare kid who didn't have at least one toe tied up in a rag, and one never has hurt until he has suffered a stone bruise.

Spring did bring a few woes besides sore tootsies because springtime was doctoring time, and one had to take his "through" of sulphur and molasses, probably the world's most nauseous dosage. A "through" lasted about a week, and by that time was supposed to have thinned down the blood. Some of the more tender-hearted mothers compromised on sassafras tea which wasn't too bad if a little sweetnin' was added to it.

Along with the vernal season came green peaches, green wild plums, wild mulberries and cactus "apples," all productive of hideous stummick aches only amenable to castor "ile" or Black Draught, about as bad as the sulphur-molasses deal. It was well known that the worse a medicine tasted, the more *efficacious* it was. If a kid was sort of puny, he might be dosed with a tonic of some other kinds of bitter "yarbs." One old doctor out our way became quite popular with the kids as he usually prescribed "sweet toddy" as a tonic. However, he didn't last long in the community as the good W.C.T.U. ladies imported another doctor who prescribed more in accordance with their ideas. We used a right smart of turpentine and red pepper for liniments. Somehow we managed to survive in spite of it all.

Our school grounds were bare dirt, usually covered with pebbles, somewhat hard on knees and bare feet. Along after shoe time in the fall, it was a rare thing to find a kid who had whole knees in his pants and stockings. We had no playground equipment, but we made do without it. Our first footballs were made out of rag strips wound to the appropriate size. They served quite well for the soccer-like game that we played. As a baseball substitute, we played town ball, using a hard, bouncy rubber ball approximately half the size of the baseball of today. Our bats were homemade out of a one-inch thick plank. They were paddle shaped and a lethal weapon when a strong boy connected with the ball. I'll bet Babe Ruth never knocked a baseball as far as a big boy could send that hard rubber missile. We had a diamond with three basemen, a pitcher and a catcher, but here the similarity practically ends. We had about three shortstops between first and second bases, a like number between second and third, and an outfield composed of all the other members of the team. We chose up sides, and every kid big enough to play made one or the other of the teams. Our basemen didn't have too much to do, as most put-outs were made by throwing the ball between the runner and his base, but the baseman could stop batted balls and touch the runner while off base. An out could be made by catching the ball on the first bounce as well as on the fly. The pitcher was closer to the batter than today, and he delivered the ball underhanded as in present-day softball. His was the most dangerous job of all. A smartly rapped ball was hard to dodge, and it sure raised a whelp when it landed on any infielder. All played without gloves, even the "hind-ketch" who stood some twenty feet back of the batter and took the ball on the first bounce. He could put a runner out by throwing between him and his base.

Thus it would seem that the side in the field had all the advantage. Don't you believe it! Most any time that wide, heavy bat connected with a ball, it produced a whizzer! Most infielders were chosen on their ability as "artful dodgers." One ingenious shortstop used a square five-gallon kerosene oilcan to handle the missiles that came his way. It wasn't considered quite sporting, but there was nothing against it in the rules. The old can was mighty well beat up by the end of the season. If a fly ball was caught in the outfield, runners had to remain on the base until the ball got back to the pitcher.

Every man on the team got to bat before the inning (ending) was over, and he continued to take his turn at bat until he got put out. As a result endings could be kind of long drawn out, and many eyes (runs) were garnered. It took quite a spell to play out an inning, and scores were rather astronomical.

We had no umpire, and you can well imagine the hassles that ensued. If the going got too tough, the teacher rang the bell for books, and the game came to an abrupt end—but not every time. I recall one occasion when the hassle developed into such a free-for-all that the teacher had to use a club. It was all good, clean fun with no carried over animosities. We could be on one team today and chosen for the other tomorrow. We never knew which side we would be on until we were chosen by one of the captains of the day. Captains, as well as players, rotated. All this evened things up and kept down real feuds.

We had one form of entertainment that seemed to be strictly a local affair, as I have never heard of its existence anywhere else, and it was called "school butter." When one of our lads became old enough (about fifteen or sixteen), he usually quit school instead of graduating. They were called "quitchuates" and most went into cowpunching. When he arrived at that status, he became mighty biggity and looked with lordly disdain on his erstwhile schoolmates, whom he called "school butters," that is, if there were not too many around, for the term was considered an obscene, deadly insult, especially when it was accompanied by a thumbing of the nose.

Our schoolhouse was right on the road to the ford across the river, and mounted men constantly passed by. If one of these squads passed by at recess or as school was turning out, hell went to poppin'! Some smart alec would be sure to yell "school butter," and the whole bunch would put spurs to their horses and take off on the run amid a shower of rocks. A plentiful supply of such ammunition was always kept piled at strategic points.

If school was out and the punchers stopped in town, the fun really began. The kids would take after them, and if they caught one, they really gave him the works. According to the code, no one in his party could come to the victim's aid. The kids swarmed him like the Lilliputs did Gulliver, pulled him down, and held him flat on the ground while a couple of them rubbed his head with a rock until he hollered "calf rope," a full and complete apology. Sometimes the victim's scalp got redder'n ary beet before he gave up and squalled apology. If he attempted reprisal, the older punchers would pull him off and make him set up the sody pop.

We kids certainly enjoyed that old sody pop as we didn't get much of it. It was put up in heavy bottles corked by a rubber gasket to which a bent wire loop was attached protruding about an inch above the bottle. The loop was struck a smart blow, forcing the gasket back down the bottleneck to make the foaming contents available. Then another good time was had by all! This popular drink came in lemon and strawberry flavors, the latter much preferred by the younger fry on account of its brilliant red color. When available, it was a prized accompaniment to picnics.

There was a cold, bold running spring at the Painted Rocks, making the site very popular for picnicking. (Incidentally, this spring hasn't flowed for the last dozen years.) One hot afternoon, when I had arrived at button status, a bunch of us had finished branding out a bunch of steers and had taken them to the river where we turned them loose. We went by the spring to rest and refresh ourselves and found a case of twenty-four bottles of assorted sody pop stashed in the spring to cool. The owners were some distance away viewing the Indian paintings, so we promptly drank up most of the pop, leaving only a few bottles of the red. We filled the empties with the spring water, pulled the wire loops back in place, thus corking the bottles before we snuck off. When the tired, hot picnickers opened their refreshments, they were mystified to find only a few flavored drinks. They indignantly returned the case to the seller and made him refund their money, accusing him of unethically substituting plain water. Cowpunchers could be dirty pranksters on occasion.

Most of our games were not so rough, but the hard, pebbly grounds were pretty hard on old clothes, especially on knees and elbows. Nobody but a sissie could go through a school term without torn britches and stockings, especially about the knees, and these caused complications on the home front. Mamas got so tired of darning and sewing on patches that some just gave up in despair and let their tattered offspring get so disreputable looking that the teacher would write Johnny's mama a note advising that he needed patching up. Incidentally, you will note that I never refer to parents as "Mom" and "Pop." Such terms were considered disrespectful. It was always "Mama" and "Papa" with only an occasional "Daddy." That idea still sticks with me, and right now I'll get fighting mad if some whippersnapper refers to me as "Pop." This propensity has caused my Wife-Mate no little embarrassment on occasions when I flew off the handle and called my presumptuous addressor a sonofabitch.

We hand-crafted most of our play gear and weapons of the chase. We would cadge a couple of leather strings and a piece of soft leather from our friend Shoemaker Ford and make slings, a la little David. Some of us became so expert with them that we could have taken on a good-sized Goliath ourselves. We also made our own slingshots (nigger shooters, we called 'em, just why, I'll never know, as our relations with the few colored children were most amicable). Some of us became so expert with these slingshots that we garnered many a lark, sparrer and rabbit for the family larder, to the unhappiness of our long-suffering mamas who frowned on such "trash" but, nevertheless, cooked them for us. No gourmet ever savoured breast of pheasant more than a budding Nimrod eating his own "trash."

The cottontail rabbit was our *big game*, and no man ever really lived unless he twisted rabbits when he was a kid. When a kid jumped a rabbit, he sicked his dog after him; that is, if he were fortunate enough to possess a dog. Otherwise, he took after him on his own. If he could crowd him enough to make him take to earth under a rock or in a shallow hole, he had it made. He cut a catclaw or hackberry stick with his Barlow knife, notched it at one end, and he was ready for business. He poked the notched end of his switch into the rabbit's fur and twisted. If it took, he yanked out his struggling, squealing prey, and no mighty hunter on safari ever experienced a greater thrill over bagging a trophy lion than a six-year-old boy did on capturing his first cottontail. He dressed the game with his Barlow and bore it proudly home. Poor, patient Mama carved it into suitable pieces, rolled it in flour and fried it; *entre nous*, it was really delicious! Most youngsters yearned to be cowpokes and scorned rabbit by the time they were fifteen, deeming them only fitten for sheep herders and nesters.

In his sub-teen years, the youngster of that day early acquired a remuda of stick horses and a herd of cow horns, salvaged from old carcasses. When he obtained an addition to his "herd," he promptly built a fire, heated his wire branding iron and burnt his brand on the horn. When two or more herds were brought together, right smart trading ensued. The new owner would "vent" the old brand and burn on his own. Some of these horns carried as many brands as the old cows did.

Each budding poke usually managed to acquire a rope, generally a quarter-inch one, which he mooched from his mother who had used it to bind up her trunk when traveling. These old trunks had such poor fasteners that a small rope reinforcement was required to withstand the rough handling by the baggage-smasher of the time. Our beginner started out on the cats and dogs, progressing onward to the pigs and milk calves. He got his tail burnt if his daddy caught him pestering the porkers or calves.

After he got a little older, he began to ride the calves, another pastime in bad odor with his daddy. I recall the sinking feeling I once experienced when my father caught me trying out a milk calf. The calf not only dumped me on my sitter, but a disapproving parent added injury to insult by paddling the same aching posterior.

We had plenty of chores to do feeding the horses, slopping the hogs, milking the cows, getting in the wood, and even weeding the garden. One chore that I especially detested was turning the grindstone for Cousin Will. He could bear down harder and sharpen an axe longer than any other man in the world.

The girls didn't have it any easier than the boys did. They started out wiping the dishes, and progressed on to washing them, cooking, sweeping out the house, making the beds, sewing (by hand mostly), and cleaning lamp chimneys, all done under Mama's critical supervision.

Our early schools, compared with those of today, were pretty sketchy operations, but they did learn us readin', spellin', writin', and 'rithmetic. We learned our ABC's and our multiplication tables, and we absorbed quite a lot from the older kids, as several grades were taught in one room. Reading and spelling were taught on a competitive basis. Our grade was called to the long front benches, a pupil was called to stand up and begin reading the lesson aloud. If he made a mistake, he had to sit down, and another kid took over. Johnny certainly learned to read that way. Spelling was taught the same way, and every Friday afternoon was devoted to spelling matches and "speakin' pieces." Several classes were lined up, and the teacher gave out the word to the pupil at the head of the line. If he missed, he was ignominiously sent to the foot, and the next one was given the opportunity and so on down the line. A lot of attention was paid to handwritin' and each pupil had a copy-book of Spencerian script and painstakingly copied each of those wise saws a dozen or more times, one of which I still recall:

> Be not weary in well doing,
> For in due season you shall reap.

By the time a pupil had finished all the copy books in the grammar grades, he was a tolerable penman. I know that such methods of teaching are now outmoded by our educational experts of today, but I wonder how many pupils they have turned out who can find a word in the dictionary, read aloud acceptably, spell even reasonably well or write a legible hand. I have known high school graduates who could do calculus, but they couldn't hold a candle to an old-time seventh-grader in these elementary subjects. A few years ago, I helped an instructor in one of our leading educational institutions grade papers. There were only a few of the students who spelled correctly or wrote a legible hand, and *these were from small towns.*

In those days of scant *divertissement*, oratory was such an esteemed form of entertainment that any speaker, from a professional, to a medicine show or even a school speakin' could draw large and appreciative audiences. In consequence, much attention was paid to "elocution" (dubbed "yellercution" by the Philistines of the community.) Every Friday afternoon of the school term was devoted to "speakin' pieces" as well as spelling matches and so on. About twice a year the trustees, along with sundry proud parents, would show up, and the kids really strutted their stuff.

Every child had to memorize a verse or so, get up, duck his head and gabble it off, to the delight of a doting parent, the satisfaction of the complaisant teacher, and the boredom of the kids who had heard him repeat it before. I recall one overgrown hulk of a boy who was kind of on the dumb side and had great difficulty in memorizing his pieces. Finally, through the combined efforts of his mama and the teacher, he came up with the following gem:

> Little birds in their nests agree
> Sugar candy does with me.
> Grandma says it make me sick,
> But I git better very quick.

This masterpiece rapidly gabbled off in singsong never failed to produce rousing applause.

My good mother, who had attended a "young ladies' finishing school," was quite an accomplished elocutionist and, on occasion, would entertain with selections from the classics. So, she assiduously trained her eldest in the fine art. School Ending—not commencement, mind you—was the occasion for really big doin's. I especially recall one occasion when I really shone. School endings were held in the courthouse, and the whole community turned out *en masse*. Dressed in a black velvet Little Lord Fauntleroy turn-out, her budding seven-year-old orator piped out:

> You scarce would expect one of my age
> To speak in public from the stage;
> And if I chance to fall below

Demosthenes or Cicero,
Don't view me with a critic's eye,
But pass my imperfections by.
Large streams from little fountains flow;
Great oaks from little acorns grow.

All delivered with flowing gestures and accompanying pos-
tures and artistic nuances, this evoked the greatest ovation
of this speaker's entire career. So much so that great things
were predicted for him by the distinguished and eloquent
guest speaker of the occasion. But, somehow, these great ex-
pectations failed to jell.

This speechifying "gift" progressed until I had a repertory ranging from "Excelsior," "Fair Bingen on the Rhine,"
to "Thanatopsis." However, by the time I had advanced to the
stature of an eighth-grader in the more sophisticated atmosphere of the San Angelo schools, such exhibitions had become *passe*; thus, an accomplished speaker and great nuisance was lost to history. However, even in sophisticated San
Angelo, such Friday afternoons were devoted to quotations
from the poets, classics and the Bible. Right here I take violent issue with those nine crusty old sinners in Washington.
Readin' the Scriptures never hurt nobody. Besides, about
the only way a lot of kids became familiar with the Scriptures
was in the reading of them in school. I shamefacedly recall
a smart alecky caper a bunch of older lads pulled in San Angelo. Our wonderful teacher varied the subjects to be memo-
rized. We were permitted to choose our own verses, from popular poets to the classics on to the Bible. Assignments were
made a week in advance, and quite a few duplications ensued. On this particular occasion we were given the New
Testament, and we pranksters conspired together. As a result,
an oversized kid got up and dead-panned: "Jesus wept." One
by one, eight or ten of his fellow conspirators arose and repeated the same. Of course, the kids tittered, and this so dis-
tressed our teacher that she wept. This shamed us all; besides,
the word got around, so the superintendent and our parents
took over from there.

When we misbehaved, we were not gently admonished or reasoned with—we were spanked both at school and when we got home. There was no rod-sparing then; consequently, no teen-age problem. The sure knowledge of prompt, condign punishment kept us from doing a lot of meanness.

Professor Glenn was the head of the San Angelo Public School System, which consisted of one stone building for all the white children, plus a small separate Mexican school. Professor (all male teachers were called "Professor" or "Fesser" for short) was a strict believer in discipline by the rod, and he didn't throw off any time he wielded it. When trouble occurred, "Fesser" called the offending boys into the "liberry" (he left the girls to the lady teachers), where he asked each boy if he was a participant. He got a straightforward "Yes, sir" or "No, sir," and he accepted the answer without question, for he knew it was true. So far as I know, no boy ever lied to Fesser. He didn't tolerate tattling but relied altogether on a true reply to his question. When the culprits had identified themselves, Fesser reached up behind the map case for a bundle of switches he always kept stashed there. Then the fun began and the dust to fly! It was a point of honor never to holler, but we did try to circumvent him during the punishment. One offender foolishly put his geography in his pants, and the switch sounded like "hell a-beating tanbark." Wise Professor detected the subterfuge, frisked the culprit, and doubled the dose.

And, thereby, hangs another tale.

I was a senior in high school, and the brightest boy in the class—the other two members being girls. (Contrast the size of this class with the one that graduated the other day, 656. Whew!) I was therefore something of a big shot and elected as a sort of a monitor and disciplinary aid to Professor. We had a good, convenient swimming hole on the North Concho River that was so secluded that we swam in the buff. (This site is now within a hundred yards of a fifteen story, high-rise apartment and a large motel complex.)

Well, anyway, when the weather grew warm, the boys were accustomed to spending their noon hour in swimming, which was all right, provided they showed up in time for class. On one well-remembered occasion, they failed to show when the bell rang for books. After a reasonable interval, Professor told me to go bring the loiterers in. They were all still in the water when I got there, and it looked so inviting that I peeled off and dove in for a quick dip—that's what I thought. I delivered the message and started to crawl out when someone threw mud on me. So I got back in and proceeded to throw mud myself. This kept on so long that we didn't make it back to school until quite a spell after the classes had gone home. So, a hangdog bunch of offenders made their way into the sanctum sanctorum, where a glowering executioner sternly waited. We sheepishly "acknowledged the corn" and meekly awaited our merited punishment. Knowing that he had a big job on his hands, Professor had sent another older boy to cut a fresh supply of catclaw switches. They were about the size of young buggy whips, and our behinds began to twitch in anticipation of the stinging they were going to get. Fesser called up the youngest boy and hit him a good lick—so good that the switch broke all to pieces. Professor apologized to the boy for hitting him so hard, selected another switch and gave him a lighter blow. After the third switch had flown to smithereens, Professor smelled a rat and examined the implements of torture. Every switch was notched in a dozen places. But trust canny Professor to have a supply of his own cutting stashed away. He excused the first boy, called old switch-cutter up and really gave him the works. (Incidentally, this culprit is now the distinguished mayor of a good-sized town, and I hope he sees this.) This proceeded down the line until I was the only one left. The others licked their chops in anticipation of what I was going to get, which we all knew was going to be a humdinger! I took a long breath and stood up to get mine. Our hot-under-the-collar flogger glared at me and told me to sit down. Thereupon, the other boys raised a howl. Professor grimly told them to shut up and listen to what was coming to me. He said that I was too old and too well advanced in high school to be whipped and ordered me to report to Miss

Horton, who would supervise my writing Lincoln's Gettysburg Address 250 times on the blackboard. My partners in sin crowed while I cravenly begged for two lickings instead. But, no, that was it, and I reported to Miss Horton who awaited my coming with pleasure. She handled the disciplinary chores other than the spankings, and I still think she would have made an efficient member of the Inquisition.

You just try to write that address on a blackboard one time and then multiply it by 250! She handed me a large printed card and admonished me to keep my lines straight, my writing tidy and to watch my spelling, capitalization and punctuation. Result—I barely finished one copy by dark as she made me erase the other attempts. I was sternly questioned at home about why I was so late, and I gave the lame excuse that I was helping Miss Horton. I had to milk the cow and do the other chores in the dark and eat a cold supper to boot. While I soon learned the speech by heart, it took me more than two weeks to serve out my sentence.

It is an old and very true cliché that wrongdoing never pays; but, once in a blue moon, the red gods kind of disremember—as witness:

A number of years later, I was a member of the exalted graduating class in civil engineering at the University of Texas. They gave us pretty free rein in those days to select our own times to take several one-year required subjects. Owing to circumstances, I chose to put off taking three freshman subjects until my senior year, Spanish among them. I had a pretty heavy load of class work and a lot of extra curricular activities, so I scamped Spanish something scandalous. I was sort of a big wheel on campus and managed to wheedle my other instructors into exempting me from final exams, but not my Spanish teacher, who sternly informed me that if I didn't make a good grade on the exam, she would bust me for the course. That would have prevented my graduating, with all the attendant train of dire consequences. So I really burned the midnight oil, and that's no figure of speech, as I had a kerosene burning "student's lamp." I crammed that dang Spanish grammer until I practically knew it by heart.

The fateful day arrived, and I approached the examination between a sweat and a swivet. In those days, examination questions were written on the blackboards. One board was devoted to the book and rated twenty percent. The other boards, covered with paper, rated eighty percent. We were told to do the grammar questions first. I happened to know each one of these by heart and rattled them off, parrot fashion. I asked for the covers to be removed from the other boards, which proved to be in Spanish. It looked tough, and I finally began to sweat. I had bumbled through only a few lines when I discovered that it was—you guessed it—Lincoln's Gettysburg Address. I tore up my first sheet and started "Fourscore and seven years ago, etc. . . ." I finished the translation in about ten minutes.

My instructor thought that I had flunked the exam and, good friend that she was, implored me to keep at it until I could at least show decent effort. I grinned loftily and informed her that I had "knocked her eye out." She said: "Alright, Mr. Smart, let your sins be on your own head." I purposely left my tablet on my desk and, after a suitable interval, returned to retrieve it. The door to the examination room was opened by a thoroughly bewildered lady. She sternly said: "You hound, here I have been worrying my head off about you, and you have just turned in the best examination I ever saw in my whole life. I just cannot understand it." I looked wise and said: "Miss Alice, I am just smarter than you think I am." She wouldn't give me 100 on the paper, but she did give me 99.5 on it and "B" plus for the term. So I graduated with flying honors even if it wasn't *Summa Cum Laude*.

A year or two later I sat with my friend at a luncheon table, and she remarked about my wonderful examination paper that she was preserving in her files. So, I just had to break down and confess the whole bizarre happening. She laughed delightedly and said: "I ought to kill you, even yet. I have worried for all this time how badly I had underestimated a wonderful student, and you don't know how much I am now relieved." I wish a few more of my misdeeds had turned out so happily.

I was graduated twice, yes'r, twice from the San Angelo High School: once from the tenth grade and once from the eleventh grade. That is probably my only claim to fame, as I am the only male ever to have done that. I "knowed it all" on that great day in history and felt no need for further education and set my sights on a career of cowpunching. My wise father laid down the law that I had to go to college, and I began to finagle. The family had not moved to the ranch, and the men were batching. I went all out to make myself indispensable. I even learned to cook a little. I was the first one up of a morning, and I built a fire in the cookstove, wrangled the horses, got breakfast, washed the dishes and did as much work as any other man on the place.

However, I sort of overjumped myself—I was just too smart (I've been that way a good many times). The home field had been enlarged until it was over 100 acres. That summer we made about the biggest sorghum crop in history. It was so thick and so heavy that it wore out most of the broad cast binders in our end of the county. (The row binder had not yet made its appearance.) We had to shock it. After it cured, it had to be stacked. My canny father put me on the stacks to assist the stacker. This expert was a lordly sort of fellow, and he really made me wait on him. I'll bet I lifted every danged one of those forty-pound bundles at least once. You just try stooping over, lifting a heavy, bunglesome bundle of cane and toting it over the soft uncertain footing to the stacker for about twelve hours, and you will be sure that old Joshua is somewhere around as the sun gets stuck in the sky about four o'clock in the afternoon. To cap it all, the cook quit, and I was elected. That meant getting up by at least four o'clock in the morning, cooking up a big batch of breakfast for a bunch of hearty hands, washing the dishes, sweeping out the kitchen, chopping a supply of stove wood for the day, and putting on a batch of frijoles and meat for the noon meal. By that time the dew was off, and the men were ready to begin stacking. You guessed it, old smarty pants had to get on the stack. I had to take off about 11:30, hop it over to the bunkhouse and fix dinner. The hands rested while I did the dishes, and the week-long afternoon was beginning. I had to get supper, and them danged lazy pups just sat around kidding me. About the time I was ready to throw in the towel, I would note a twinkle in my dad's eye, and I knew he was trying to burn me out on ranching.

We finished stacking along in August, and an outfit was making up for a trip to the country below Rock Springs where Father had bought a herd of cattle. He had to leave, and I got my mount together, rolled my beddin', sneaked it into the chuck wagon and showed up at the big pens just as Mr. Bob Morris was allotting their mounts to the men. He started to give one of my horses to one of the men, and I set up a howl. He said, "Your Paw didn't say nothing about you going along." I innocently replied that I guess he had just overlooked it. Wise Mr. Bob grinned beneath his luxuriant mustachios and let it go. The outfit had to pass through town, but I sneaked around it lest my papa might be there. Mr. Bob stayed in town to meet him, and they came out to join the outfit in the buggy. I kept pushing the remuda so that we were a fur piece when noon came. When the two bosses rode up, they just grinned wisely, and I was mighty proud how I had outsmarted them.

We picked up the herd and encountered all sorts of aggravations and delays. The cattle were hard to handle, and our open country waddies did not function any too well in the heavy brush. We had to count the cattle every morning and were always short, so we had to drag it out while our best hands went back and rounded up the strays. These delays didn't bother me one whit. Every day that we were out meant just another obstacle toward meeting the deadline of school opening. My father left us as soon as the cattle were delivered to us, and the younger, meaner hands took it out on me. They hazed me so unmercifully that the boss finally had to put a stop to it, but that didn't keep him from giving me the humblest and dirtiest assignments, due, no doubt, to my dad's instructions. We finally reached the San Saba River two days before the University was to open, and all was clear on the San Saba as well as on the Potomac, at least, that's what I thought. We arrived at the water about two o'clock on a very hot afternoon. The thirsty cattle were cantankerous, and I had ridden my horse down, hazing them back into the herd. The dust was about as thick as a London fog back with the drags. When we finally got the tail-end on to the water, I was pooped but good.

Most of the men had eaten and were back with the herd. As I rode up to the wagon, there was my smirking father. I turned my tired horse loose, since another one of my mounts was tied nearby. After a leisurely lunch, I noticed that one of the men was putting his saddle on my horse, and I yelled at him: "Hey, Chappie, that's my horse." Grinning, Chappie replied: "Your Pa told me to," and he mounted and rode away.

Father cocked a cold eye at me and said: "All right, Mr. Smarty, get your clean clothes out of the buggy, go down to the river and take a good bath, and while you are at it, throw your old clothes away." I protested that my old clothes were still good even if they were a mite dirty—I'll say they were, they were absolutely filthy. Papa said I wasn't going to need those clothes anymore, and I knew what he meant. With a sinking heart, I made my way to the water, contemplating taking a powder. But I was tired and afoot, and my old run-over boots were dealing my feet misery. I had forgotten to get my shoes out of the buggy, so I had no choice but to accept the inevitable. I dawdled so long over my ablutions that an aggravated parent sternly bade me to get going, as we had to drive to San Angelo that night.

We had made only about ten miles when one of the horses got sick, and how I prayed that he would die or sumpin'. My captor just drove to a nearby ranch and borrowed another horse. We drove all night and reached Angelo well after sunup. Mother had my trunk packed and a new suit laid out. I tried just one more fling—I took the studs. I just flat refused to go to Austin unless my father went with me. He threatened and stormed, but I continued to sull. He finally gave in, and I still think that he had a fleeting sense of pride in my hardheadedness—a sort of chip off the old block, as it were. So, I was pitchforked into an education, and all down through the years, I have thanked God for wise and foresighted parents.

The University of Texas probably had a thousand students that year, counting the medical branch at Galveston. Austin was just a big country town of some ten thousand, but it looked bigger'n all outdoors to a scared, bewildered freshman from out in the sticks. I was fortunate to have C. C. Cole of Dallas as my roomie at the boardinghouse. Lum was a big wheel on the campus, fullback on the football team and knowledgeable in the ways of the big school. He oriented me, and I soon fitted into the routine of college life.

Football was pretty primitive in those days with little of the padding and trappings of the present. Lum's uniform consisted of a jock strap, a rubber noseguard, an unpadded jersey and kneepants, and they let their hair grow long for helmets. They played thirty minute halves with no substitutions unless a man was knocked out for good. It was a rough, tough power game—no forward passes or razzle-dazzle. You just ducked your head and hit the line, which made it plenty rough on the fullback. They had no trainer except old Henry, a kind, old colored man who doubled as a campus caretaker under Mr. Beck.

So I was elected Lum's trainer. The coach gave me a huge bottle of arnica and witch hazel, a bunch of red flannel squares and a flatiron. After a game, Lum would repair to our room, all covered with abrasions and contusions and aching in every fiber. He would strip and sprawl out on the bed, and old "theraputist Sims" would go to work. We had a fireplace in the room, and I would set the iron up in front of the fire and let it get good and hot. I would soak a flannel rag with the liniment, put it on a sore spot—and he had 'em from the crown of his head to the soles of his feet—and start to work with the hot iron. Steam would rise along with Lum's anguished howls. It was heroic treatment, but it did the work. Doggone, if I don't believe that men were tougher in those days. We had a broken arm or leg now and then, but no serious injuries. If a man was knocked out, Henry sloshed a bucket of water in his face, and if he had an extra bad lick, Coach might slip a sly dollop of raw whiskey down his gullet, grab him by the collar, jerk him to his feet, give him a kick in the pants and tell him to get back in there and pitch. *Ay de mi!*

All this seems a fur piece from cowpoke doin's, but it does give a picture of college life at the turn of the century.

Orland L. Sims at the University of Texas, 1904

I went on to graduate in civil engineering and proceeded to cripple myself the next day. After months in the hospital, I came out with a "flat wheel" which I have with me to this day. So I had to go back to the ranch and take over the office chores. After a couple of years, I was so out of touch with engineering that I perforce settled for a ranch job after all, and, you know, I have not regretted it too much. I probably made more money than I could have made as an engineer, and I daresay that I have led a more varied and interesting life as a "layman." I never practiced my profession, but I'll say this: I have done more free work than any other engineer I ever heard of. I never charged my neighbors for the countless hours I have put in for them at the drawing board and out in the field. One rooster I didn't 'specially like gave me twenty dollars for about a $300.00 job I did for him, and, you know, I have regretted it ever since as it sort of ruined my record. My father, as a youngster, got four bits for working one day for a neighbor, and he always considered it a blot on his escutcheon.

Now in my "sere and pantaloon" days, I am sitting around hotel lobbies, listening to my arteries hardenin' and authoring books. This latter activity can turn into drudgery, but it sure does keep your mind offen the Far and Middle East and hydrogen bombs as well as the miniskirts.

After I graduated from high school, the family moved back to the ranch where a large, rambling house was built. We had our own water and sewer systems installed, and we got along as well as the city folks in Angelo. These headquarters developed into quite a complex and became very popular with every kind of preacher. We always had a smokehouse full of home-cured hams, bacon and sausage, a large chicken yard, and an irrigated garden. Our housekeeper, Miss Emma Kanter, was known all over for her cakes, pies, hot biscuits, roast turkeys and fried chicken with its accompanying fritters and cream gravy. M-M-M-M! Every preacher who put up at the ranch, and they all did regardless of their "flavor," became Methodists when the great platter of fried chicken came onto that twenty-foot dining table.

The home became as popular with the laity as with the clergy. My parents were the soul of hospitality, and everyone, even the wayfarer, was welcome at their board. It was seldom that the family ever sat down to the table by themselves. If someone rode up, he was invited to get down and come in, whether he was known to them or not. Later on this hospitality became abused by total strangers so that it got to be a burden. After I took over, it became so bad that traveling salesmen would make it a regular stopping place. Two of these birds became so especially offensive and demanding that I cussed them out and sent them packing. It felt so good that we closed the place to these modern grub line riders.

After the sons entered college, never a summer passed without a full complement of college chums. That called for parties, and things really got to jumping. Mother had a Chickering grand piano, and there were singings and dancings out on the long porches. Mother had the firm conviction that Missouri gals made the best wives; consequently, there were always two or three of them spending the summer at the ranch. But her matchmaking just didn't jell: her uncooperative sons refused to cooperate and all settled for Texas mates.

The high points of the summers were the house parties, when twenty or more visiting youngsters held high carnival for a full week. I just wonder how we ever got any work done, what with the fish fries, picnics, barbecues, dances and high jinks. As the weekly newspaper was wont to say: "And a good time was had by all." These parties became so well known that there was considerable finagling for invitations.

But the young folks had no monopoly by any means—the old folks had their innings too. Mother was very active in the Methodist churches of Paint Rock and San Angelo, and she gave many parties for the Ladies' Aid. These middle-aged, dignified and socially prominent matrons really let their hair down when they came to the ranch and had as much fun as their sons and daughters.

The highlights of such parties were the barbecues in the

large pecan motte across the Concho River from the ranch house. We had a number of Mexicans on the place, and there was always an expert barbecue cook among them. On one well-remembered occasion, Juan DeAnda, our sheep boss, his segundo Jose Vela, et al, including myself, really put on a show. We butchered a fat calf the afternoon before, built a big fire in the barbecue pit, let it burn down to coals, and put on the meat. We spent the night basting sizzling cuts, concocting a savory "Son-of-a-gun" and doing considerable feasting on choice morsels and various innards of the calf. Juan suggested that we cook the calf's head, *con el custumbre de los Mexicanos*. We dug a hole some three feet deep and built a rousing fire in it. After it had died down, we covered the coals with about six inches of dirt. The thoroughly washed head with the skin intact was wrapped in damp cheesecloth and put on top of the dirt. Another six-inch layer covered the head, and another big fire built.

When dinner was served, Juan, resplendent in a large, spotless white apron, dug up the head, removed the hide and proudly bore the *piece de resistance* to the table. Of course, he left the eyes intact, considering them the choicest tidbits of all. When those old ladies took a gander at those staring eyes, they promptly lost all desire to taste Juan's masterpiece. Finally, one of the more daring declared that she would try anything once. She made such a to-do about its delicacy that the others timidly tried a bite. Before they finished, they had really cleaned up that calf's head, leaving only the eyes and some gristle for poor Juan and me.

The river ran so deep that we had to ferry our guests across in a wagon. We would cover the bottom of the wagon bed with straw, and our passengers sat flat on the floor with the guest of honor occupying the spring seat with me. Most of the ladies had on their best bibs and tuckers, and had to borrow more suitable raiment from Mother and Emma. Now Emma was very large, and there were shrieks of laughter over some of their turn-outs. But they all had to wear their good shoes. The passage over the river was a gala affair!

On the day of the calf's head, a shower came up a couple

of hours after noon, so we had to make tracks back to the house. The river bank was pretty steep, and the brakes sort of failed as we started down to the water (it may be that I did not put them on very hard), so the wagon ran down against the team. These horses had not been worked for some time and were a mite skittish, and we hit the water all spraddled out amid the screeches of the passengers. This frightened the team all the more, and they ran away, but not far. The bottom of the river was slick bare rock. One of the horses slipped down and managed to get himself caught under the wagon tongue. The shrieks of laughter turned into screams of terror, and hell broke loose in Georgia! Of course, I had to jump down into the hock-deep water to try to untangle the team. I was joined by the Mexicans, and we had to cut the now unmanageable horses loose from the wagon. There was so much noise and confusion that we couldn't get them back in the water. Fortunately, we were only about six feet from the far bank, and the wagon tongue made a passable foot-log to shore. With her shoes removed and a man on each side of her, a squeaking, laughing lady would make her tottering journey to terra firma. That is, all but one—she just flat refused to trust herself to such a slippery bridge, so Jose and I formed a packsaddle by interlacing our hands and carried her out. She was no wispy sort of gal, and her straining carriers made a stumbling progress over the rough river bottom. Then one stumped his toe, and down came the whole kapoodle! We were up to our necks in water, and innocent me, I was always falsely accused of doing it a-purpose. By that time, it was really pouring down and all got well soaked before we reached the house. But that didn't dampen the fun, and I think they got the most fun of the trip out of this fool *contre temps.*

Sic transit gloria mundi.

PART III

WOOLIES

THE SHEEPMAN shared the disdain with which the cowpoke held the nester, only more so. In addition to the superiority the mounted man has always felt toward the lowly foot-slogger, the cowpoke had a monumental repugnance for the smelly, runny-nosed, bleating charges of the shepherd. This aversion was shared by the cattleman who feared the range-destroying hordes as the Israelites of old feared the swarms of locusts. These aristocrats of the range had the unshakeable idea that no self-respecting cow would ever touch grass that had been defiled by woolies. It just didn't stand to reason that the twain could ever meet and amalgamate. No wonder that the cowman hated to see sheep invade his territory.

My father, who trailed the first flocks into our immediate section, had to meet this aversion and suspicion of the cow-men who had preceded him to the open range on the Concho River. At first, he was a sort of a pariah, but he stayed on his side and kept his nose clean; so he was finally accepted as a "pore misguided, ignorant pilgrim" who meant well, even if he did have the zany idea that cows and sheep could get along well on the same terrain.

He stayed on the job and somehow managed to tough out those first sterile years until he mastered the mechanics of the sheep business and began to prosper mildly. He bought a few cows and found that the twain could run together and sort of complement each other. After he fenced his range, he stocked it with both cattle and sheep and prospered. The die-hards fell into line, and the practice became general. The cows ate the tall grass, and the sheep ate the short grass and weeds.

Although this combination made money, my father grew to share the widespread aversion the cowman had for the woolie. So, when he got sort of prosperous, he would sell off his sheep and run cattle exclusively. Then, just before the cattle broke him, he would go back into the sheep business. He just flat hated a sheep, even if they did save his bacon periodically. I heard him say many times that he would "walk a mile to kick an old ewe in the side even if the critter did put wool on his old cows' backs."

There was certainly no glamour in running the pesky critters, and the dumb clucks could get into more kinds of trouble than one could shake a stick at. All sheep had to be kept under herd until the advent of net wire many years later. Naturally, this caused all kinds of complications. One had to find herders, and no self-respecting Anglo would stoop so low as to take such a job unless he was flat broke and hungry.

Being crowded together day and night created all sorts of health problems. One old sheep could get the epizootic, and the whole mess would come down with it. Screw worm cases were most difficult to locate and treat among so many closely packed bodies. Sometimes they became so bad that strips of red rags were tied around the "wormies'" necks, and I have seen flocks that were so decked out that they resembled a Shriners' parade. The sharp hooves of so many close-herded animals played hob with the range, and the flocks had to be moved frequently. It will take many more years for our de-pleted ranges to recover from the beating they took under the early herding and later overstocking. Of necessity, our

younger sheepmen are beginning to display the sense we oldsters didn't have, and I believe that the young squirts will
eventually lick the problem.

HERDERS

PRACTICALLY all the old herders were Mexicans who put in
their whole lives herding the woolies, and I take off my hat
in respect, affection and admiration for the old breed. These
wise, patient, serene, kindly, dedicated men were devoted to
their charges and guarded them as jealously as Caesar did his
wife. They were weather-wise and knowledgeable in the
ways of nature, animals and men. When I wanted to know
something about the weather, I would go to one of these wise
old men and say, in my pidgin Spanish: "Abran, Juan, Jose
(or whoever), *que pense el tiempo por la manana?*" He
would squint knowingly at the sky and reply: "*Pues, quien
sabe, señor, pero mebbe-so he rain.*" Then I knew that I had
better keep my slicker handy. I always got their forecast before I set the date for a barbecue, and my prognosticator only
missed it one time. One Fourth of July it rained like cats
a-fighting, much to Abran's embarrassment. When I kidded
him about it, he just grinned shamefacedly and said: "Mebbe so, El Senor Dios, He change He mind."

These men lived so close to nature that they sensed weather changes well in advance of the signs known to us lesser
mortals. If one of our modern meteorologists had one old
herder on his staff, he could throw away his maps, radar, and
the like, and he wouldn't get caught like the prognosticator
of a local T.V. station did when he announced that the
weather was warm and dry when, if he had only glanced
out the window, he would have seen that it was raining
pitchforks.

Our pastores lead lonely, solitary lives, sometimes going
for a week without seeing another person, so they had plenty
of time to meditate and to "study" their charges. Although
every flock had its "markers"—belled sheep, black or crippled ones—these men soon learned to recognize individuals

by their features. So they rarely had to have their flocks counted unless they missed a few markers. I don't see how they did it, as all sheep, as well as Chinamen, look alike to me.

The sheep learned to know their herder about as well as he did them so that they quickly reached complete rapport. It was amazing how an experienced shepherd could control his flock of 1500 or more, and I never tired of watching them. Very few of them had dogs—they just didn't need them. He would stroll along in front of the grazing flock and turn it by a shout, gesture or a rock thrown in front of straying individuals. He had plenty of water, so he would "noon" and shade up there. The herder would eat his "lunchie" and take a short siesta. After an hour or so, they would move out for grazing, and along in the shank of the afternoon head towards camp, arriving about sundown. Then he would pen his charges for the night with a few whistles, shouts or well-thrown sticks or rocks. You just try to pen a flock of those hard-headed, opinionated critters by yourself, and see what you get into. Some of the real old-timers disdained pens for the night, as they did not like to have their charges crowded up so closely. The sheep stayed put unless a storm came up or coyotes ran into them, but old pastor slept with one eye open and soon rallied them back on the bed ground.

At first sheep were penned in brush enclosures something like an African "boma." It was quite a job to build one of these pens, especially if the brush was scattering. One had to chop it down, drag it into place by the horn of the saddle and pile it in a circle with the butt ends on the outside. It could turn into real work, and I'll bet that I have built miles of those danged brush fences. Later on, panels made of 1x4 lumber eliminated much of the work.

RUSTLERS

OUR CAMPS were usually covered wagons (similar to the cowpoke's chuck wagon), as they were easier to move than tents. The "rustler" (sheep boss) would ride one horse, lead the other one to the campsite, harness up and start out. He would go by the water hole, fill up the water barrel and move on to the new campsite. If it had been formerly used, all he had to do was to patch a few holes in the brush pen, but he had to build a lot of new ones. Then he would ride by the flock, gossip with the herder and get his order for supplies. A rustler could be quite a busy guy if he had several flocks to look after.

He kept constant check on the herders and their flocks, keeping his eyes peeled for wormies, crips, strays, invalids, checked the markers and examined carcasses to ascertain whether the animal had died from disease or been killed by predators. If markers were missing, the flock was counted, a very demanding job that called for vast concentration, poise and quick thinking. You just try counting a couple thousand of those goofy, bleating, unpredictable critters running by about four deep and kicking up a cloud of dust, and you will know what I mean.

I tried it many times, but my head would get to swimming so that I would lose count and become utterly bewildered. I well recall one time my father sent me and another cowpoke out about daylight one morning to count a flock out of the pen. We opened the gate a bit, but the crowding critters kept pushing it more and more open. We finally became so befuddled that "we couldn't find our back pockets with both hands." One of us would slam the gate shut, compare notes and begin all over again. Result: we counted the flock some 300 short, to the old herder's disgust. He said we were loco and ordered us off. We high-tailed it back to the ranch and reported the shortage. Father failed to get excited and sent me out with Juan de Anda, the sheep boss, the next morning for a recount. I did a little better as I counted them out only 150 short. Juan's count showed them all there. He reported to my father that "Mr. Orlie, she's pretty good boy, but she no can count dem old sheeps." Incidentally, Juan spoke the best Spanish I ever heard, but he was so proud of his English that he used it when talking to any of us. However, through him I learned the accent, pronunciation and nuances so well that I have been complimented for them in every Spanish-speaking country I have visited. It may be sheep camp Spanish as to grammar and so on, but they say it sounds fine.

This Juan was cute as a bug and got along well with everybody from the cowpokes, nesters, visitors and, above all, with his temperamental and oft-times cantankerous herders. He was a psychologist and a diplomat. When we went out of the sheep business for good—that's what we thought—Juan decided that he wanted no part of farming or ranching chores. So we fitted him out in good clothes from top to toe, gave him a new saddle, a good horse and a generous severance stipend and sent him on his way farther west. He got a good job with one of the big sheepmen and remained with him until he got *tan viejo* to work. He visited us as an honored guest shortly after his retirement, nicked us for *poco mas dinero* and went back to his kin in Estado Coahuila where he ended his days. He was *muy hombre.*

In our outfit the boss tried to see each flock as often as possible. We fed our herders, and they were constantly running out of something. One day it would be "Leetle Joke" smoking tobacco, the next "bermacil" (vermicelli) *arroz* (rice), *patatas* (potatoes), *cebollas* (onions), "garlickes" (garlic), bacon, flour, lard, sugar and *muchos frijoles*. Frijoles (red beans to you of the uninitiated) were old "Juanito's" prime comestible. He always cooked them in a gallon lard or molasses bucket with a tightly fitting lid in which several small holes were punched to let out the steam. The dry beans and a little fat bacon and water were dumped into the cooking vessel, which was placed in hot ashes, never on the fire. Thus, the beans simmered slowly day after day until consumed, and the longer they simmered, the better they got. They were eaten at every meal regardless of what other food there was on the menu. Most of them fried their beans for breakfast. Bacon fat was put in a frying pan, and some simmered beans added and mashed into a paste with a pestle, usually whittled out of a root of the algerita (agarita) which was preferred because it had a beautiful yellow color and was supposed to add a touch of exotic flavor to the beans. Then our break-faster would add a liberal supply of chili pequin (petine)—hotter than the hinges of Sheol—break off a piece of *pan* (bread), pour himself a cup of hot coffee and hop to it. He would put some frijoles and *pan* in a can for his lunch. This can was carried in a canvas satchel slung over his shoulder which contained as wide a variety of things as a modern woman's handbag. These old boys used enormous amounts of chili—chili petine preferred—and woe to the uninitiated Anglo who incautiously dived into a plate of beans well laced with that fiery little berry. My first sampling might nigh ruined me! I finally got to where I could handle a right smart of the stuff (in fact, I still do), but never like one of those old veterans. These pastores were dried up, thin men (I never saw a fat one), and I always thought that the inordinate amounts of red pepper they consumed had something to do with it. It was legendary that if a Mexican herder died out on the range, no coyote or other varmint ever touched the body because the chili had so permeated his whole system that the body was impalatable. They rarely got sick, and they always said it was the chili that kept them well. Now that vitamins have become recognized as playing such an important part in our physical well-being, perhaps the vitamins in the pepper had something to do with the Mexicans' rugged health. *Quien sabe.*

Their *pan* was made from slightly leavened flour, patted out thin into a cake the size of the Dutch oven, and nicely crisped. *Frijoles con pan caliente* made mighty scrumptious eatin', and the college boys who used to infest the ranch during the summer dearly loved to stop by a sheep camp and fill up. This thin patty also went well with some "mollasa" laced with hot bacon drippings.

A sheep was never butchered unless the rustler ordered it, so the pastor was somewhat dependent for fresh meat on what wild game he could take on his own hook. Practically all these old herders had leather slings and became quite expert in their use. It was no trick at all to knock over a cottontail rabbit, an armadillo, or even a wild turkey. We had lots of wood rats which occupied large nests of cow chips, sticks, dried prickly pear leaves, and so on. The nests were built above ground in catclaw bushes or clumps of prickly pear, so that it was not much of a chore to take a pole, tear up the nest and roust out the occupant. These *ratas* were an esteemed addition to the herdsman's menu. The rat was skinned, dressed and tied by its tail to a stick and toted back to camp. During the interval, it acquired a glaze that was supposed to add to the flavor of the meat. I recall one instance when I saw an old fellow who had four *ratas* tied to a stick. He was near camp, and he invited me to supper. But I just reneged, and I have been sorry that I didn't accept. And, thereby hangs another tale:

My good friend, Mr. A. M. Slator, who ranched in the border country near the Rio Grande, gleefully related an incident in point. He had been out on the range all day and came by one of his sheep camps about dark, hungrier than any wolf. The herder courteously invited him to eat supper with him. These old boys were most hospitable and treated their guests with the exquisite courtesy of an old Spanish Don, a heritage from their Castilian forebears. My friend accepted the gracious invitation and pitched in. In addition to the frijoles and other eatments was a frying pan full of fresh meat. Mr. Slator said that he never in his life tasted better meat, and he really feasted! When he had finished, he asked his host what that delicious meat was and was told in one word *ratas*. He said that he tried his best not to become nauseated, but just couldn't make it. Although he thoroughly enjoyed his *rata*, he never again tackled fresh meat in sheep camp without first asking what it was. But, it's all in a name, and I'll bet that wood rats would be a highly esteemed delicacy if they had some fancy name rather than "rats." We are bound to miss a lot in life by being so persnickity.

Practically all of those old herders were bachelors. Señoritas just naturally didn't cotton to sheep camps and the lonely life. So, two or three times a year, old "Juan" would kinder hone for the bright lights and company other than his woolly charges. He would then announce that he was going on *pasear*, and the rustler would provide a temporary substitute. Old Juanito would draw all his pay, scrub himself up good, break out his town clothes and make his way to town. For a week or so he lived the life of Riley, playing some monte, visiting the *señoritas* and drinking a lot of "wheeskey." About the time his money gave out, the law would step in and haul the amiable and undemonstrative inebriate to the pokey.

When Jaunito sobered up, he would have the law call in the *factor*, a knowledgeable countryman who spoke good English and knew the ropes. He would spring the culprit and get word to the employer who would send a man after the deflated celebrator and pay the factor for the fine together with commission, and Juanito was ready to go back to work again. He took it all in stride—just "come easy, go easy"—and did not regret his impoverished condition one whit. For, like Old Cooper, he had had a mighty good time.

The net wire fence put the herder out of business, and we have lost a worthy figure from the Western scene.

SHEARERS

IN THOSE DAYS the shearing season was a time of excitement and bustle for all. A *patron* (or *capitan*) would assemble a great bunch of shearers and start on tour. All shearing was done with hand shears, and the larger sheep ranches required a lot of shearers, each of whom usually had a family, a bunch of burros, horses and mules which he brought along.

One of our best known *capitans* was Juan Flores who did our shearing for a number of years. He was a good businessman and thoroughly reliable. His men also liked him, and he always had more hands than anyone else. Our shearing pens were located on the river and the range had not been heavily stocked, so it was a most popular place with the shearers and their *familias* and animals. Everything would be in readiness, even to great piles of wood for the cooking fires. The day before shearing was to start, the large entourage hove into sight with all its wagons, carts and loose stock which were immediately turned loose on the good range and plentiful water. The fires were lighted, and all was set a-bustle.

The pens were shaded by large pecan trees, and the men really enjoyed the shade and the water with its swimming and fishing. A bunch of sheep were penned: each shearer would pick out a sheep, grab him by the hind leg and lead him backwards to the shearing floor. It was quite an art to keep a reluctant *borrego* on his feet. If a shearer dragged in a sheep lying down, Juan would roar at him, and the embarrassed captor would maneuver his charge back on its feet. These men became quite expert in the work, turning out a quick, clean, smooth fleece in one piece. When he finished a sheep, he would yell "checkee," and Juan or a segundo would hand him a tin check about the size of a five-cent piece with Juan's name stamped into it. At the end of the day, checks were counted, turned in and the proper notation made on the *capitan*'s ledger. These "checkees" were legal tender around camp. Every afternoon along about four o'clock a cook would bring in small hot cakes, pies and coffee which the hands purchased with "checkees." These checkees also served as chips in the nightly monte game. Juan was considered a very good monte player, and he usually cleaned up. The next morning, when shearing started, the other hands would josh the losers about working for Juan for nothing. They took it in good part and 'lowed as how there was always another night and another game.

I even now recall with deep nostalgia the busy scene in the shearing pen with the clicking shears, the gay banter of the men and the general air of bustle and excitement. Every now and then, a shearer would burst into song, and the others would take it up. Those haunting Spanish melodies are with me yet! "Adios, hermos' Alena," "La Golondrina," "La Paloma," and an occasional bouncy ribald one which would cause all the señoritas in hearing to clap their hands over their ears or run, thus adding to the enjoyment of the men.

When a sheep was finished, the fleece was rolled into a tidy package with the flesh side out, dumped on a table, bound securely with heavy twine and dumped into a long jute sack hung from a frame. After a few fleeces were deposited in a sack, a tromper would jump down in the sack and pack the fleeces tightly. Those handlers and trompers became about the greasiest persons imaginable as the oil in the wool soon covered them from top to toe. They all had wonderfully smooth complexions and hands because of the lanolin in the wool. A man would sew up the open end of the plump sack, roll it over to the freight wagon, and it was on its way to the warehouse or a railroad.

FREIGHTERS

THE SACKED WOOL was turned over to the freighters who always delivered it in good order to the railroad point. These old roosters were also sort of *sui generis*, themselves. They were a hardy, self-sufficient breed that could extemporize themselves out of most any dilemma, and, believe me, they encountered many. They also made do with what they had.

The first freighters in our section mostly drove ox teams, and I can dimly remember them coming through Paint Rock with long strings of plodding oxen teams amid cracking whips and shouts of "whoa," "haw" and "gee." Old trail drivers told me that when passing through the Indian Nations, they were always confronted by a band who demanded "wohaw" as tribute. It was blackmail of a sort, but it paid off in freedom from molestation.

With the coming of the railroad, San Angelo became the distributing point for a wide area, and my earliest impressions of the town were of the swarms of freight outfits all over the place with the attendant bustle, confusion, congestion and noise of yelling, cussing drivers, popping whips and braying mules. On a busy day, it took a lot of skill to maneuver a rig of a dozen draft animals and two or three heavily laden "wains" through the traffic jams—comparable to rush hour on a modern freeway, only they never had any pile-ups or blood-spilling.

These freight rigs ranged all the way from modest one-team, one-wagon to a dozen or more assorted animals and two to four wagons trailed one behind the other with the junk or plunder cart, loaded with horse feed, grub, bedding, cooking outfit, repairs and spare harness bringing up the rear. All wagons had wooden bows over which the protective wagon sheets were stretched. At least one wagon would have a water barrel lashed on the side.

Wool wagons in San Angelo, 1898

Most teams were hooked two abreast with the largest, strongest animals, known as wheelers, in the rear. Then would come the swing teams, and finally the leaders. The wheelers and the leaders were the important members of the team, for upon their strength and intelligence depended the smooth operation of the rig. It was interesting to see how a smart pair of leaders could react in a tight spot. A big team was useful in breaking in a bronc. He would be tied close to his gentle teammate, and there was nothing much that he could do except to go along with the team. If he sulled or lagged, he could be cranked up with a whip or a nick on the root of his tail by the clicking teeth of the irritated wheeler immediately behind him.

With three teams or more, the driver rode the near wheeler controlling the brake by means of a rope attached to a long brake lever. A good brake on the lead and heaviest laden wagon was a most necessary piece of equipment, especially in hilly country. If a brake failed on a downhill, one could get into real trouble when the wagon ran onto the heels of the team. Most wagons carried chains to lock a hind wheel on steep hills.

The mounted driver controlled his string with the various combinations of lines, and it was something to see an expert driver control a long, spread-out team with a single jerk line. (You can get an idea of that contraption by watching the Borax advertisement on T.V.) He also carried a long whip mounted on a long, limber wooden whip stock with a popper of soft leather on the other end. How those drivers could make a whip pop—louder'n ary firecrackers. Some of them were so expert in handling a whip that they would boast that they could flick a hoss fly offen the leader's butt without ever touching the hide. Many a driver had a sack of good-sized pebbles hung on his saddle horn and could really perk up a laggard by bouncing a rock off his caboose.

Mexicans were especially expert in handling large hook-ups, some of which were weird affairs with horses, mules and burros all intermixed. It was remarkable what heavy loads could be handled with burros and how well the drivers could control the stubborn little beasts. They might be sort of pokey, but they always made it through. However, they really had some foul-ups with a long, strung out burro team. One of the worst I ever saw happened one drizzly, foggy night when I ran head-on into a team of a dozen burros pulling two big wagons loaded with wool. I was on my way to the Howard Draw country on a deer hunt. I had a hunting partner, a buggy whip salesman and torn-down prohibitionist, and Abe Mayer's Negro bunkhouse cook as passengers. Old Eph struck me in Ozona and bummed me for a ride to the ranch, so I piled him, his plunder and a bird dog in the back of the Model T. I had been held up by car trouble and wanted to make it into hunting camp that night. The cook had plenty of whiskey and broke out a bottle and passed it around. Being the driver, I declined to partake, but my dry

JUDGE ORLAND L. SIMS

An early West Texas cattleguard, 1914

friend made up for us both. A cold norther blew up, and my two companions really began to fortify themselves against the cold drafts whistling through the open touring car. As a result, they became so happy that they raised their voices in song, which drew accompanying howls from the dog. I was mad and tired and hungry, so I was really pushing that Model T. The dirt road wound down the canyon, and Ford headlights were not so good then. I just knew that no one would be out on such a night. I roared around a sharp turn, and there, right spring in front of me, was the long, strung-out team of burros—the great granddaddy of all foul-ups ensued. Fortunately, I stopped a few feet short of the leaders, who promptly turned back through the team. The wagons stayed upright, and no one was hurt; but, in all my born days, I never saw such a mess of ropes, harness, kicking, braying jackasses! My befuddled companions were so little help that I banished them back to the car, where they opened another bottle and serenaded us. Between the Mexican, his teen-age boy and myself, order was finally restored with little damage even to the harness, which was mostly rope. I was reaching for my billfold to pay off, when old Eph grandly offered the Mexican his bottle. "Old Juan" took two or three snorts and courteously waved my proffered money aside. So, we parted with many handshakes and expressions of mutual esteem.

In about an hour, I delivered Eph, his dog and his plunder to the bunkhouse. When I left, Eph had broken out a fresh bottle, to the delight of the awakened cowpokes. I doubt if Mr. Mayer got much work out of his hands the next day.

While feed for the teams was a prime necessity to the freighter, water was his principal problem. If grass was short, grain and even hay could be carried on the wagons, but water was something else. Some outfits carried a barrel or two swung on the sides of each wagon. Some freighters in extra dry country trailed waterwagons on behind, but these were a nuisance and added a lot to the loads the teams had to pull. So the freighter knew his watering places and always tried to space his journey so that he would be on water by night-fall. Good watering places almost always had several outfits camped at them every night. I have camped with these men a good many times, and I always enjoyed their company. "The lids of the flesh pots clattered high" at a dozen or more campfires, and the wayfarer was always welcome. If one had a bottle of whiskey along with him, he passed it around for each man to have a dram out of it—no pouring it into a cup or mixing with water. They always arose before dawn, built their fires, got up their teams and ate hasty breakfasts. Practically all of them fried bacon for breakfast, and I know of no sweeter aroma than that diffused from a dozen frying pans in a chilly dawn. The coyotes also appreciated the smell, and I well recall one morning out in the Big Bend. It was a large and popular camping place with a whole bunch of rigs. The wind was just right, and the coyotes came in droves. They formed a circle all around camp, sat on their haunches and gave out with a weird cacaphony of eerie howls. As the last wagon pulled away, the hungry predators crowded in for the scraps of food left on the ground for them.

It was a chore to take a big team loose for water before the night stop was reached, so each rig carried some galvanized water pails. The animals were trained to drink out of the buckets, and it was a lot handier to tote the water to them. And, thereby hangs another tale: An especially irascible and profane old codger ran a freight line west of Menardville (Menard, now), and he always stopped at a ford on the San Saba River to water his teams. He had acquired a mule that was so wild that he couldn't teach him to drink out of a bucket. So he led the mule behind the wagons on a trip to Menard. He tied the critter up short to a tree and left him there. The next afternoon, on the way back, the team was stopped and watered from buckets, and water was taken to the dry and famished captive. The mule would sniff the water, stick his nose in it and then jerk back in fright. Old cusser would patiently trudge back and forth to attempt it all over again. An old preacher drove up about the beginning of the operation and watched it with intense interest. Finally, his curiosity got the better of him, and he asked the exasperated "gentler": "Brother, why do you go to so much trouble to water the animal out of a bucket when you could so easily lead him down to the river for a drink?" Old cusser set his buckets down and roared: "For the best blankety, blank, blank reason in the world: *because I want to.*" That got to be a stock reply to silly questions hereabouts, and it never failed to shut up a presumptuous questioner.

I also belonged to this honorable guild, but I didn't follow it much. I have hauled many a wagonload of freight from Ballinger and San Angelo to the ranch, but I wasn't much punkins as a driver. I could handle two horses about as well as the next man, and I could barely get by with four if they were gentle and knew their business, but I just couldn't manage six. My old friend, ex-governor Coke Stevenson, freighted when he was a boy, and he still considers his ability to handle a "six-up" team as one of his major accomplishments.

When I returned home for summer vacation after my freshman year at the University of Texas, I thought I could do anything and volunteered for a freight trip to San Angelo as my first job. My father bought a load of registered rams at

Angelo, and for my mother, a Chickering grand piano. My lead wagon had a long, let-out coupling pole and a slatted bed for the sheep. A regular wagon was tied on behind, and a team of big horses, fat off the range, was chosen for the job. One of these horses, named "Banjo," was about the meanest horse I was ever around, and there wasn't any meanness that stinker wouldn't do. To begin with, one of the hands helped me hook up my team out on a high, treeless flat. Banjo promptly balked and reared up and fell over on his side. The hand put his foot on the hames and held Banjo down while I gave him a good licking. The man held him down until I got all set and then turned him loose. Banjo hit the ground running, and I circled the team until its wire-edge had sort of worn off. The hand rode on ahead and opened the pasture gate for me. Everything went smoothly until we neared the gate. Banjo stampeded again, and we went through the gate like a bat out of hell. I really poured the leather to my team, and they were pretty gentle by the time we reached Angelo. The next morning I loaded the sheep on the lead wagon and the crated piano on the rear one and set sail for the ranch. A few miles out of town, I tied the lines to the set brake lever and got out to examine my cargo. I was tightening a lashing on the piano box when old Banjo looked around and saw me. So he took off again. I just had to stand there and goggle at my runaway train. Fortunately, a cowboy was passing by, and he stopped the runaways without damage to the cargo. About a third of the way home, I had to get down and open a gate, and as I started through, the wind blew the gate to. It hung on the hind wheel of the lead wagon and broke the long, flimsy coupling pole. There I was all by myself on a lonely road with small chance of anyone coming by for a day or two. I fastened my team and found some bailing wire nearby. After dint of much straining, I finally got the two broken ends of the pole together and fastened them with a few nails and the wire. My repair held, but the hind wheels were out of line with the front, and the wagon ran sort of whomper jawed. This made the load harder to pull, and I had a give-out team when night fell. So I improvised hobbles out of some rope, turned them loose, rolled up in the wagon sheet and tried to sleep. But the danged coyotes smelled the tired, dry, hungry bleatting sheep and held a singing convention all around me. Consequently, I got very little sleep. I had a few morsels left from my lunch, but they only whetted my appetite. The next morning I had to cross a creek with very steep banks. I had no brakes on either wagon, so I tied one wheel with a chain and started down the hill. About halfway down the chain broke, and away we went. We had to negotiate a curve, and, as I looked back, I saw the wagon carrying the piano teetering on two wheels. I gritted my teeth, closed my eyes and waited for the crash. Fortunately it did not turn over, but it was such a traumatic experience that I still shudder at the thought of what might have happened.

I finally arrived at the ford across the river near the ranch house, and, of course, the river was up. I decided I could cross it, and one of those fool horses fell down as we neared the far bank. So I had to fall out into that cold water and help the Mexicans unload the sheep. We finally got the rig out: a wet, hungry, weary and sleepy lad delivered the freight. To cap it all, my good mother, usually one of the kindest and most understanding souls, was so perturbed about my late arrival with her precious piano that she berated me soundly for not getting home the day before. That did it! I was about the most put upon freighter in the country. One good thing about it—it cured me of freighting.

However, my troubles were still not over for the piano and crate were so heavy that it took all the men on the place to unload it and carry it to the house. Even then we dropped it on a Mexican's foot which crippled him for weeks. When it was uncrated, we found that it was too big for the door, and a side of the house had to be torn out. But we got it set up, and it well repaid all the blood, sweat, and tears expended in its delivery and installation.

Mother was an indifferent performer and none of her offspring could play, but we always had visitors who could make plenty of music from ragtime to classical. We had lots of playing, singing and dancing, all of which afforded much pleasure to the family and to the whole community. I had a little aunt who could really knock fire out of that old box, and I'll bet I danced all the way from Paint Rock to Del Rio to her toe-tickling performances.

The highlight of it all was when Oscar Seagle, the famous gospel singer with the gorgeous baritone voice, and his wife were in our country. They came to spend a night at the ranch and stayed for more than a week. Mr. Seagle and I hunted ducks and quail in the daytime, and we had a real *soiré* every evening. The Seagles were most generous with their talents and provided much joy for us music-starved West Texans.

They seemed to enjoy it all as much as we did and always referred to their visit as their "honeymoon." Many years after Mr. Seagle's death, Mrs. Seagle and their son John, a great musician in his own right, made a sentimental journey to the ranch, and I never saw anyone get such a kick out of a visit.

At the break-up of the old ranch headquarters, the piano was given to one of the daughters-in-law who later sold it. Wherever it is, I trust its aged bones are still furnishing enjoyment.

The old freighters were pretty cute, and one picaresque character once told me some sneaky tricks of the trade. One that I especially recall was how he got his drinkin' whiskey for free. He hauled a lot of the creature in barrels, and he came up with this shenanigan. He procured a gimlet, stopped by a field of wheat and gathered a sheaf of the stalks. He would bore a hole in the barrel head, stick in a straw and suck to his heart's content. He said that it was surprisin' how much better whiskey tasted through a straw.

There is still a lot of freighting done, but mostly by trucks. I haven't seen a real, old-time freight outfit in years. Freighting may be a lot more efficient now, but it sure has lost its flavor.

Like everything else, modern progress tolled the bell for another picturesque, salty, self-reliant old character. The automobile flat ruined the old-time freighter. The first trucks were bob-tailed affairs running on solid rubber tires and were the butt of much ribald laughter and sour disgust of the old freighters who 'lowed as how the "ol' stink-pots were only fitten to get broke down and scare hell outen a man's teams." I wonder what old Daddy Gann thinks as he peers down from his cloud and sees the endless procession of forty-foot monsters roaring down the highways at seventy miles an hour. Anyway, the old freighters sure started something.

RAILROADERS

ALONG WITH THE WIRE FENCE, the drilled well and the windmill, the railroad was the prime developer of West Texas. The cowman and the sheepman could now ship their products to market and get supplies without the long, time-consuming drives, and the tempo of living speeded up. People came in, towns sprang up all along the line, and wild-eyed promoters flourished. Every village had its quota and each one dreamt dreams and saw visions of metropolitan grandeur. The railheads quickly developed into distribution centers, and San Angelo did "really go to town."

The event of each day was train time. Every person in the village would turn out to the depot to see the train come in. When the whistle sounded, someone would always yell "There she comes," and everyone would crowd to the platform with frantic mamas desperately trying to shepherd their young 'uns away from the tracks. How many times have I heard screams of "Now, Jimmy, don't let the train run over you"; "Sally, don't you dast get too close to that dirty old engine and get your pretty dress all dirtied up!" The puffing locomotive, with its clanging bell, clanking driving gear, its puffs of black smoke pouring from the smokestack and clouds of steam all over, would come to a dramatic stop. The lordly conductor, resplendent in long-tailed blue coat and gold-braided cap, would swing off, followed by the not-so-resplendent brakeman and grinning porter. The dudish drummers and other important-looking passengers would

Shipping cattle from the Sims' switch to Kansas City, 1920

gaze superciliously out of the windows, and the baggage-smashers would tumble off luggage, mail and express. Last good-byes were exchanged with abjurations of, "Now be good to yourself and be sure to write." The out-going passengers would scurry aboard, the porter pick up his stool, the conductor haul out his large hunting-case watch, scrutinize it, yell "'Board," and wave "high ball" to the engineer. That worthy would give two tremendous blasts of the whistle, the engine would puff and snort, great clouds of steam would spew all over the place, the clanking driving gear would begin to revolve, and another exciting episode was ended!

The old locomotive was the most interesting part of the train and was a noisy, clanky, hooting affair, but it carried an aura of romance that makes the modern diesel seem sort of sheep-like. An old cowpoke and I were riding beside a railroad track early one foggy, drizzly morning when a train passed us with the old "pot" emitting great clouds of smoke and steam, whistling, with the bell wildly ringing for a crossing. Old poke gazed awe-struck and said: "Ain't a locomotive a majestic lookin' dam' thing!" And, you know, I still agree with him.

The old passenger coaches were also something. They were garishly decorated, and the seats were practically all upholstered in red plush. The smoking car, always up next to the baggage car, was plainer and shabbier, and no lady ever rode in it—ladies just didn't smoke in public, if at all. Each seat had its own spittoon (cuspidor), a most necessary accessory as practically every adult male chawed terbacker. The chair cars were nicer, with each complicated, reclining chair always topped with a snowy (at the beginning of the run) headrest. If the weather was hot and humid, the coal smoke and cinders from the engine poured in the open windows so that the white headrests became pretty grimy along towards the end of the run.

The sleeping car (called the Pullman) was the acme of luxury. It was decorated in wood paneling, something that looked like mother-of-pearl, and all kinds of cupids and curlicues in various hues, with gilt predominating. Even the spittoons were ornate, tall, brass affairs, shining like a full moon. Each car carried a mysterious unpronounceable name in large letters on its sides. The porter, with blue cap and shining, white starched jacket, was a smiling, affable, and helpful man who assiduously looked after his passengers. At the end of his run you always gave him a quarter; that is, if you felt sort of affluent, and somehow one always felt that way when riding on the Pullman. As the train approached a station, the brakeman would walk through the train bawling out the name of the next station. As the train left each station, the conductor, closely followed by the brakeman, would start at the front end and take up tickets. He was a lordly looking man in immaculate blue uniform with gold braid and stars or "hash marks" on his sleeves indicating his years of service to the road. He had a shiny puncher wherewith he punched holes in the ticket, stuck it in his coat pocket, punched a cardboard slip with a series of holes and stuck it in one's hatband (every self-respecting male wore a hat in public). The number or arrangement of the holes indicated the passenger's destination. He would stroll through the cars eyeing these slips and take them up as one approached his destination. One had better take care of that card in his hatband; if one didn't have it, he might be put off the train. Any kid under twelve years of age rode free, and it was amazing how big some twelve-year-olds got to be, which caused a right smart of discussion between the parent and the conductor. If the parent was a woman, she always won the argument, but the father usually lost and had to sheepishly fork over the kid's fare. I recall one old woman who came aboard with a great, overgrown hulk of a boy and a blanket. She made the kid squat down on the floor in front of her and covered him and her lap with the blanket. When the conductor came through, he asked her why the blanket, and she replied that she was sort of puny and didn't like drafts on her feet. The conductor looked wise and took up her ticket. After he left the car, the kid came up for air. It looked pretty good until they got sort of careless and allowed the blanket to become disarranged. The conductor spied the big feet and ankles of the kid, but didn't let on. When they arrived at their destination, he jerked off the blanket and lectured the woman soundly, to her intense mortification.

A passenger didn't pay too much attention as to where he was, as the conductor would wake him up when his hatband ticket showed the right number of punches. But, on rare occasions, he might overlook the ticket, and one was carried past his destination. One time my father, a very sound sleeper, failed to wake up at Temple and was carried halfway to Fort Worth before he discovered where he was. As a consequence, he was a full day late getting home.

One time an old lady, sitting just in front of me, had a good long snooze and waked up just after we had passed through a station. When the conductor came through, she agitatedly asked if we were on "this side of Lampasas." When the conductor assured her that we were, she peacefully went to sleep again only to discover that we were on the wrong side of Lampasas for her. So, they took her on to Temple and sent her back to Lampasas on the next train.

Another most important member of the train crew was the "butch" (candy butcher or seller of various wares). He had all kinds of candy, the most popular of which was fabricated in small, multicolor pellets and housed in a glass replica of a pistol. Every kid wanted one of these, and poor mothers were sorely beset between the wheedling butch and her bellering offspring. She usually had to give in. Butch always had a supply of bannaners, a most popular and messy comestible in the hands of a tired, sleepy child. He also had the latest papers and popular novels of the time. My father had to do a lot of traveling, and he nearly always brought home a book. Once he brought back the *Museum of Antiquity*, a ponderous tome all lavishly decorated in gilt designs and portraying the ancient Greek and Roman mythology. I was an omnivorous reader, and early acquired a knowledge of the subject, much to the amazement of my teachers. He also introduced me to the delights of H. Rider Haggard when he brought *Allan Quartermain* home. I read *Allan* about as many times as I did *Huckleberry Finn*. After I was growed up, I obtained a full set of Haggard books, which I still say are the bloodiest and most informative historical novels ever put out by an author.

The male urchins of that far-off time had three ambitions as to what their calling would be when they growed up: a cowpoke, a railroad man, or an actor in a circus—most wanted to be a railroad man. No kid ever saw the lordly engineer sitting at the throttle without picturing himself in that station. These men were usually large, sort of fattish, and dressed differently from us lesser mortals, wearing white and blue striped "overhauls" (overalls), a peaked cap of the same material, and great gauntleted gloves. At every stop, he got out, inspected his engine and doused sundry bearings with a great, long-spouted oil can. At night he usually carried a flaming kerosene torch instead of a lantern when he made his inspections.

Each engineman had his own particular and individual tune on his whistle—flourishes, trills, pauses, nuances—all produced by delicate manipulation of the whistle chord. If one lived near a railroad track, he soon learned to identify the engineer by his whistle. I especially recall one engineer of the 10:00 P.M. *I & G N* passenger train as he whistled for a crossing in Austin. That feller was a real virtuoso on a whistle chord. Somehow, the diesel men of today don't seem to produce any distinctive sounds on their blatting air horns, which remind me of the bellering of a bull in distress.

His fireman was a lowly soul clad in dingy, soiled blue duckin's. He had to heave coal into the flaming maw of his boiler, look after the water and do sundry other menial tasks on his side of the old "Tea Kittle." He was the worker of the train crew, and he really had to keep his heavy scoop shovel clanging when they were going up a long grade. But "firing" was the only way he could get to be an "engineer man." Both of these enginemen were pretty soiled critters at the end of the run. Contrast them with the present breed. Not long ago, I saw the engineer and his *three* firemen clamber down from a diesel, and every one of them had on a regular suit of clothes, with the engineer sporting a white shirt and necktie. He did bow to the old tradition in one respect—he had on that peaked blue and white striped cap.

The brakemen, denominated "Shacks" or "Brakies" in railroadese, were the active men of the crew. They usually were younger men beginning a railroad career. They wandered about a lot working for different roads. Such a wanderer was called a "Boomer," and the "stay-puts" didn't think too much of them.

The front shack rode up at the smutty end relaying signals to the rear end and opening switches when the train went into a siding. His was the tough job on the freights as he had to stay topside in all kinds of weather, on the engine or tender on a passenger and on top of the front car on the freights.

The rear brakie on a passenger train was the busier of the two. He had to watch for and relay signals, close switches, ride the rear platform a lot, and take care of signals to a train that might be following. These signals were fuses, flags or torpedoes. The bang of a torpedo could set the air mighty quick—it meant STOP and no foolin'. On passenger

JUDGE ORLAND L. SIMS

trains this bird was the conductor's *aide de camp* and followed closely on that worthy's heels, especially when taking up tickets or when trouble seemed to be brewing. The two of them could usually handle any bum or drunk, or quell fusses. Another of his duties was to call the names of stations as the train neared them, and each had his own way of singing them out. Somehow, he always found time to visit with the passengers, especially the gals. He was quite a boy!

The rear brakie on the freight had his roost in the doghouse cupola of the caboose when he was not walking the train or throwing bums off. He watched things fore and aft and yelled down information to the conductor below. I can still hear him sing out "clair board" if we had a clear signal at a station or siding.

Both brakies had to keep watch for "hot boxes." The axles on the old cars always ran on babbit bearings that were lubricated by oil-soaked, waste cotton strings wadded up. Dirt and grit or lack of oil could heat up a bearing mighty quick and could cause serious trouble if not detected in time. One could smell a hot bearing if conditions were right. But, if the weather was bad, and the doors and windows shut, a hot bearing might not be detected until it burst into flames. If the box was flaming, water had to be toted in a hurry. The blaze could well set fire to the car, and this could be really serious if the car were loaded with inflammables or explosives. I recall one night when a box really flamed up. They had a car of dynamite in the train, and we could not tell from the caboose whether or not it was the car on fire. I had helped work on these fires before, and I grabbed a couple of buckets of water. The conductor sternly bade me stay put. It was their job and they had to do it. They bravely went forth and fortunately found that the fire was on another, but almost adjacent, car. They doused it and made the necessary repair. I was up in the cupola when they returned and got another scolding from the conductor for being up there while I should have been way back and lying flat on the ground. They didn't seem to think that they had done anything especially heroic: it was all in the night's work.

When a hot box was detected, signals were given and the train ground to an immediate halt unless they had to make a closeby siding or another train was following too close behind. Considerable cussing ensued at such times, as it was nearly always a hot, nasty job that had to be done in a hurry. If the hot box went undetected to the point of flaming, new bearings had to be installed, and this really ran into work. The rear brakeman had to close switches and set flares several hundred yards back if an emergency stop was made.

If he and the "hog head" were at outs, he might have to hurry when he closed a switch as the engineer might keep going. So he developed into right smart of a foot racer who rarely failed to make it to the caboose, which could be a frustrating and humiliating happening. On two occasions, I saw the conductor have to set the air for a brakie who had been outrun. Then cussin' really turned the air blue, with all kinds of threats as to what would happen to that blankety blank old hogger when he caught up with him. If the front and the back ends were at outs, a real feud could develop with each end dealing the other all the misery they could. Most of the settled crews got along amicably among themselves, but there was nearly always some kind of hassle going on between these crews and the earth-bound workers, but they were all railroaders, first, last and all the time. They were a salty bunch whom I still love and cherish.

You only found the full flavored railroader on the freight trains. They were really *sui generis* in looks, mannerisms, dress and vocabulary. They were a tough, independent, hardworking, profane and scrappy lot, jealous of their skills and secretly looking down their noses at the sissies who stayed at home. Whenever two railroad men foregathered, they talked "railroadin'," and no other topics, not even "wimmen" held their attention too long—they always went back to railroadin'. They had a weird sort of argot and a sign language all their own. One of their most frequently used words was sonofabitch. They called each other that freely and thought nothing of it. On the other hand, this was the fightin' word among the cowpokes to whom it made no difference if you did smile. Smile or not, you either had to run or fight if you called a cowpoke that, and I well remember my amazement when I heard a man so addressed without his displaying any resentment. One old cowpoke friend of mine decided that he wanted to go to railroadin'. But he didn't last too long at it. I asked him why he quit, and he replied that he didn't like being skinned up all the time. He matched a fight every time a railroader called him that, and he said that most of them could whip him.

My real interest in railroading began after the family moved to San Angelo. I hung around the yards, watching the switchmen, the engine drivers and the brakemen do their stuff. San Angelo was a great shipping point for livestock of all kinds, and things really hummed around the yards during the shipping rushes of spring and fall. The shipping pens were located a mile or so out of town, and it was a great experience to ride a freight train out there. The Kelly boys had a friend (a kindly soul) who ran a switch engine, and he let us ride with him when there weren't any officials around. I doubt if I experienced thrills in all my later years comparable to those times on John's engine. Now, I do say so, as shouldn't, that I was not a very bad boy, but I must shamefacedly admit that I just couldn't help playing hooky now and then when the shipping season was on. I think that the most envied boy in San Angelo was the kid who had the "Sancho," (the lead sheep). He had raised this wether from a dogie lamb to a well trained Judas sheep, trained to lead the others into the cars. Probably the most striking characteristic of the sheep is his following of a leader, and old Judas really tolled his followers in. This lad would lead his pet up the steps into the caboose and nonchalantly take a seat therein. He got ten cents for every car he helped load; consequently, he was about the most affluent kid in the community during shipping season. He would lead his sheep into the chute pen, take off the leading string and shout: "Andale." Old Iscariot would push his way through the other sheep and start up the chute. If his dupes were slow following, he would stop, bleat a few times and take off. The rest would follow him into the car, and he would work his way back through them and slip out before the door was closed. He was frequently rewarded with a chaw of 'terbacker or a tailor-made cigarette, which he purely relished.

When we got barred from the engine, we took to sneaking aboard the rear platform of the caboose as soon as the train started for the stock pens. Two unfortunate youngsters made the mistake of getting on a caboose of a train that had already been loaded, and they had to ride the caboose platform into Brownwood, 100 miles away. They were there corralled by the law and shipped home in ignominy and terror of what they were going to get when they had to face their parents. What broke me was the time I got kicked off the caboose while the train was under pretty fair speed. It skunt me up something awful, ruined a pair of new britches and caused all kinds of complications at home and at school.

I was a proud and happy young man when I reached the glorious status of "stock tender" (accompanying stock to market). Those old railroaders were tough, mean old devils and made life a misery to a caretaker aboard their trains. But, if he kept his nose clean, asked few questions and stayed out from underfoot, he would be tolerated. Let me say here and now that I had rather ride an old-time stock train than the finest vista dome, slick, stainless job of today. There was romance and high adventure on a stock train never equaled by any other form of transportation I have sampled.

With the passing of the years, the old, hard-nosed train men were superseded by a gentler breed under strict instructions to cater to the shippers' agents aboard their trains. Competition for business changed the breed. Besides, after the road built into Paint Rock, we became known as one outfit that always had a chuck wagon at the shipping pens, and how those railroaders enjoyed that fresh beef, hot biscuits, freeholie beans and all the trimmin's. After a few years I got to know practically every Santa Fe man from Paint Rock to Kansas. I always carried a box of "Seegars" and a bottle of "Four Roses" along. It was an iron-clad law, and rightly so, that no crew man could take a drink while on duty, but everybody looked the other way as the men went off duty. Just before we reached a division point, I would ask a crew member in a whisper if he would like a little snort before he got off the train. He would usually accept and call another member of the crew; but every man always turned his back as the other took a pull out of the bottle. Consequently, neither I nor he ever saw a crew member take a drink.

These courtesies paid off, and I could get anything I wanted from any man on the line. If I ran short of grub, they would wire ahead to the next stopping place where a hot lunch and plenty of coffee would be awaiting me. They would unload and take care of my stock at the feeding stations, and they always gave me the run of the place. I loved to ride the engines, and if conditions were right, I would be invited to share the seat behind the engineer.

But I finally got my fill of riding the "smutty end." One morning, up in the hills of Arkansas, I was asked how I'd like to make the run on the engine, and I gladly accepted. It was up hill and down dale, and we were pulling a heavy train. The hogger had to really let her out going downhill so that he could maintain a fair rate on the upgrade. An old locomotive was a rough riding piece of machinery, and it really swayed and bounced at full speed. If there were a lot of curves mixed along, it would lurch and lean over, making it a lot scarier to the uninitiated. On that particular morning, we had a "clair board," meaning that we had the right-of-way and could highball it. In addition, that jokester on the right-hand side went all out: he really had "her over in the corner," and I hung on for dear life. I never hollered a single time, but, you bet, when we stopped for a passenger train to go by, I sure hot-footed it back to the caboose, and stayed there.

It was hard, demanding work looking after a trainload of stock, and a stockman had to know his stuff. The conductor would tell him how long the train would be on the siding, and he and his helper (if he had one) would light out up the train looking for anything in bad order. If he had stock down, he tried to get them up with his long, steel-tipped prod pole. If that didn't work, he had to crawl in the small door at the end of the car, get down among them and tail 'em up. This didn't amount to much with sheep and young stuff, but it could certainly run into politics if he had big stock, especially when they were wild and had plenty of horns. He took his life in his hands when he got down among them. If he was still up the train when time came to start, the engineer would give two sharp blasts with the whistle, and he clambered up on top of the first car he could get to. If it was dark or slick with rain or snow, he just had to set there until the train stopped, and that could become uncomfortable.

If it were on a warm, bright Sunday morning in Kansas, a stockman rode on top by preference. Not only could he see a lovely countryside, but he could wave at all the farm girls along the way, and they always waved back. If everything went smoothly, he really enjoyed it unless he was hongry. I doubt if a stockman ever took enough food along with him, and he usually ran out well before he reached his destination. When I first started riding the stockers, I got no sympathy and danged little cooperation from the crews or even at division points, but after I got acquainted, I had it made. On several occasions, I received the top mark of friendly courtesy when a crew man would build a fire in the heating stove in the caboose and make a pot of coffee. I was really *in* when that happened.

It was pretty rocky at first, and two or three missed meals could get one mighty lank before he could get unloaded. One soon learned to hustle into a restaurant, grab all the pies and stuff in sight, pay plenty for a can of coffee and scurry back to the caboose. (Those "railroad" restaurants always kept a good supply of tin cans on hand for such emergencies.) That reminds me of Jack Westmoreland's prize story. Jack and a young helper left San Angelo on a through train, and, of course, forgot their food. They traveled all day and arrived at the Temple yards way in the night, might' nigh starved. A kindly trainman told them of a small "quick and dirty" in the yards where the switching crews got coffee and light refreshments. They would be there about thirty minutes, so they had to make a quick trip to the eatin' place. It was a hot, muggy night, and the little one-room shack, right in the midst of the dust and smoke of many trains, was pretty grimy. In addition, it had no screens and the flies were swarming. The place was lit by a couple of dim electric drop lights and was presided over by a most untidy, sleepy young man, who ran the back of his grimy hand across his runny nose and drawled. "What'll it be, gents?" Jack took it in stride, but his neophyte gagged and said: "Gimme a piece of that raisin pie and a cup o' coffee." The *garcón* waved a languid hand over the pie and said: "'Tain't raisin, it's custard." His guest ran outside right quick, and you know why! The waiter turned to Jack and said: "What'll be yourn?" There was a big bowl of hardboiled eggs still in their shells on the counter and three coconuts on a shelf. So Jack said: "Leave the eggs in the shell and put them and the coconuts in a big sack, you dirty S.O.B!" They had enough grub to last them to the feeding point at Arkansas City, but neither ever cared much for hardboiled eggs or coconuts after that.

Let me tell you about one trip that was fairly typical but rather on the rough side. Every teen-ager in our community wanted to make a stock trip with me. It was high adventure, and they had a return free pass, where they could ride in style on a passenger train. At this particular time, we had some three trainloads to take to the Flint Hills of Kansas, so I kinda had to scatter my usual helpers out among the other experienced men. I selected a big old green kid who had never been farther away from Paint Rock than San Angelo. He was totally inexperienced, but he was dependable and would listen to me—at least that is what I thought.

We carried a lot more baggage than usual, as I had to stay in Kansas for some time in order to settle the cattle on pasture. In addition to several packages of grub prepared by our respective mothers, we had to take along plenty of clothes, as the weather was still pretty cold in Kansas. We also had the customary lantern, two prod poles and our slickers, together with my saddle, making a lot of plunder to tote about in poorly lighted railroad yards at night.

We had a solid trainload of the biggest steers ever to come off the ranch. These cattle were so lengthy that we had trouble placing them crosswise in the cars, so I knew we were in for it. However, we made it fine as long as we had the number of cars we had started with. But, when we got on the main line, a lot more cars were added. The stock were on the front end almost half a mile away from the caboose, necessitating considerable footwork to check on them. We had all kinds of delays, and I got left at Paul's Valley. I knew that we would not be there long, so I made my helper stay with the caboose in case they started up before I could get back. Sure enough, when I was about ten car lengths from the caboose, the engine hooted twice and took off like a turpentined cat. The two cars immediately in front of the caboose were gondolas loaded with crossties standing on end, making the most hazardous situation a car-walker could face. I didn't want to sit atop the cars for some hours, so I waited to swing on the caboose. But the old hogger was mad at the conductor (as usual), and he really picked up speed. I turned and ran with the train, not noticing that we hit a high ballasted stretch of track. Consequently, the caboose mounting rails were clear out of my reach. My compadre was standing in the door watching and when he saw that I was left, he started to throw off our baggage and jump. I yelled to him to stay with the train and that I would catch a passenger train and join him up the line. The conductor, a friend of mine, heard the commotion and yanked the air rope. This stopped the train long enough for me to climb aboard with the assistance of the two of them.

We had trouble with the unloading at the feed pens and had to stay up most of the night; so we were a couple of tired, wore-out stockmen when we resumed our journey. They had added more cars to our train so that we could barely see the engine, which had a hard time moving along at a very slow gait. These long trains dealt misery to the occupants of the caboose by reason of the tremendous amount of slack that ensued at starts and changes of pace. On a long train like that, the caboose could well be jerked ten feet or more, so one had to keep a constant lookout. I cautioned my helper, time and again, about this slack and made him sit tight on his bunk and stay away from the open side-doors. I went to sleep, and when I waked up, I saw that he was standing in front of the door watching the great chunks of ice drifting down the Kaw River. I yelled at him to get th' hell away from that door. We were just creeping up a long grade, and the train was bucking. Just as he started back to his seat, the train broke in two, the air set and we stopped in our tracks. The jerk threw my apprentice some ten feet, end over end. Luckily, it didn't hurt him, but it split his new khaki britches from waistband to waistband, front and rear. (As Juan de Anda would have said: "It broke his pants!") He had a coat and a clean shirt along, but no more pants, so he had to get along kind of sidling. He did stay put after that.

A number of cattle were knocked off their feet by the break, and when an animal of that size got down in the car, that's all she wrote! The train could not be stopped, and just the two of us would have been unable to get the downies back on their feet anyway. So, when we got to the division point at Ark (Arkansas) City, we had several cars of stock in bad order. We changed crews here and had plenty of time to beat it to the yard office and report our dead and injured animals.

The yards were a-swarm with trainloads of cattle and the loading pens were full. The regular yardmaster, whom I knew very well, had been up forty-eight hours and had gone home for some rest. His place had been taken by an assistant —a young squirt "dressed in a little brief authority"—and he was really feeling his oats. He flatly refused to give me any help or to unload the bad-order cars. So, one tired, hungry, and mad cowpoke riz up on his hocks, and a cuss-fight ensued. Finally, I told him that the Santa Fe Railroad had bought a trainload of steers and that I was turning them over to him. He gentled down right quick and called the superintendent over the phone. The super had him call me to the phone and told me that the Road would assume all responsibility for the dead and injured cattle, as they had no room to unload them, and that he would get me moving right away. We went into the coffee shop to refresh ourselves, but before we got started, old smarty pants rushed in and said for us to get aboard the train as they would be ready to pull out in five minutes. We grabbed all our plunder and made tracks back to the train. When we reached the caboose, they had already coupled on and had the air pumped up. They had cut off our loads and hooked on to a passenger engine—and then occurred the wildest ride I ever experienced! We reached the "Y" a couple of times from Eldorado, where we changed roads. A switch engine was waiting for us, and the train crew heisted our belongings up to us on top of the rear car. It was dark by the time we backed into the station, where a reception committee awaited me, consisting of two live-stock agents, a trainmaster, a yardmaster, the stationmaster, the conductor and the rear "shack." They coupled us on and told me that they also were full up at the pens and would assume all responsibility for the stock if I would give them permission to pull out. Of course, I was glad to do it. We clambered aboard the "way car" (as those damn Yankees called a caboose) accompanied by a young livestock agent who had an enormous hot meal and a big bucket of coffee for us. The depot agent handed the conductor his "flimsey" (orders) and said: "You barely have time to beat the Flyer to your unloading point, so get going." And we got! I never saw any seventy-five miles of road with so many curves in it. We were running light, and the hogger "put 'er over in the corner." We sat on the bunk to eat our supper; but after we hit the first curve, the agent, my helper and I sat flat on the floor and tried to eat. The conductor, a droll-looking old fellow, had on an old straw sailor hat and sat at his desk trying to do his paper work, but he never finished it, even though his chair was securely anchored to the floor. The rear shack was up in the doghouse hanging on for dear life and begging to come down. But he was denied permission, as he had to sit up there and look for signals from the front and watch behind us for the Flyer. That old caboose really played pop-the-whip all the way down there. We got slung about so that we could hardly finish our supper, and our coffee spilled all over the floor. There were five frightened individuals in that car, I tell you! I'll bet that conductor looked at his watch a hundred times in that seventy-five miles. After an eternity, ol' shack yelled: "I see the switch lights," and the whistles howled for the switch as the train bucked and jumped under the air. The switch was open, and we rolled up to the pens. I daresay, we made a world's record for speed on that stretch of track: we had two cars unloaded before the passenger roared by doing at least seventy.

Our pasture man and his waddies were there to help us unload, which didn't take too long. We just sat around the fire the balance of the night, drinking coffee and shivering over recollections of that wild run. My partner had enough of railroading and beat it back home as soon as he could get a new pair of pants. If you want to have a good time and if you want to jump the devil, just jine a shipping crew.

As a finale to my railroad experience, I became a member of a railroad family, myself. My own daddy became president of a railroad "system" hisself.

Shortly after the turn of the century, a veritable rash of railroad building broke out all over the state, and West Texas experienced its full share. It became the happy hunting ground of the promoter, and most of our towns had visions of becoming railroad centers. The usual procedure was for a promoter to dream up a railroad and get the towns along the projected route to make up bonuses. Paint Rock got into the game when a railroad was headed south from Abilene and raised a bonus of $50,000 for the first road to build into the town. But the canny railroad committee in a town north of us tied up its bonus with a proviso that the road would have to stop there for two years. We had the money raised, and like Olie: "Ve yust couldn't vait." So, we found a promoter of our own.

I think that he was one of the most impressive-looking individuals that I have ever seen. He was tall, handsome, distinguished, and confident. He fairly oozed opulence. He even dressed like J. Pierpoint Morgan, complete with white piping on his vest, black patent leather, buttoned shoes, snow-white spats, and a flat-topped derby hat. (It turned out later that he was a traveling salesman.) He had no trouble selling us yokels on the idea of building a railroad ourselves. A charter was obtained for a railroad bearing the grandiose name of "The Concho, San Saba and Llano Valley Railway Company," projected from Sweetwater on the T & P to Llano, with its ultimate destination Corpus Christi on salt water. The stock was subscribed and a board of directors elected.

The promoter established an office, and we scurried all over, talking big and soliciting bonuses. But we didn't have much luck, and I shall never forget the awful, let-down feeling I experienced when the board called me before it and told me that they could get nobody else to build the road and had decided to build it themselves. They would start at Miles Station on the Santa Fe and build the twenty miles into Paint Rock. My father had been elected president and the promoter, general manager. They then offered me the job as chief engineer, which I turned down in holy horror, as I was totally without experience on location or building. I had an even greater sinking spell when they laughed and said that I didn't have anything on them, for they had no experience either.

They secured the services of a competent engineer, and the road was completed in good time. They put in two switches on the ranch, and the pens and a good, long switch were named "Sims Valley." The train stopped on flag, and we sure rode it. As a gag, the Miles office sent an annual pass to the president of the Santa Fe, requesting a pass for Father on the Santa Fe system. The president returned his pass with a tactful letter explaining that it was hardly fair to expect a pass over such big mileage in return for one of only twenty miles. Father just wrote, in his scrawling hand, on the bottom of the letter: "Dear Mr. ———, In reply, I will say that while your road is longer than mine, mine is just as wide." This amused the man so much that he sent Father an annual pass over the whole Santa Fe system.

However, it looked like that pass was to cost him dearly,

for the material notes were coming due. Only a half-dozen of the stockholders had any resources, and the burden of payment would fall on Father and two or three others: they were plenty worried. About two weeks before the due date, a bunch of Santa Fe officials called Father and his fellow officials to San Angelo for a conference. We heard nothing from him for a day or two, so we were on tenterhooks ourselves. I was a couple of miles away from Sims Valley, but I saw the train stop. I got back home as soon as I could. The rest of the family was away. I put up my horse and came in the back way. As I entered the house, I heard singing—you guessed it—"Amazing Grace." So I knew that he had sold out. He was rocking in his hammock out on the front porch, and I never saw such a beatific expression on anyone's face! He had got the monkey off his back.

The Santa Fe operated the road, mostly in the red, until the 1936 flood that destroyed their big bridge over the Concho River. We got back the right-of-way that we had nodated, together with a bunch of half-rotten ties that must have cost us twenty bucks apiece, counting our part of the bonus and our stock in the company. But we did get to enjoy a railroad for some twenty-five years, and it didn't break us—that is, except from building another one.

When a railroad headed for a village, its inhabitants immediately got the big-eye and envisioned it as a coming metropolis. Consequently, promoters and "townsite" men flourished. Many acres of good land were laid out into town blocks, lots, alleys and streets, bearing all kinds of high-falutin names. Nearly every town had its "Broadway."

Even Paint Rock was not exempt, and we laid out enough lots to warrant the name "Broadway." The railroad company located a townsite midway between Miles and Paint Rock and named it "Lowake" after two farmers named Lowe and Schlake who donated the land out of their good farms.

Being a draftsman, I was saddled with the job of drawing the maps of many of these subdivisions, and more than a few of them are still on file in the various county clerks' offices as mute reminders of the "glory that was once Rome's."

We sold many lots, practically all on credit, and finally had to take them back. I was secretary for at least three town-site companies. I did all the work and never received one thin dime for my services. Most of the land finally reverted to the original owners, and I have some acreage that ain't fittin' for anything on account of a lot of dilapidated concrete curbs and sidewalks. Oh, well, live and learn.

Contrary to the dreams of the promoters, development was slow, and the railroad did only so-so. We did not have the people or the freight to produce the expected revenue. However, the railroads managed to get along pretty well, and traffic increased for some twenty years. But "there was something dead up the creek," and none of us had the gumption to sense it. It was a noisy, chattering, smoking, stinking contraption known as the horseless carriage, an object of derision and raucous jokes, but what it did to the railroads was a-plenty.

AGUA Y PAPALOTES

WATER HAS ALWAYS BEEN THE DOMINANT FACTOR in the occupancy of any land by man or beast. *Homo Sap*, the most adaptable of all mammals, just has to have water, and so do his animals. Texas, west of the 100th Meridian, is pretty much on the dry side. The Indians and wild game, including the mustang, adapted very well by having developed a tolerance for dry country and scant waterings, together with high mobility and a sort of a sixth sense for locating water. But these aptitudes are woefully lacking in the dumb, driven, domesticated critters. Consequently, large sections of West Texas were slow settling up.

Five miles was about the limit of a cow's ability to walk for water, and even that was plenty hard on her. The sheep couldn't make it that far, although they could manage on water every other day. There was a lot of water, but it was "downstairs," beyond the limit of the dug well. Thus, the land over five miles from water was unoccupied and of little value.

Most of the old army men were sort of tenderfeet who took a very dim view of West Texas, calling it a part of the Great American Desert and totally unfit for civilized man to inhabit. General Phil Sheridan, in a report to Washington, was purported to have stated that if he were offered a choice between Hell and West Texas, he would unhesitatingly choose Hell. This statement didn't endear him very much to West Texans, especially the unreconstructed Confederates.

In context is a yarn told me by an old West Texas friend, Mr. Chas. Hobbs of San Angelo. He had become the owner of a good-sized spread in the dry area, but soon decided that he was no ranchman and put the place on the market. His first prospect was a young Englishman who he showed over the place. As they were leaving, a chaparral cock (road runner) fluttered across the trail in front of them, and the young man interestedly inquired the name of the bird. Mr. Hobbs facetiously replied that it was a "Bird of Paradise." The young man grinned and said: "I s'y, Mr. Hobbs, has he not strayed from his habitat?" During the trip to San Angelo, the prospect made no comment as to how the ranch impressed him. Mr. Charley made a last desperate attempt to make the sale, winding up his pitch with: "The place may be a mite dry, but this is a great country, and all we need is a little more water and a few more people." The young man dryly replied: "I dare s'y, Mr. Hobbs, that is true. Hell would, no doubt, be a desirable spot it if it were not for the climate and the association." Mr. Hobbs was glad he did not make the sale as oil was later discovered on that section of "Paradise."

All those dry acres of good grazing and farming land remained desolate and unoccupied until old Mother Necessity hatched out a couple of birds with the answer—the well driller and the windmiller. The early wells were dug by hand and were limited in depth. Also, the West Texas rock is as hard as Beelzebub's head is supposed to be. There were few hard-rock miners in our country, and most men were mighty juberous of high explosives. So, the ingenious Yankee did it again: he came up with a machine that would drill a hole in the ground.

At first it was a crude conglomeration of cogs, gears, levers, ropes and what-not that raised a heavy drill stem and let it drop kerplunk. It was actuated by a "horsepower." This was a large, heavy cast iron ring gear attached to a long pole, or sweep, which was pulled by a dejected horse plodding around in a circle, urged on by a bored youngster follering him around and around. This gear turned a smaller cog attached to a tumblin' rod which conveyed the power to the drilling machine. A hole was started with a crowbar, water was added, and the drill was raised and lowered. The hole was cleaned out with a long "slush bucket" with a valve in the bottom, raised and lowered by a rope running over a pulley on the mast. The drill cuttings mixed with the water formed the mud, or slush, that could be picked up by the bucket and dumped into the slush pit. Water was poured in the hole, and the drill thumped away again. It was a slow go, but it eventually got the job done on down some two or three hundred feet. If water was struck, tin or galvanized iron casing, something like an elongated stovepipe, was placed in the hole, and it was ready for the pump. This pumping business was operated by hand or horsepower or even a rope running over a pulley and attached to the saddle horn of a disgusted horseman. I have done it during emergencies, and I know just how monotonous a job it could become.

Drilling rigs and techniques have also been identified with our technological explosion. I can well visualize how an old driller's eyes would bug out at the sight of the latest mobile, self-contained rotary unit complete with motors, compressors and hydraulic gadgets, all mounted on one ponderous truck. This rig can make more hole in an hour than the old horsepower could in days, and they can drill much deeper.

Recently, a 1966 model rig left San Angelo one morning, drove forty miles to location, spudded in, completed, tested and cased a 150 foot well and got back to town in time for lunch. The clean technician, dressed in spotless, permanently pressed khakis, has a tough job: he has to pull an occasional lever and let the hydraulic systems do the rest. They don't even have to haul water for drilling: there's no slush as they just blow the drill cuttings out of the hole with compressed air. How smart and how lazy can we get! To these loafers and hard workers West Texas owes a big debt.

The job of getting the water out of the hole has also kept pace with the drilling techniques. Wind has long been recognized as a source of energy, and for centuries man has harnessed it to his machines. We have an ever-present, inexhaustible supply of that power in West Texas just howling to be utilized. Consequently, when the drilled well was a *fait accompli* in West Texas, it didn't take long for Yankee ingenuity to tinker up an adaptation of the European windmill to raise the water to the surface. Boy, that did it!

These first windmills had wooden wheels with narrow, slat spokes set sort of slonchwise. They caught the wind and turned the wheel which raised and lowered a wooden rod connected to a cylinder pump in the bottom of the well. The oldest mills that I remember were the Perkins and the Eclipse, ponderous, heavy clanking affairs with inadequately lubricated cranks and gears that squalled and squeaked so loud that one could hear a mill operating about as far as one could see it, even if it was mounted atop a tall wooden tower in order to ketch the wind. (It took a right smart of a breeze to start the wheel to wheezing.) They took a lot of looking after, but they got the job done. If a ranch had a half-dozen or more mills on it, most of one man's time was required just to keep them going. The "windmill man" had about the dirtiest, nastiest, greasiest job imaginable, and it rubbed off on him so that the other hands all swore that his disposition was as nasty as his appearance.

The modern steel mill, turning on roller bearings within a sealed gearbox, requires little attention and once-a-year change of oil. It is about half the size of its wooden prototype and operates in a breeze gentle as a "Maiden's Breath"— leastways, that's what the advertising matter says.

The old-time ranch windmill man has about become extinct except on the largest ranches. Now a man will drive by in a pickup, take a quick gander and drive on about ninety per cent of the time. But, with all this, the windmill business ain't what it used to be. R.E.A. lines are building all over, and when a mill does finally wear out, it is more and more frequently replaced by a motor, jet pump and pressure tank that keeps the water flowing as needed, even in a long spell of calm weather. We didn't have too many dead calm spells, but when we did, things really fouled up. We were not too well equipped as to storage, and we soon ran out of water when the mill stopped turning. Seemed like this always happened in hot weather when the cattle needed the most water. It was something to see how much water one old cow could drink when it was short. When the supply failed, one had to start snaking out water by slush bucket and rope tied to the horn of the saddle, rig up the old horsepower or couple on a cranky gasoline engine. I have lost several nights' sleep chaperoning one or another of these devices. After about a week of this, no sailor ever whistled as earnestly for wind as did a wore-out cowpoke. But the wind, like the rain, always came just before things went to hell.

Conquering the Great American Desert called into being two new professions—the well-driller and the windmiller. They were also sort of *sui generis*, with skills, customs and mannerisms all their own—fiercely independent, salty and sot in their ways. They knowed their jobs and they done 'em. I knew many of these men to whom our country is so indebted, but most of them are now helping out folks over there in the Great Beyond.

There have been endless arguments about which of these two old roosters was the most valuable in the development of our water facilities. "If it warn't for the driller, we'd have no water; and if it warn't for the windmiller we couldn't get it out of the ground." Argumentation was a source of much entertainment among loafers in those days of scant divertisement.

One of the great windmillers is my good friend, K. B. Logan of San Angelo, a skilled artisan, no mean hydraulic engineer, and truly one of the old breed. K. B. has in all probability put up more windmills in West Texas than any other living man, and his experiences and accomplishments would fill a book a whole lot bigger than this one. He has seen the same great improvement in mills as in all our other machinery. His territory reached from Uvalde to Lubbock and from San Angelo to El Paso—a right smart strip of country, believe me. For years, he made his own towers out of lumber, using six by six scantlings thirty to forty feet long for the four legs. I'd like to see you find a piece of timber like that nowadays. These legs were slanted towards the top and were fastened together with large nails and bolts to cross pieces and sway braces of 2x6 or 2x8 lumber. This heavy tower was built prone on the ground and raised by means of "block and tickle" with the rope running over long shear poles, some two-thirds the length of the tower, attached to a team of horses. Later on a truck or pickup replaced the sometimes skittish and unpredictable teams.

Part of the gears were fastened to the tower and raised with it, and the rest, together with the wheel and tail, were hoisted by means of a gin pole and "block and tickle" operated by hand or horsepower. The tail was attached and the wheel assembled by the windmiller sitting astride the tail. One had to be a pretty good peeler to stay with that tail when a whirlwind hit. One of my most hair-raising experiences occurred when I was straddling a tail some sixty-five feet above ground. I locked my laigs around that whirling windmill tail and almost tore the galvanizing off of it with my bare hands. It's remarkable what one can do when he has to!

As drilling techniques improved, wells kept getting deeper and deeper, but the windmiller kept pace with it all. It can be right smart of a job to install a pump and mill over a really deep well or pull pump rods and cylinder on a 700 foot well, but he could do it easily enough even with the crude means at his disposal.

Another most important individual in our water development was the water witch. Of course our geologists and scientists snickeringly raise skeptical eyebrows, but I again say unto them: "There are more things in Heaven and earth, Horatio, than are dreamt of in your philosophy." For years, I also "hurled the critic's ban," but I sure don't any more.

Like the old nester lady who caught her husband in dalliance: "I know what I seen."

I live in a "dry streak" of country where underground water is in small veins, and it is a big gamble when a hole is put down. I am sure that we drilled fifty dry holes and got only two wells, one of them pretty weak. One summer I was mighty short of water and got me a driller. Some of these old boys were pretty fair rule-of-thumb geologists, acquiring their experience by observing the lay of the land. This man picked out a favorable looking spot and went to work. While he was hammering away, I met an old friend who had about the same kind of country that I did. He had just struck a fine well which a water witch had located for him. He bragged on him so that I rather sheepishly went to see the witch. He said that if I had any water, he could find it. So I told him to go to it. We went to the drilling well the next morning, and he stuck his forked switch over the hole and announced that I had struck all the water I was going to get even if I went 1000 feet. I told the driller to tear down his rig and move to another location. The witch asked me where I'd like a well, and I said just any old place, so he went toddling up the turn-row, grasping his peach tree switch. I had the morning paper with me and sat in the car reading. Before I had read half the front page, I heard the witch holler. He was all smiles when I drove up and said: "I've shore found a good 'un. It's forty-five foot deep and a strong vein." I told the driller to set up at the location, and in less than one day's drilling, he had a good well. He also found me two more—you see why I believe.

This man prevailed on me to try my hand at witching, and, to my surprise, the switch worked for me. I cannot explain it, but when I find the right spot, the switch will turn down despite my strongest efforts to control it. I have even had the bark twisted off the switch in my grasp. I have found several good wells, but I don't guarantee my work, and I have no more idea than a hant how deep the water is supposed to be.

And thereby hangs another tale: one extra dry summer my

tanks played out, and I desperately needed the grazing in that pasture. I got my driller, but my witch was out of pocket, so I did the witching myself. Some days later I was delivering a bunch of steers to some Kansas buyers when the driller drove up to the shipping pens where we were loading out the trucks. As the last truck pulled away, old driller announced with a grin that he had made a well, but that it was oil instead of water. I disgustedly said: "Dadgummit, I wanted water, not oil." I never saw a bunch of men get more kick out of a fool incident than those Kansas Jayhawkers did out of my reply. Some years later I met one of these men, and he was still laughing about the guy who was mad because he struck oil instead of water. For the record, I might remark that it was a "stinker" and just enough oil to mess things up, as I had had every reason to suspect.

Another source of water is the stock tank (stock pond or farm pond if you hail from Yankeeland). Practically all tanks are "of the earth earthy," either holes scooped out of the ground, impoundments behind earthen dams or a combination of both. One was in luck if he was in a country where the soil is clayey, but he can hub the devil if it is sandy or gravelly. He may even have to coat the sides and bottom with concrete sprayed over net wire or use some of the drilling muds of the oilman.

A good holding tank is an asset on any ranch, no matter how well it is watered. Even if one does not need the stock water, it can provide a good fishin' hole. You have no idea how hungry a man can get for fishing if he has to go a couple of hundred miles to wet a hook. These dry country folks always order fish when they patronize a restaurant in a big town, and the fellow who lives in a fish country always orders steak when he is at Lowake or similar steakhouses. You can spot 'em across the dining room.

The old tanks were pretty skimpy, but they did help piece out the water if they were good holding. One just couldn't make a very big tank with our primitive dirt-moving equipment—a turning plow and a "slip."

One picked out a spot in a small draw (ravine). He daren't

select too big a one or it would carry more water after a rain than his flimsy dam could handle. He hooked a couple of horses to the turning plow and ploughed up an area the size of his projected tank. He then hitched the team to the slip (truly an invention of the devil), a sort of glorified sugar scoop fabricated out of steel. It had a heavy "bail" attached amidship to which the team was hooked. It had a couple of straight wooden handles, some three feet long, attached to the rear. He draped his let-out lines over his right shoulder, passing these around under his left armpit, clucked to his team, bent over and grabbed the wooden handles, tilted the scoop, and took off. When he reached the dam, he stooped over, grabbed the handles and dumped it by main strength and awkwardness, and on and on in endless cycles. It only carried a shirt-tail full of dirt, but it required a good deal of strength to dump it. Twelve hours of plodding through loose dirt could become mighty tiresome along in the shank of the afternoon, and it could be dangerous if he had a fractious team or hit a rock or stump when filling. If his team tried to run away, he held on to one line, sat flat on the ground and circled them over the loose dirt until they gave out. It was a good way to break a wild one, but it was hard on the driver. He just kept on ploughing and scraping day after day. If he stayed with it long enough, he got a tank. A tanker surely had well-developed muscles, and I have often thought what a good conditioner tanking would be for a football player.

Sometime later the Fresno was developed. It was a rotary affair pulled with four animals and operated by a long steel lever actuated by a rope held by the driver. It handled a lot more dirt and was somewhat easier to operate.

Then came the caterpillar tractor, and the tanker had it made. The modern scrape can handle twenty yards or more at a time, and the latest models on ponderous rubber tires can really fly. So it's no trick now to build a big tank or a great lake with miles of high earthen dams.

Bureaucrats are pretty cute people, and it didn't take them long to latch on to the tank-building ploy. So they tied it into their conservation program. I guess we are all hipped on getting something for nothing, and we West Texans really went to town on tanks. Now they are thicker than fiddlers in Gehenna! One old acquaintance of mine had a little place without a single draw on it, but he had a big tank stuck up on the side of a hill. I asked him if he had ever caught any water in it. He sheepishly replied that he had not and said he knew it all the time, but that the government feller said that it was a good spot for a tank, and it didn't cost him nothin' so he let them go ahead and build it.

I also jined the band, and I now have from one to half a dozen on every draw on the ranch. They are all good tanks, and they supply plenty of water, but I sometimes wonder if I did not pay a pretty high price for them in the area of self-reliance and a bit of self-respect. You just flat don't get somethin' for nothin'.

THE HORSELESS CARRIAGE

THE NEXT FACTOR in our development was the gasoline engine, and I wonder how we ever got along without it. The first ones were heavy, noisy, temperamental and undependable, but they had it all over the steam engine in convenience and mobility. One could haul the smaller ones around and adapt them to farming and ranching chores, such as drilling wells, pumping water, grinding feed, sawing wood and everything else requiring comparatively light power.

They kept improving them until wild-eyed tinkerers conceived the idea of using them to propel vehicles, and the horseless carriage was born, a lusty offspring that has about taken us over lock, stock and barrel. It's kind of interesting to speculate as to where we would now be if it were not for that horseless carriage with all its variations and impacts (no pun intended) on our lives, limbs, mores and economy.

At first, this bizarre contraption was nothing but an annoying plaything of the foolish, idle rich who had little to do except to pursue the fad of the moment. It was expensive, unreliable and fit for little except to scare our horses into conniption fits, and it sure did that! I daresay that the horse-

Orland L. Sims in one of the earliest "horseless carriages" brought to West Texas.

less carriage caused more runaways than all the other boogers combined. After the monstrosity became more common, our legislature produced all sorts of measures regulating its operation. One law provided that if the driver of a horseless carriage met a horse-drawn vehicle in a lane or a narrow road, he had to stop, kill his motor and assist the teamster to pass. And, thereby hangs another tale.

A friend told me the following and swore that it was true. He was driving a car down a narrow, sandy lane near Giddings, when he met a large, excitable woman and a sandy-haired kid of about ten riding in an open buggy behind a sleepy old horse. The driver of the car could not pull out of the ruts he was in, so he stopped, killed his motor and got out to assist in getting the rig by. The old woman was standing up in the buggy, waving her arms and squalling her head off, while the kid and the sleepy old horse paid the car no mind. The motorist politely asked: "Little man, shall I lead your horse by?" To which the grinning kid replied: "No s'r, just lead Ma by. I can manage the horse."

But some horses never did get used to them, and I have had to do some tall old riding if I met a car on a narrow road. We had one old grey horse who went crazy as a loon if he got within 100 yards of a car. He never did get over his phobia although he lived to see cars all around him.

I always was a sucker for new things, and I got hold of an Oldsmobile, circa 1903 vintage. It was a great disappointment, and we soon got rid of it. It was a tiny, one-seater, constructed along the lines of a small courtin' buggy, even to a leather dashboard like a buggy and equipped with a socket for a buggy whip. You needed a whip, for you had to haul it in via "horsepower" ever once in a while. It steered with a tiller, and its wheels were something like glorified bicycle wheels, equipped with tubeless tires that even a grass burr could puncture. The motor of only a single cylinder was amidship under the one seat. It was started with a wooden-handled crank that looked something like a glorified coffee mill handle. Power was transmitted to the rear axle by an overgrown bicycle chain running on exposed sprockets. This exposed chain drive was what broke me from wanting that motorcar. Most anything would cause it to jump off the sprockets, and when it did—oh brother! It just flat flew to pieces and scattered links and pieces all around. My tool compartment was a towsack hung on the side of the body which contained a claw hammer, cold chisel, punch, screwdriver, monkey wrench, wire pinchers, a gallon lard can of chain links and rivets, and the bottom of a disabled flatiron.

When the expected happened, it sounded like all the innards were being torn out of her, but it stopped quick. I got out, gathered up the useable chain parts, opened my lard bucket, sat flat on the ground and placed the flatiron, bottom up, between my knees and went to work. When I got enough chain assembled, I had to inch my way under the car, flat on my back. The old outfit was pretty drippy, and I usually got several drops of oil on me. That didn't bother too much unless a drop got in an eye. That could be downright uncomfortable. It also took some doing to maneuver the chain onto the sprockets. I then inched out from under, dusted my clothes off as best I could, wiped my face and hands on a discarded flannel petticoat, gathered up my plunder, and then began the real chore—that of starting the motor. That one-lung engine had considerable compression so there was a petcock on the cylinder to relieve some of the pressure. One opened the petcock by means of a rod attached to its cut-off and cranked away. The heavy, exposed flywheel picked up momentum until you could close the petcock and spin the crank. If the spark and gas levers were set just right, she caught hold and began her satisfying popping—it didn't have a muffler.

The driver got in and pushed up the gas, and the whole thing began to shimmy and shake. He grabbed the tiller and put her in forward gear (it also had a reverse gear) and away he went, sailing down the road at least six miles an hour. I put up with all that, but I just couldn't take any more when a nester in a wagon passed me at a trot and yelled: "Git a horse!"

We laid off automobiles, as they then became known, for several years. Mr. Charlie Hobbs of San Angelo, our banker and wool factor, had a four-cylinder car with a high topless body, called the "tonneau," entered through a door in the back. Choctaw George, master craftsman and mechanic, drove Mr. Charlie and two wool buyers down to our pens while we were shearing. When they left, Father got in the car, ostensibly to help push it up the considerable incline near the pens, but secretly because he wanted to ride in it. He rode with them for about a half a mile and walked back to the pens in an enthusiastic mood. He said: "Son, it went up the hill just like it had a team of horses pulling it. I think that we had better get one." But I had had my fill of motorcars and didn't encourage him any.

This lasted until the Model T Ford appeared on the scene. I was on a bank board, and we loaned a man money to go into the Ford business. When he went broke with six cars on his hands, we were in the automobile business ourselves. We managed to get out rather cleverly: we each bought and paid for a car. The bank didn't lose any money, and we were the owners of the first workable cars to come to our section.

Mr. and Mrs. D. E. Sims, parents of Orland Sims, with their car, "Animosity," 1912

And here beginneth the saga of old "Animosity." It was customary to name cars, and I chose the name after a fool tale that I had recently heard. A local cutie busted a bottle of soda pop on a fender and christened her "Animosity."

"Annie" was a black touring car, which was the only kind that Ford turned out then, its number was 4440. It was called a "phaeton." It had no doors, but the coach work was better than on the finest American car of today. The fold-back top was anchored by two leather straps fastened to the front frame. The windshield was a straight up-and-down heavy plate glass, and it folded in the middle. Its radiator was solid brass, as were the kerosene headlights and dash lights, which were shaped like the front door lamps of a house.

It was quite a "gal" car, and when I got all that brass shined up, she looked like a million dollars. So I never had any trouble getting dates. There are several staid, portly and whiteheaded "Grammas" in the area who cherish fond memories of "Animosity."

Annie wasn't good just for socializing alone: I still think that she was the best car I ever owned, even to my late model Cadillac all dolled up with the bucket seats, red leather upholstery and every accessory except a pipe organ and a powder room. All one needed to keep her running was a pair of pliers, bailing wire, tire tools and a lot of tire patches and dope. She might be a mite cantankerous about starting up on cold mornings, but all one had to do was to "tie up a hind leg" (jack up a hind wheel), pour a teakettle of hot water into the radiator, grab the crank and spin her. She was the best mud car I ever owned and could go about anywhere a burro could.

There was only one drawback to her: I had to send to Dallas or the factory for repair parts. I had a friend, who owned a bicycle shop in San Angelo, whom I talked into taking the Ford agency so that I could get parts and help in putting them on. He bought one car and got the agency for most of West Texas. He ran that car for more than a year and cussed me every time he saw me. He managed to sell it just before he went broke. He then bought another car and that did it. He made more than a million dollars out of the agency.

After the new wore off "Annie," we turned her into a ranch car, and I could do might' nigh everything with her that I could do with a horse. I drove up the milk cows a jillion times with her and rustled horses until the brush got too bad. Once I got to bragging what I could do with her, and one of the hands bet me that I couldn't rope a calf with her. I tied a rope to the steering column and eased up to a big bull calf who trotted along beside me. I made a lucky cast, and when the rope tightened around his neck, things really picked up. I tried to get that blasted rope loose, but I was kept so busy trying to stay right-side-up that I couldn't get my knife out of my pocket. Before I knew it, we "forked" a tree. As a result, yearling, Annie and I all met head-on. Strange to say, it only knocked some hide off the calf's head and bunged up a few of Annie's radiator fins. But it sure cured me of trying to rope from an automobile, and I wouldn't recommend it to anyone.

Of course, roads kept pace with the motorcar, and they began to dig into the railroad's revenues. Paved roads and increased speeds cut the passenger traffic down to a dribble, and trucks began to compete for the freight. What really hurt the railroads hereabouts was the trucks' taking over the livestock shipments. It took about thirty-six hours for a railroad to deliver a load of stock to the Fort Worth market, while a truck could make it in about twelve hours, a substantial savings in time and shrinkage of the animals.

The first road-building tractor brought to West Texas

These early stock trucks were pretty small, flimsy affairs, but they got the job done. Many a cowpoke or nester boy, tired of agricultural pursuits, went into trucking. He could buy a small truck on the installment plan and build himself a stock bed on it out of 1 x 4 lumber. They were kind of shackeldy affairs, but they got the stock to Fort Worth quicker, cheaper and in better shape than the railroads could possibly do it. Besides, they could come to the shipper's own pens on short notice, so he had no problems such as driving his stock to a railroad point, waiting for cars, and experiencing all kinds of delays. He simply called his pet trucker, told him how many head of stock he wanted to send, named the time and location for loading, and old Ollie or Joe had trucks Johnny-on-the-spot.

Just one example of this convenience: I had a bunch of lambs that didn't get fat, and I had to hold them over. This upset my plan of operations, and I sure needed to get rid of those sheep. We had some good summer showers, and I decided to double up on some pastures and rest the others. We rounded up a pasture, and as we were putting the sheep through the gates, I got a good, close look at them and was amazed to see what gains they had made. It's funny about a fool sheep: he can change condition quicker than any animal I know. He can either go to pieces or get fat in a couple of weeks if conditions happen to be just right. I hadn't seen these critters in two or three weeks, and in that time, they appeared ready for shipment.

I had the men start them for the shipping pens while I high-tailed it to a telephone. My commission man in Fort Worth said that the market was strong on that class of sheep and advised a trial shipment. I called Ollie, and he had a couple of trucks at the pens at 4:00 p.m., and they were in Fort Worth by midnight. The market was up a dollar that morning, and Swift & Co. bought the rest of the bunch by phone. Result: within two weeks, I had cleaned them all out at a profit of more than $10,000 where I thought I would have to take a loss. Good old trucks!

Of course, I wanted to sample what a trucker's life was like, and made a trip to Fort Worth with Joe. We left home after dark for Fort Worth with a load of sheep. The truck was underpowered and overloaded, so I am sure Joe had to change gears at least a thousand times that night. Changing gears in those old trucks was a complicated procedure. They had several more gears than a passenger car, and the driver had to go through the whole train from "grandma" (low-low) to high-high every time he changed gears, and he had to double-clutch at every change. It was an accepted fact that the calf of a trucker's left leg was twice as big as the right because of all that double-clutching. We each drank about a half-gallon of coffee that night, and I ate two or three suppers. Joe declined to eat as he said it made him sleepy. Anyway, we got the sheep unloaded just before daylight, and he turned back for another load. But he went without me. I went to bed and would have slept the clock around if the phone hadn't rung.

Threshing grain

These old truckers were tough, salty critters with mannerisms, customs and an argot all their own. They had a complicated set of signals, either by hands or headlights, whereby two meeting truckers informed each other as to what to expect up ahead. If the "do right" boys (the highway patrols) were out, they met a sedate procession of trucks trundling along at moderate speed. If a trucker was overloaded, he pulled off onto a side road, turned his lights off and went to sleep.

Once I met my friend Ollie out on the highway in the daytime. I wanted to deliver a message, and I tried to wave him down. I evidently made the wrong signal for he did not stop. There was a good deal of traffic; consequently, it took several minutes for me to turn around. When I did, Ollie was nowhere in sight. A dirt road turned off the highway, and Ollie was really kicking up a dust! It took me a couple of miles to overtake him, and, even then, I had to get in front of him to stop him. He had failed to recognize me, and my signal had told him that a cop was nearby. He had on an overload and wanted to dodge a fine.

It was nip and tuck with these men whether they could pay off a truck by the time it wore out. Livestock constituted most of their loads, and the shipments were more or less seasonal. So they had to "make hay" during the shipping season. It was absolutely amazing what one of those men could stand. He would unload his shipment some hours after midnight and stop by the side of the road for a couple of hours' nap. When he got home, his wife would have a good hot meal for him, let him sleep for two hours and roust him out for another trip. He got only about four hours sleep and one square meal each twenty-four hours, pieced out by a scattering hamburger and much black coffee. These spells happened about twice a year, and the rest of the time they had to rustle around for scattering loads. They made a living, but they dead sure didn't get rich. Like retired railroaders, these old truckers continue to truck long after retirement. When two or more get together, that's all they talk about, and some of their tales are pretty tall.

Like everything else, the whole picture has changed. The modern stock truck is a forty-foot behemoth with a steel and aluminum body and is covered over. The sheep trucks may carry three decks. They have plenty of power and most of them are equipped with automatic transmission, power brakes and power steering. About all the driver has to do is to sit in his comfortable, air-conditioned cab, turn on the radio and roll down the road at about sixty-five. He may even have a bunk where he can get a good snooze while his "swamper" takes over the driving chore.

These birds may have sort of sissified jobs nowadays, but they sure do deliver the goods. A shipper can now call his trucker and send any kind of a load anywhere in North America in insured, bonded trucks. Most of the business is now in the hands of corporations. It just costs too much for the little fellers, who had no small part in the development of West Texas.

You may be old and stove up now, fitten only to sit around playing dominoes and squirting tobacco juice, but you shore done your part, amigos.

OIL & OILERS

OF COURSE, all the foregoing, from the Injun-chaser to the truck man, played an important role in the development of West Texas, but I wonder if any of them had as much of a finger in the pie as the "oiler." If that feller could provide water out here as plentifully and as widely as he has oil, I know most votes would be cast for him. In any event, he's the guy who put the money here.

Despite a good country and a lot of hard work, the weather and our own danged foolishness had just about broke us cowpokes and nesters. We just can't keep robbing our soil and overstocking our range, disregarding the laws of nature and the conservation of resources, without the patter-rollers catching up with us. They had might' nigh caught up with us by the time the oil people came along. Although they developed our whole state, I refer herein to the country west of the 100 Meridian.

Droughts, depressions, foreign competition and our own mismanagement had us just about hanging on the ropes when the Santa Rita well was brought in. This happened in the early twenties, and I doubt if there is a landowner in all West Texas who has not benefited from the oil business, even if he never got a drop of oil on his place. Leases and rentals have paid off about as well as actual oil royalties. They have paid off our mortgages (and most of us had them on our land), educated our kids, built our roads, our cities and towns, brought in industry and made more rich widders and old maids than you can shake a stick at. I wonder how many of us would be playing golf, drinking $12 Scotch at our country clubs, going to Europe and around the world, and getting all kinds of nice divorces if it had not been for oil. Probably a lot of us would now be digging ditches or trying to make a living on a dry cotton farm if it hadn't been for the fantastic chance of somebody else's bringing up the black gold through a hole in the ground that just happened to be located on the land that we and the mortgage companies owned.

However, I wonder just how much oil has contributed to our happiness and our spiritual well-being. I once heard a wise old lady remark that she hoped that they would not strike oil on any of her considerable landholdings because of what it might do to her children. I also knew of another one who sadly said on her deathbed: "I wish to God that they had never struck one drop of oil on the Pecos River. We were a poor, hard-working family, but we enjoyed life and each other. Now look at us, scattered all over the world, fussing, quarreling and hating each other."

So, I have about decided that no landowner is any happier by having oil struck on his land; however, I would be mighty willing to try it. In all of West Texas I am on one of the very few ranches that does not have an oil or gas well on it. However, leases and rentals have helped a lot, and a good country has not been ruined by having a lot of *nasty oil wells* on it.

At first, people thought that an oil well would produce forever, and they spent their money as fast as it came in. Now, a lot of them are having a tough time getting by on their Social Security. Later on, folks, profiting from such experiences, called in financial experts, and under their guidance have socked away their money in tax-free securities, trusts and foundations. That's just fine, but I am wondering if they are not pointing a bunch of children and grandchildren toward lives of cultivated idleness. Despite my gripes, grumblings and moralizings, I have the sneaking feeling that I would have enjoyed being one of those cultivated idlers.

I should be somewhat familiar with the history of the oil business in West Texas, for I have lived right spang in the big middle of it as landowner, dabbler and observer since its inception down to this very hour. For some reason, Concho County was one of the first to attract the seekers for oil. In the late 1890's and early 1900's, several "deep prospectors" for artesian water were drilled in and near the county. Practically every one of them found some water, but it was either salt water or contaminated with oil. Small gas shows were also encountered, and I remember one well, that never was plugged, which for years produced enough gas to burn when we threw lighted matches in it and ran.

In those days of primitive geology and absence of practical experience, such streaks of oil and gas were considered sure indications of the presence of an oil field. The lay of the land, especially if it resembled that of fields in other states, was also prime evidence. An old driller or a wiseacre would find a landscape that recalled others where oil had been found. How many times have I heard the expression: "I shore like the way them hills run down into the flats . . . just like Californy." And there were just pure D hunches of these "experts," all of which found ready credence with us gullible landowners. Hence, we were sitting ducks for promoters, treasure hunters, gyp artists and owners of rigs who were seeking jobs.

The major companies of Texas were somewhat infantile, and limited their activities to proven areas in deep South Texas. So, we got the small fry. It's a funny thing, but most of our early discoveries were made by these small visionaries. By the same token, even today, the majors are prone to sit on the corral fence like a bunch of buzzards waiting to see if the old cow is going to die, while the small independents are out prospecting on a shoestring. When a good strike is made, the big boys swooped down on it like a bunch of *Aasvogels* on the African veldt.

Locations were made on rule-of-thumb geology, hunches, witching and superstition. One successful old wildcatter in East Texas swore that he located his wells with the aid of an old cross-eyed Negro. When he found a favorable looking area, he would mount his "finder" facing backwards on an old blind white horse, and turn them loose at exactly midnight in the dark of the moon. He would smite the horse a hearty blow on the rump to start him off. When the horse stopped, his rider would throw a rock over his left shoulder, and where it struck the ground was the location for a well!

This was the era of the "doodle-bugger," and those of us who believed in water witching had great faith in him. A doodle-bug was any kind of a contraption that a man "with a feel" used to locate oil pools. We fell for one of these birds ourselves. Some friends who had struck it rich in the Brecken-ridge Field had a doodle-bugger that they swore by as he had located every well that was discovered on their lands, which were plumb lousy with oil.

This "Bugger" was a tall, gangling, precise-talking individual with all the earmarks of the treasure-hunting zealot, and he had a weird contraption of batteries, gauges, switches, etc., with a remarkable story behind it. According to the operator, the device was developed by a young geologist-engineer who was employed by a major American oil company in the Baku oil fields in Romania. This man had a theory about bouncing echoes of electric impulses off underground formations, something like the radar of today. He experimented around, drilling wells in production areas until he pinpointed the proper echo from each stratum, whether rock, shale, water or oil-bearing sand, the oil formation giving a most distinctive reaction. He finally worked out a device that would pick up only oil "vibrations." He had to make the device out of whatever materials he could find in the fields, mostly junk. It was a rough job, turned out by someone who was not very efficient at handwork.

He had located several wells for his company when World War I broke out. He was tipped off that the Germans would overrun the area within a few hours, and he hid his gadget in a small cave. He finally made it to Constantinople and thence to the United States. But his health had become so impaired that he was in hard straits. Our old fellow, a long-time acquaintance, befriended him during his illness. After the war, he returned to Baku, retrieved his brain–child and came back to the States. He did not live long and left his invention to his benefactor.

The story so intrigued my "scientific mind" and my credulity that I swallowed it, hook, line and sinker, and communicated my enthusiasm to my father. So we hired the old gent at the fabulous rate of $300 per day (big money, then). He insisted on complete secrecy because of "professional ethics." So, Doodler, my father, my very skeptical brother and I set out in a Model T for to explore.

The mechanism consisted of a 12x12x18 inch box, sealed with a pitchlike substance, with switches and a gauge resembling a thermometer tube that went into a hole in the box. One could hold this gauge over a pail of crude oil, and a dark liquid would rise in it, probably due to the heat of the operator's hand, but to our bemused eyes, it was a sure indication of its reaction to oil.

He would set the box on the ground and attach it by two heavy copper strips to a large wet battery from which led off a couple of small brass chains some four feet long, each attached to a brass knob about three inches in diameter. In retrospect, the chains appear to have come from an old-fashioned hanging kerosene lamp, and the knobs resembled the "ornaments" on the posts of the old metal "bed-stids."

The knobs were buried in holes about a foot deep and some three feet apart, and dirt would be moistened and tromped on top of them. Our scientist would take out a big silver, open-faced watch about the size of a turnip and scrutinize it for fifteen minutes. No fluid in the tube—a dry hole. We put in a couple of days setting up all over the ranch and never got a smell! Well toward evening of the second day, I was tired of digging holes and lifting the heavy components of the "finder," as well as fed up on the jibes of skeptical brother; besides, a heavy rain storm was coming out of the Northwest. I wanted to call it a day, but our explorer insisted that we set up one more time. After about ten minutes, I happened to be looking at the gauge and saw the liquid begin to rise in the tube and remarked, "Thar she blows!" My father and the "witcher" were seated on the running board of the car some twenty feet away, and when they heard my exclamation, our old fellow sprang to his feet, took a look at the gauge, and gave out a regular Comanche yell. He excitedly danced around and screamed: "Mr. Sims, there is your oil!" He either believed implicitly in his device, or he was the best actor I ever saw. After an interval of shouting and prancing about, he took a reading on the tube and triumphantly announced that it was a 1500 barreler at 2200 feet. Despite my demurs and the gleeful joshing of my brother, he insisted on making a dozen more tests to stake off the width and direction of the "vein." It ran north-northwest by south-southeast and was some 200 feet wide. He insisted on staking it off for some hundreds of feet. It began to rain, and we were a thoroughly soaked bunch of explorers by the time we reached the ranch house. It rained all that night, and we gave up testing. We didn't get a well, but we sure got a good rain! Comment: Some years later, when the real geologists had taken over, a well was started on that location. However, the wildcatter went broke when he had reached only a few hundred feet, so we still don't know.

With our inexperience and our gullibility, we were prone to believe any representation made to us by any "oilman," so it's a wonder that we have any clear land titles today. We would sign most any kind of a lease stuck in front of us by a lease hound, so we had to learn the hard way. As a result, "oilmen" kind of lost their standing with a lot of folks in West Texas, and it has taken a long time to erase that feeling of suspicion. As a case in point: just a few years ago, the perfectly ethical representative of a major company was assembling a drilling block in our area and needed some acreage controlled by a local banker. I introduced them, remarking that the man was assembling a block under a drilling contract and a sizeable bonus. The banker scowled and grunter, "Did you ever see an oilman who would do what he said he would?" I was so embarrassed and so mad that I stalked out of the bank. But the leaseman, evidently better conditioned than I was to such rudeness, stayed on the job and got the signature.

The first real test in our county was drilled by local people who formed a stock company in which neighbors invested. They got in an old, wooden cable rig, something like a "Star Rig" water well outfit of today (only larger), secured the services of an experienced California driller and slogged away. One Sunday, when they had got down some 2500 feet, three of us stockholders visited the well which was being drilled "tight," *i.e.*, under strictest secrecy. They wanted a chance to buy leases if they made a strike. And thereby hangs another story told to me with a straight face by one of our early Texas pioneers in the oil business.

A man from Pennsylvania, drilling a wildcat in deep East Texas, was called home on some emergency just when they had reached an "interesting" depth. He wanted to buy some more leases if it was a well and instructed his driller to telegraph him the following message in code if oil was encountered: "Pine trees grow tall." Within a few days, the promoter got this message: "Pine trees grow tall . . . she's squirting clean over the derrick." Needless to say, he had plenty of competition for the leases.

Anyway, we were sitting around the rig with the three principal promoters, one of whom owned the land being drilled. The profane old driller was "making little hole," and he couldn't understand why as he had just sharpened the bit. After considerable squirting of tobacco juice and some lurid cussing, he pulled the drill out of the hole, ran his fingers over the drill bit, licked them and shouted: "By the Jumping Jesus Christ, there's your oil!" In all my put-together, I have never seen a bunch of men so excited. The crew sent the bailer down in the hole, and it came up brimfull of beautiful green, very high-grade oil. One of the prime stockholders, a real "man of the world," a polo player and a wide traveler, completely lost his head. He grabbed an empty five-gallon can, had the crew fill it with oil, hugged it to his bosom, ran down the steps to the ground and around behind the drilling floor, and slyly hid the can under it. Later on, I kidded him a lot about it. He confessed that he was so excited that he did not realize what he was doing and only came to when he saw us laughing at him. We were solemnly sworn to secrecy and went home considerably stirred up ourselves. Well, that night an inexperienced driller was on "tower," and he managed to hang the bailer in the hole. The old rag-line parted, and the well was "jimmed up, for fair." They fished that hole for months, but they could never get the bucket out. It's still there, and we don't know what else is, but I have a pretty reasonable conclusion that there is little oil. They drilled another hole not too far away and on better geology. It came in about like Number One. They shot it with nitro, and it looked like a field. However, it turned out to be a "stinker" (a small producer) that soon petered out.

They have struck some oil and some good gas wells in Concho County, but nary a drop on me, although I run over into Runnels County which is reputed to have more oil wells than any other county in the State of Texas. But, dadgummit, like every other landowner in the area, I just know that they would strike big oil if they would only drill to the "Farmer Sand," a most prolific legendary horizon just fifty feet below where they stopped drilling!

I think our own experience was so nearly typical of the majority of landowners in our area that it is worth the telling. Somehow, through sheer luck (in all probability) we managed to avoid serious entanglements with shysters and leased our country to an ethical explorer, Tom Slick, the well-known and highly successful wildcatter from Oklahoma.

Together with adjoining landowners, we gave Mr. Slick a ten-year lease on more than 40,000 acres simply on his promise to drill a 3000 foot well somewhere on the block. After a lot of prowling afoot over the block and two-bit geologizing, he located the test on my father's land and adjacent to two other of the larger landholdings. I kidded his superintendent about the location, maintaining that he had located it near the creek so that he would have plenty of drilling water. Mr. Slick contracted with a Californian to drill to a depth of 3000 feet, and a big cable rig was set up. Although larger than most of the local rigs, it operated on the same principle, and a description is in order.

The contractor made a trade with a local man to dig a cellar of about 10x10x10 feet and scrape out a good-sized slush pit. Heavy timbers were shipped in, and a great wooden derrick, some ninety feet high, was erected. A drilling floor, made largely of heavy lumber, was built for the drilling machinery. A small steam engine supplied the power through heavy hempen cable-belts to a large wooden wheel which actuated a walking beam by means of a wrist pin and connecting rod. This beam raised and lowered a heavy drill stem with a cutting bit screwed on to the bottom. Some large pulleys (the crown block) were placed atop the derrick, and a heavy hemp cable ran from the top of the drill stem, over the crown block down to the walking beam and thence to a large winch. By this means the drill bit was raised up and down to drill the hole. Another winch and rope over the crown block handled the bucket or bailer for cleaning out the hole. The hole was spudded in, water was added, and the drill began pounding away. After an interval, the drill was pulled out, and the bailer sent down for the drilling slush. It was raised to the surface and emptied through a valve into the slush pit. When the hole was cleaned out, water was poured down the hole. The drill was lowered and starting to pound away—just as simple as digging a deep post hole. But it "ran into a lot of politics" that were anything but simple, and it took a bunch of he-men to do the work.

The crew consisted of a driller, a tool dresser, and a bunch of roughnecks. A crew worked a twelve-hour shift called a "tower". These were strong, tough men who put out an amazing amount of pure D physical labor and effort. Ever so often they had to sharpen the bit which called for strength, stamina and know-how. The bit was heated in a portable forge, placed on an anvil, and the two top men began pounding away with twelve-pound sledges to reshape and produce a cutting edge on the bit. They really had rhythm as they alternately swung their sledges. The bit was screwed back on the stem by ponderous wrenches held up by cables and a lot more sledge pounding. That bit had to be tight, plenty tight, so that it would not come off in the hole. If it did, the crew was in real trouble. They had ingenious devices for fishing stuff out of the hole, but it all added up to loss of time and added labor.

The cables were hemp ropes (known in the vernacular as raglines), large in diameter, easy to foul up, and prone to wear out. These men were expert splicers, and the way they could patch up a line was a caution. But every now and then a rope would break and a lot of frustrating fishing could ensue.

West Texas oil rig, 1920

Steel cables soon supplanted the "rag," and they were so much easier to handle. However, when a steel line broke a strand, it was harder to splice and was cast aside. They were practically valueless for junk, and the driller was glad to give them to us ranchers. I got several thousand feet of old cable that came in mighty handy on the ranch. It made good corral fences, and so on. I built several dams and small bridges using such cable for reinforcement. This was against engineering procedure of the time, and local engineers predicted all kinds of failures. One of my dams is still standing after nearly fifty years. Also pre-stressed, high-tensile steel cables are being used in the latest bridge construction. So, Old Smarty Pants can still snigger and say, "I told you so." You know, I have about concluded that those four words provide more incentive for achievement than most any other motive. La, me, it's simply a soul satisfying thing (especially to sister woman) to be able to say, "I told you so."

The throttle of the steam engine was operated by a braided, wire clothesline running over a grooved pulley on a post set near the hole, and that old driller could really play a tune with it, one hand on the drilling cable and the other on the grooved pulley. The winches were equipped with steel band brakes worked with a long pole lever as a brake pedal. That driller had the touch of a virtuoso, and he knew what was going on by merely feeling the line.

It was a ticklish job to handle the throttle and brakes when there was heavy strain on the cable, when the hole caved in on the tools, or when casing was being set. I was at the well one morning when they had about 2500 feet of hole and the drill stem was being lowered. There was some sort of trouble about the rig, and the driller put a green man on the comparatively simple job of lowering the drill. This greenie was letting the drill down too fast, and the driller yelled at him to slow it down. The man lost his head and jammed the brake. The cable broke and the heavy stem whistled down that hole like a heavy artillery shell. It seemed to take many minutes for the bit to hit bottom, and it jarred the ground like a high explosive when it struck. The poor driller flopped down on the floor, and I never heard such a picturesque and copious flow of Oil Field English. He cussed the world out by sections and never repeated himself once. The air was blue—really.

He fortified himself with a prodigious chaw of Mail Pouch, fired his inept helper and set about retrieving the mess, which took some two weeks of grueling labor. When he did get the drill stem out, it was twisted like a gigantic corkscrew.

Oil field cook shack, 1924

When things were going smoothly, a crew member might snatch a bit of rest on the "lazy bench." Many are the hours I have spent on that long bench listening to picturesque English and trying to chaw Mail Pouch with them. Smoking was taboo around an oil rig as the holes were drilled "blind." Nobody knew anything about the underground formations and, consequently, never knew when they might run into a pocket of gas or oil. If a visitor wanted to get the bum's rush, just let him start smoking on the drill floor. So, all crew members chawed, and their favorite brand was Mail Pouch, loose tobacco leaves, black as sin and stronger than sheep dip. They tried to learn me to chaw it, but I had to give up after several disastrous bouts with it. I think that is why I admired those old toughies so much—their ability to handle Mail Pouch. This tobacco was put up in sort of yellowish heavy paper sacks, just the right size to fit in a convenient pocket. One of these experts could stash a heavy chaw in his cheek and never miss a lick in what he was doing. And he didn't have to spit as much as the Navy or Brown's Mule chewers did. There wasn't any sweetnin' or "lickerish" in it to make much spit, just pure D tobacco.

Just the other day, I was talking over old times with my friend Mr. Charlie Hickox (more about him later) who saw it all as a roughneck, driller, tool pusher and district superintendent for a big company. The conversation turned to the picturesque old drillers and their idiosyncrasies, including addiction to Mail Pouch. Charlie ran into one of these real, old-time cable drillers, and an argument started regarding the relative virtues of the old cable rig and the latest rotary. . Old Driller snorted that the only real way to drill a well was to use the old cable rig. Charlie chuckled that there hadn't been but two improvements in cable tools in the last forty years: substituting steel cables for the old rag lines and putting Mail Pouch in cellophane pouches. Whereupon old argifyer triumphantly exclaimed, "Well, ain't that sumpin'?"

They hammered along on old Sims No. 1 for more than two years, and they encountered several shows, but it never made a well. How many times did I wake up in the night and hear the rig pounding away! As I drifted off to sleep, visions of Pierce Arrow cars and easy dates with blondes drifted through my head. The first thing I did of mornings was to take a long gander to see if she was squirting over the derrick, for hadn't two celebrated fortunetellers predicted lots of oil?

Finally, the contract depth was reached and the well plugged and abandoned. That sort of put a scab over my heart that took years to heal. Which reminds me of another tale. It is customary to designate a well by the name of the oil company followed by the name of the landowner, *i.e.*, Slick Oil Company, Sims No. 1. Our newspapers carry a full page of oil news, and sometimes there is so much of it that they resort to abbreviations. One very proper lady took great umbrage at such an abbreviation when a paper ran the following squib: "Mrs. ———— plugged and abandoned."

They have made about as much progress in oil exploration

and production as they have in the realms of other industry. Gone are "by guess and by God" methods of yesteryear. The present geologist is a wise "guinea," an educated scientist who is up to the minute not only in geology, but in chemistry, paleontology, engineering and other related subjects. He no longer relies on surface geology, as he can now get a good picture of the subsurface by reading the reliable logs now kept on wells and running them through a computer. But, with all the present-day knowledge, men can only find what is really underground by drilling a hole, and they can now do that in a hurry.

The latest model rotary rig can put down a hole five miles deep quicker than one of the old cable rigs could complete one three thousand feet. The geologist sets a stake, a bulldozer is hauled in, and the necessary surface excavation is made in a few hours. Ponderous trucks haul in the giant, jackknife, welded steel derrick, and raise it into place in less than an hour's time. The drilling floor, the giant diesels mounted on it, and all the rest of the heavy and intricate drilling equipment can be assembled in a day. The drill no longer pounds up and down; it rotates, and a complicated bit made of the hardest steel cuts through ordinary formations like a hot case knife through butter.

The men who operate this intricate machinery, while maintaining the traditions of their forerunners, are a different breed of cats. While they only work eight-hour towers and have every kind of mechanical aids, don't put them down as a bunch of sissies. They have to be tough, muscular technicians with split-second reflexes and intricate technical skills undreamed of in the early days. In addition to all their skills, they must possess an amazing amount of concentration. If a man ever lets his mind wander while he is coming out or going down the hole, he not only endangers his own life but that of his fellow as well. As the cowpokes used to say: "He has to keep his eye on the indicator."

They have gauges and gadgets all over the place, and it is truly amazing to the uninitiated how much these men know about what is going on down below. The highly skilled driller has a depth gauge right in front of him so that he can instantly tell just how deep he is. He knows when he changes formations and when to tell a roughneck to take a sample of the drillings, which he gets at the discharge end of the "mud pipe." These drillings are washed and put in small cloth sacks with name of location, time and depth. They are then handed over to the trained scientist in the field office, a trailer house equipped with microscopes, chemical sets and various weird instruments. He can usually identify the formation at a glance or under microscopic examination, and from the tape of the electric log, he can tell how it is running, whether high, low or level.

If one of his tests indicates a show, the rig may be shut down and a radiophone call made for the drill stem tester. This worthy is on call all the time, and he gets to the rig in a hurry and takes over. He is like the pilot of a ship entering harbor: he is the boss, and the crew members hasten to obey his commands. This expert makes use of gadgets of his own and indulges in a good deal of black magic to the uninitiated, but he is pretty scientific and amazingly accurate.

If conditions warrant, a core test is made by another expert operating a diamond drill—yes, madam, I said, "diamond." These drill bits are studded with real diamonds of industrial grade, as hard as but without the color and sparkle of the jewel grade, but they are expensive, nonetheless. I have seen drill heads containing more than $50,000 worth of diamonds stacked on the concrete floor of a warehouse. The bit is screwed on to the end of the drill pipe, sent down the hole and rotated at speed. At intervals, depending on conditions, the pipe is pulled, and the core, a real cross-section of the rock, is removed for examination by the geologist. He usually breaks the two-to-four-inch core into short sections which he examines for signs. He may shine an ultraviolet light on the chunks, scrutinize them under a magnifying glass, sniff and even taste them by licking with his tongue. A core may have globules of oil oozing out of it, and then business begins to pick up, especially if the landowner is present.

I recall one such test made late at night on a well drilled on the Sims' spread. The young geologist on the job was newly married and had been away from "Sweetie" since early morning. He broke up the core, shone his light and so on, announced that it was dry and told the driller to go to drilling again. Sometime later, one of the disappointed ladies present went out to the pipe rack, shone her flashlight on the core and discovered blobs of oil big as a frijole bean oozing out of it. The contractor on the job was sure we had a well, and I suggested that he shut down until morning. But shutdowns are costly, and he had a deadline to meet on another hole. Of course the oil drops had all evaporated by the time old Romeo returned the next day, and he quickly dismissed the whole thing, indicating that we farmers were seeing visions. I tried to get him to send the core into the laboratory for testing, but, of course, he refused, knowing full well that it meant his hide if his superiors discovered his dereliction. Love may be the greatest thing in the world, but I have always felt that it beat us out of an oil field.

To get back to our knittin', the geologist may send a chunk of the core to the home office for laboratory examination. A very thin slice may be cut from the core by a small diamond rotary saw and the slide examined microscopically. The paleontologist may discover a tiny fossil no larger than the head of a pin that may identify the formation and the chance for a show.

But, with all their know-how and their gadgetry, they may overlook a show owing to human frailty, such as the bridegroom above. Once, a dry hole was thought to condemn an entire area: later, it only condemned the hole itself. Developing techniques warrant frequent reentries. A number of nice little fields have been discovered by such reentries. A geologist may be poring over a subsurface map and discover a "wrinkle" previously overlooked, and his company may decide it is worth a reentry or a new well. Then, there is always that old "Farmer Sand" again.

Oil people are funny folks to us uninitiated, and we just can't savvy their capers. A "hot" area may suddenly become colder than a frog's tummy and remain so for years. Then a company slips in and picks up a bunch of leases. Every company has men who periodically drop around to county clerks' offices and run the records. He may find where a rival has taken a block of leases and report it to his company, which immediately begins taking leases, figuring that the other fellow has run into something. The rest of the boys follow suit, and the area becomes hotter'n a pistol. One wise operator once remarked to me that oilmen are like sheep, for they follow a leader. All of which is just fine for everybody, as we landowners can cash in on bonuses and rentals, and the companies get a write-off.

I went into the oil business once, but all I ever got out of it was one $13.20 royalty check—and it all came about this way. A number of friends who had struck it rich during the Breckenridge oil boom moved their families to Paint Rock to get away from the turmoil of the oil fields and to enjoy the fishing which was so good on the Concho River. We became fast friends, and they just knew that I should go to Breckenridge and "get my feet wet." So, together with some other friends including our very conservative banker, we went to see what we could see.

The oil boom was just beginning to peter out, only nobody suspected it. Breckenridge, formerly a placid country town of some 600 inhabitants, had burgeoned into a madhouse of activity with some 30,000 people, all kinds. They were drilling on single city blocks, and the town was a veritable forest of wooden derricks. It had been raining, and the streets were loblollies. All hauling was done by teams, and I never saw so many good draft horses in one place in all my born days. The teamsters were getting astronomical prices for their work, and they took great pride in the condition and appearance of their teams. I especially recall two teams, six horses each: one was beautiful dappled gray Percherons, and the other, bright bay Clydesdales with bald faces and stocking legs. They had the finest harness I have ever seen, and how well the teams obeyed their proud drivers.

Everybody was getting top money, and how they threw

it around! Fifteen dollar silk shirts were all the rage, and nearly every driller and roughneck sported one, usually red and white striped. These rough, tough, unshaven fellows were covered in oil and mud, but that didn't make any difference—their shirts had to be silk.

One could walk a block and see more kinds of people than he could see in weeks in other places. There would be a dignified city banker dressed like J. P. Morgan, an oil-covered roughneck, a preacher-lookin' fellow, and a shifty-eyed thug, a hustlin' lease hound, a pitchman, a lawman toting a big gun, and a gambler, or a painted practitioner of the "oldest profession" publicly and brazenly soliciting business. Diamond-studded bootleggers and whining panhandlers hit you up at every turn (and the law was purported to always look the other way). Just name it, and that character was there.

We went out in the field, and our friend took us to one of the family wells, flowing 1000 barrels a day. We really got the big-eye when we saw that eight-inch stream of oil spurting into the storage tank. We finally found an old fellow who had 160 acres just a little off the main pay. He had bought an irrigated farm in the Rio Grande Valley, and he had to meet a payment on it. While he had no production on that particular tract, two wells were going down on it, and oil was being struck on all four sides of his plot. We made him an offer for his royalty, and he took us up. But his wife refused to sign the deed and the trade blowed up. That's what we thought! The old man kept the unsigned deed and went back to work on his wife.

They were fixing to shoot a well nearby, and we were invited to watch. The glycerin wagon drove up, and the shooter nonchalantly picked up some tin torpedos containing enough nitro to blow up the whole place. He tied them to a line, lowered them into the hole and jiggled the line up and down after his lethal charge rested on bottom. Although I was 150 yards away and stashed behind a barricade of automobiles, I could feel the short hairs on the back of my neck squirming around! He raised the load well above the bottom, dropped it, and calmly stepped back a few yards on the rig platform. There was a dull, muffled bang, and the earth jarred under our feet. The shooter climbed down from the platform, kind of dusted off his hands and strolled over to us. After what seemed an interminable wait, there was a deep, rumbling roar, and out she came: water, smoke, mud, and rocks shot up well above the crown block, and I crawled under a car just as rocks showered down all around us. One, about as large as a man's two fists, hit just a few feet from me. Then, as suddenly as it started, the flow stopped, and the driller and the shooter indulged in some choice oil field English—the blankety-blank hole had "bridged" (stopped up by the detritus).

In testimony of the awesome heat and power of the explosion, the casing had expanded some four feet above where it stood before the blast. There was nothing to do but to go back into the hole with the tools and drill out the bridge. This would take some time, so we went to supper. After a while we went back to the rig, and a man met us and made us leave our matches and smoking materials in the car as the hole was making some gas. They were pulling the tools up and invited us to the drilling floor. Just as the tools came out of the hole, I saw a glimmer of gas and decided that I had better be elsewhere. Just as I started down the steps, I glanced back over my shoulder and saw oil begin to flow over the top of the casing. I started to run when, with a whoosh and a roar, a solid stream of oil was mounting towards the crown block. One of the members of our party was a sort of a dandy and was dressed in a handsome, light-colored suit, topped off by a new Stetson. The others beat him to the steps, so he was delayed long enough to be drenched by the oil spray. It took some time to get the well under control, and we gazed, bug-eyed, at the beautiful stream of black gold going to waste. Incidentally, drilling techniques have become so improved that they can now bring in a well like that without a blast and without wasting a drop of oil.

As an example of the awesome force wrapped up in nitroglycerin, witness an experience of my brother who was an oilman. He was going west from Mineral Wells when he overtook a glycerin wagon—an enclosed truck, painted fire-engine red with lurid yellow signs all over it, warning that it was carrying explosives. The road was full of potholes, and the driver was pushing his truck regardless. My brother managed to pass and poured the gas to his car. His passengers remonstrated with him about driving so fast over that bad road. But he was frightened and wanted to put as much distance between him and the truck as possible. Sure enough, they had only gone a few miles when they heard a dull boom and a heavy blast of air hit their car. When they returned that afternoon, they found that the truck's cargo had exploded, making a deep hole all across the highway. All the officers ever found were pieces of the truck and a few scraps of flesh and clothing. My brother estimated that they had been a good two miles from the truck when it exploded.

We were so excited over seeing all that oil come out of the ground that we went back and tried to get the old lady to sign our deed, but she still sulled. We went to bed in an oil field rooming house—a large, jerry-built barn of a wooden building with very small rooms partitioned off from each other with beaver board. We could hear the snoring of tired men through those flimsy partitions. Naturally, we didn't get much sleep, and when the other roomers began to stir, about 4:00 A.M., we gave up in disgust and got up ourselves. When we got to the door of the building, there sat our old man with the signed deed in his hand. He and his wife had battled through the night, and he finally wore her down. We gladly paid him the money and went our way rejoicing. We just knew that we could not keep from making a pot of money out of the deal.

We had good production on all sides of us, and the two drilling wells on us were running along with the logs of the other wells around us. In comment as to how easy it is to lose money in the oil business, one of the wells got jimmed up and was abandoned. The other came in, all right, but it was a stinker. We paid a sizeable sum for our lease, and all I ever got out of my part was one royalty check for $13.20.

The business is full of disappointments, but the returns are so great that men still keep bucking the game. I once had a well going down on me, and things were running high and looking good in the parlance. Late one night, my phone rang, and an excited voice informed me that I had a well. I bellyached considerable about their waking me up at that time of night, but, secretly, I was happy and excited. Early the next morning, I lit out for the ranch. I was met at the cattleguard by a smiling nephew who informed me that it looked like a nice one. Presently, the "brass" arrived, and the crew turned the valve on, and the well just went PFUI— another dream was busted.

We had a pretty good gas show farther up the hole that they were getting ready to test sometime that night, but, considering myself a "Jonah," I went home. Early the next morning, the same nephew met me with a still broader smile and informed me that I really had a good gasser. This young man had "sat on" several good gassers on the properties of other members of the family, and he assured me that mine was just as good as any of theirs. They had run a "bleeder" pipe well away from the hole as a fire precaution, and the gas howled and screamed out of the upright end. They ignited it, and it lit all the surrounding country. They shut it off and retired with the firm assurance that they did have a good producer. The "brass" finally showed up and they turned the valve on: as before, the danged thing just spewed a little water—that's all she wrote. Ah, me, again—into each life some rain must fall. Mebbe it's all for the best, as a big gas field would probably have made of me a bigger fool than usual, and it got me out of paying a lot of income tax.

Of course, I just know that they perforated the casing too high up and let water in, thereby killing both shows. Also, they could have gone on deeper to the "Farmer Sand," but they got the limbertail, plugged the hole, turned my leases back, and left me sitting there with production all around me—and I'm still a sittin'. Somebody else will probably come along and probably make a field there. Well, probably, but it will be too late for me to do my kicking up of heels.

But I did get something out of the experience. I got to see them perform a real feat of modern technological legerdemain. I got to see them shoot the casing in two, just off bottom, by using about an eighteen-inch nitro torpedo. They plugged and abandoned, cleared off the rubbish and leveled off the pits. I now have a smooth piece of terrain again that will probably produce some grass along about the year 2000.

SANTA RITA

THE OIL BUSINESS is chock full of drama, as anyone who has witnessed the bringing in of a gusher or a dry hole can testify. To me, the Santa Rita and Yates discoveries top them all.

At the close of World War I, the University of Texas found itself between a rock and a hard place. It was swamped by the influx of young men returning from military service and had no place to put 'em. The legislature could appropriate money for operating costs, but not for buildings. While it had millions of acres of land which were supposed to provide the revenue for that purpose, precious little was being realized. Most of this vast acreage was located in arid West Texas and could be leased only for grazing purposes at ridiculously low rates, so, they were forced to put up a lot of wooden shacks on campus which resembled a concentration camp more than an institution of higher learning. And then oil was struck!

The university geologists were well aware that these lands had oil potential and had cautiously recommended exploration. Some independent geologists had mapped and defined the Santa Rita and Yates surface structures, but no major company would touch them with a ten foot pole. So, the small fry, short of money and experience, but long on guts and dreams, had to do it.

Many of the young veterans were loath to go back on the farm "after they had seen Paris" and cast about for something that promised high adventure and wealth. Among them was a young captain named Rupert P. Ricker, possessing a law degree and "the big eye," who conceived the idea of leasing large chunks of university land for oil exploration at ten cents per acre. He just flat didn't have the $43,136 to pay the lease on 4,136,000 acres, so he scurried around for an "angel" to underwrite it, and that angel turned out to be a former sergeant of his named Frank T. Pickrell, who was fed up with his lackluster job of operating his confectionery shop in El Paso. Frank interested Haymon Krupp, a substantial merchant of the city, and they took over. Legend has it that Captain Ricker received $500 for his lease and his dream. Parenthetically, Ricker stayed in the oil business and made his pile.

These men were short of practical experience in the oil business, but they could think big, and they had the enthusiasm of ignorance. Mr. Krupp had to stay close to his own considerable business, so Mr. Pickrell had to do most of the leg work, and the things he did are legendary. They not only had to raise the money, but they also had to drill a test well under a deadline. Frank proved a sort of a wizard at finding this money and attending to all the multitude of details incident to putting down a test in a desolate and forbidding land, short of water and far distant from supply depots.

The tales about these almost legendary improvisers are legion, but I have tried to sift out the real facts of the operation. I not only witnessed a good deal myself, but I am well acquainted with a number of men who had a finger in the pie.

Pickrell developed as he went along and worked out many complicated methods of financing. Among them was the formation of blocks of some 16,000 acres in which the investor would get a share in accordance with the amount of money he put in. Some years after the Santa Rita field had developed, I was living in Fort Davis. One day a handsome, intelligent lady, somewhat past middle age, was a guest in the Hotel Limpia where I lived. We became well acquainted, and she told me of her experience in the oil business. She was a teacher in the schools of one of our big northern cities and had invested her savings in the Santa Rita Companies and had become wealthy. I asked her how she came to invest in something she knew nothing about, while we wise guys on the ground refused to take any dish in the operation. She replied that Mr. Pickrell had such an honest face and amazing enthusiasm and faith in his promotion that she just had to go along with him.

In context, I shall indulge in one of the tales that has circulated around all these years, not only because it's a good story, but it's one that I believe to be true. Frank had sold a number of shares in his operation to some good Catholics in New York City. They compared notes and decided that they had been hasty in making such a sight unseen venture. So they laid the matter before their parish priest, who, after listening to their story, dryly suggested that they had better take the matter up with Santa Rita, Saint of the Impossible. Two of the good sisters asked Frank to name the test "Santa Rita" and gave him a red rose, with the request that he scatter the rose petals over the rig and christen it "Santa Rita." After the derrick was up, Frank climbed to the top and performed the christening rite, and "The Impossible" came to pass.

Pickrell formed the Texon Oil and Land Company in April, 1919—2,000,000 shares at par value of $1.00. Santa Rita Block H 1 comprised 10,240 acres and was divided into 685 shares at $200 each.

After a lot of backing and filling, the state authorities set the deadline for spudding in a well at midnight, January 28, 1921. This was sooner than expected, so Frank really had to get on the ball. He bought a small, rattletrap Star Water Well rig some forty miles north of San Angelo, hauled it across country to San Angelo and arrived so late that he barely got it loaded on a flatcar in time to hook on to the westbound train. The car was set out at the Best siding, some ninety miles west of San Angelo. The rig was skidded off the right-of-way, and the water well spudded in shortly before midnight. Two men came along in a car, and Frank needed them as disinterested witnesses that he was actually drilling before the "witching" hour. So, he had to follow them into San Angelo to get their notarized statement, which they were reluctant to give as they feared a shenanigan of some sort. Frank had to get a lawyer to assure them that all was in order.

Pickrell found Carl Cromwell, who had a dilapidated oil rig at Cisco, and contracted with him to drill the actual oil test. The rig needed some parts, which they secured from Trapshooter Riley, who had just finished a dry hole near Sheffield, west of the Pecos. Incidentally, the crew drilling this well "saved the lives" of myself and three other deer hunters. We were returning from a hunt in the Davis Mountains and could find no place where there was enough wood and water for us to make camp. We were driving open Model T's, and a blue norther hit us about nine o'clock at night. We wrapped up in soogans and just had to keep driving. We reached the well about ten o'clock and beat it to the drilling floor to thaw out. The crew had plenty of wood and water and invited us to help ourselves. So, I had a little something to do with the Santa Rita well.

There have been many versions of the whole operation, most of them out of "whole cloth" and embroidered by the fanciful stories told to wide-eyed reporters by jokers of the area. One, having the widest credence, was that the train hauling the rig broke down, and that Pickrell said, "Unload her here, boys, and spud in. It's as good a place as any to get a dry hole." But I got my version from my friend Charlie Hickox, mentioned before, and I know that it is correct.

Mr. Pickrell did have geology on the tract, and he drilled the hole at the stake set by Hugh Tucker, a well-known geologist who probably knew more about the geology of West Texas than any other geologist of the day.

The oil rig was shipped in and the eighty-four foot wooden derrick erected July 6, 1921. All this time, they had pounded away on the water well and never got a drop of water, which is absolutely necessary for drilling a well. They assembled the oil rig regardless, jacked up one side of it, drilled a water well in the northeast corner of the 8x10x20 foot cellar, and this time found water, but it was like the old lady's butter, "plenty of it, such as it was." The oil well was drilled with this water, but they had to ship in water for drinking and domestic purposes. They built a couple of small wooden huts on the style of boxcars for the driller and the tool dresser, but the roughnecks, of which Charlie was one, had to make do with tents and cooking out in the open. But that didn't make any difference to these cowpokes, they were used to it.

The well was finally started July 6, 1921. Mrs. Cromwell gathered up her small daughter, a few household necessities, and accompanied her husband, remaining right by his side during the almost two years that it took to drill the well. Much has been written about the hardships that these early oilmen endured, but I have yet to see a real tribute to their womenfolk. These valiant souls stayed by their men, living under the adverse conditions of that wild, Godforsaken country, unthinkable and intolerable to our pampered dolls of today with their push-button households.

I passed by this drilling operation a number of times, and I marveled at the fortitude of the wife who was hanging out the wash in the hot wind of a dry alkali country ninety miles from a real grocery store, electric lights and running water. One time, an old puncher from the ranch was with me, and as we passed by the disreputable-looking setup, I made a snide remark about the goofy guys who would try to get an oil well in such an unlikely looking flat, greasewood, alkali country, absolutely fit for nothing except to hold the world together. John grinned his slow, dry grin and offered to bet me five dollars that they would strike oil, averring that the good Lord never made anything for no purpose, that the land was no account on top, so there was bound to be something underneath. And they had a sweet time finding that something! Money was coming in in dribbles, so that they were hard put at times to get enough to pay the help. They even had to ask the roughnecks to wait at times, and Cromwell even borrowed money from them to pay small, pressing bills. But these men had confidence in the boss and played along with him—they always got their pay. Carl later told friends that he drilled most of the well by himself without even the aid of a tool dresser, even drafting his wife as helper on the drilling platform. She could handle the lighter chores such as operating the throttle like a veteran driller.

Finally, on Sunday evening, May 27, 1923, they found that something underneath. It was getting along toward dark when they encountered the slight show, so they shut down for the night to await instructions from the boss. But Santa Rita didn't wait! The next morning about six o'clock, Mrs. Cromwell heard a hissing noise and told her husband that there must be another rattlesnake outside the door. Carl stepped out to investigate, and "she was spurting clean over the derrick." His reaction was: "Well, I'll be damned." His wee daughter took a look at the dark spray and squealed: "Daddy, your lala is spoiling." So were Mrs. Cromwell's garden, her white leghorn chickens and the milk cow. It was a good thing that she had taken her wash in.

There are many stories as to Mr. Pickrell's reaction when he got the news, and probably all of them are apocryphal. One of the most widely circulated had it that he was notified by phone that he had an oil well, and he replied: "Quit your kidding." But he said that it was a canard as he never made any such of a "doubting Thomas" sort of a statement.

Anyway, Santa Rita, the Saint of the Impossible, had done the impossible, and a new era for West Texas and the state university was ushered in. The discovery of that 200 barrel well sure made a lot of people and the university rich. I dare say it has, in one way or another, affected practically every landowner west of the 100th Meridian.

Business picked up immediately. Newspapers carried front-page banners. Booster trains were run out to the switch, and nearly everybody came to goggle. The *Aasvogels* really swooped down, and within a few days, oil people were thicker than fiddlers in Hell, while starry-eyed landowners went around in a trance. The promoters cleaned up after a fashion, selling off most of their holdings and retaining their interest in the Texon Oil and Land Company. They paid their debts and became comfortably well off, but I have always held that they never received adequate remuneration for the tremendous service they rendered to West Texas.

They sold a large part of the Santa Rita block to the Big Lake Oil Company, another to the Benedum and Trees Company. These topflight wildcatters had a finger in nearly every pie where there was oil production in the Southwest, and they sired a spate of subsidiary companies. They sure cleaned up on the Big Lake deal. Fortunately, the Santa Rita block, although comparatively small, split the structure practically in half, and they prospered accordingly.

The University of Texas has really blossomed out from a sort of a jerkwater institution to a "university of the first class," no longer dependent upon the whims of niggardly legislatures. (I think that I can use the word "niggardly" without fear of reprisal, for I served therein myself.) The original forty acres are as crowded with splendid high rise buildings as downtown New York. What a pity our founding fathers, in spite of their forethought, couldn't have visualized the explosion and have set aside 4,000 acres instead of forty. Why, the university is spreading out all over Austin from Waller Creek to Bull Creek, and it is still hard-put to take care of the hordes of students swarming in. At the present rate of growth, it will soon take forty acres to accommodate just the touseled-head, the beardos and the leotard set.

But with all that mazuma, they are branching out so fast that they are still putting the bee on us alumni for everything from a new stadium to a neutron splitter or some other way out facility dreamed up by our eggheads atop Mount Olympus. But more power to these dreamers, even if I am on their sucker list.

Old Santa Rita No. 1 can still produce a few barrels of oil after forty-four years and stands as a landmark for the gents who are not afraid to attempt the impossible.

Owing to the nine near-sighted folks in Washington who are so lost in the forest of the constitution that they cannot distinguish the trees of common sense, the university cannot erect a statue to Santa Rita. But they have removed the old rig to Austin and set up the drilling mechanism on a lot near the campus. It is planned to erect the old derrick and move the machinery to an honored spot on the mall in the midst of the original forty acres—a monument to the "impossible," at any rate.

When it was apparent that the Texon-Big Lake area was a real oil field, the majors put their geologists into every nook and cranny, even into the Trans-Pecos region, which all "knowledgeable" oil people knew was drier than a bone. These were smart young cookies, graduates of our most advanced universities, and familiar with the the latest discovery tools of the profession. They located many surface structures, but they did not have the data for subsurface mapping, owing to the absence of deep wells.

Among these young men were Jack Hagen and John Emsch who located and mapped the Yates structure. But the big boys were still leery about investing their funds in rank wildcat territory, and the small fry hopped in where the angels of the industry feared to tread.

Among the spate of Benedum & Trees subsidiaries was a small, impecunious outfit known as the Transcontinental Oil Company, which grabbed off part of the acreage atop the Yates structure—all it could handle at "four bits" an acre. That took their available funds, and they sold their acreage to the Mid-Kansas Oil Co., itself a subsidiary of the Ohio Oil Company, really the Standard Oil Company. Mid-Kansas had drilled several dry holes on the young geologists' locations and were reluctant to tackle the Yates site, but Transcontinental had 'em sewed up in a drilling contract.

My friend, John I. Moore, eminent geologist and an independent oil producer, newly graduated and employed by a major company, was familiar with the Yates "hickey" and recommended that his company take acreage, but true to type, they held off. John I. scouted the well and became deeply interested in it as he saw that it was some 2000 feet "high." He got a room in Rankin and drove back and forth to the Yates test every day. He spent many hours on the lazy bench with Mr. Yates, and they became friends. One day, Yates offered John I. any amount of royalty that he might want at $10 per acre. He had the money in the bank and wanted to invest it, but it was the policy of his company that its men should not buy leases or royalty on their own. John I. liked the prospect, but he also liked his good job and turned down the offer—another man who was filthy rich and didn't know it! Later, when the well came in, his company bought leases on the nearby Smith acreage at the unheard of price of $2 per acre, and they did all right with their purchase!

A number of those young geologists who toughed it out in that rough country had like trouble with their companies. It is legendary in "pseudo" oil circles that there is constant feuding in the big companies between "Land," conservative and pessimistic, and "Geology," starry-eyed and optimistic. "Land" has a budget to watch, and they have to be chinchy. But they have been penny-wise and pound-foolish in many instances, while "Geology" snickered, "We told you so."

Another geologist friend in San Angelo, Mr. W. P. Ray, had a similar experience with his company. He wrote them repeatedly, urging them to buy leases in the Yates area, and they turned up their noses at him. When this miracle field came in, they jumped on Bill for not having grabbed off acreage. He had the copies of his letters photostated and sent them in without comment. There were plenty of red faces around the head office, and they pestered him no more.

Many men had like opportunities to hit it big like Moore. One of the tales I love about these misses was one related by Mr. Ray. He was talking to a mighty well-heeled ranchman who had much oil production on his own large holdings. One day, Bill asked him what he considered the best trade he ever made, and his wry reply was: "The time I turned Ira Yates down when he offered me his whole spread for $3.50 per acre."

The Yates discovery intrigues me most of all because of its personal implications. Mr. and Mrs. Ira Yates were old-timers in the San Angelo country and were close friends of my mother and father. I knew the Yates kids, and there was a passel of them. I liked the whole family, being especially fond of Mr. Yates because he always noticed me when I was a kid.

Things were tough in West Texas: the weather was dry, prices were skidding, and the banks were getting tender-footed. Along in the fall of 1926, my father made a business trip to San Angelo and came back worried and upset about something. As soon as I could get him alone, I asked what was the matter. He had seen "Old Iry," as he called him, in town and learned that he was in sore straits financially. He had had some big feed bills and owed a lot of money on them. Land payments were coming due, and a Kansas City bank was making threatening noises. He broke down and told Father that he was going broke unless something turned up. And that something sure did—beyond all bounds of the imagination.

Father and other friends were casting about for means to tide Mr. Yates over until spring, for they were plenty worried. We knew that they were drilling a well on his land, but none of us had any faith in it. The mail got into Paint Rock late in the afternoon, and someone always drove in for it. After supper, the family gathered in the living room to read the mail, and it was Father's prerogative to get the daily paper first. It was a cool night. A big fire was roaring in the fireplace, and we settled down to a cozy evening of mail reading. I was in the midst of a pleasing letter from a current "flame," (incidentally, the one that is still blazing brightly) and was brought out of a rosy haze by a wild yell from my father who jumped to his feet, waved the paper and howled: "Old Iry has struck oil!" I just know that he would never have made that display of emotion if he had struck a big field himself.

A San Angelo banker told my father of a similar experience. At its regular meeting, the board of directors was discussing what should be done about the Yates line. They were all friends of Yates, but they were worried for fear that the bank in Kansas City would crack down. The board was divided on what should be done, and there was a lot of discussion. They ran out of cigars, and this man went out to pick up some. Just as he came out of the cigar store, newsboys ran by yelping, "Extry, extry." So the banker grabbed a paper. He took one look at the headline and hustled back to the directors' room, laid the paper on the table, pointed to the banner screaming across the page: "Oil discovered on Ira Yates' ranch," laughed aloud and said: "Gentlemen, we are sort of previous, for Ira Yates could buy out this bank this minute and never miss the money. I recommend that we table indefinitely further discussion of his loans." And that was the picture from then on out.

Mr. Yates was a typical old-time ranchman, modest, kind, generous and credulous. "He told it straight," and he expected the same from other people. Naturally, he was totally unprepared for the blaze of publicity that burst upon him together with the army of newshawks, promoters, shysters, toadies and moochers that descended upon him, and, naturally, he "put his foot in his mouth." Perhaps his greatest booboo was his reply to a presumptuous question from a newsman who flatly asked him what he was going to do with all that money. Mr. Yates unguardedly replied that he wanted to put it to good use and would help worthy young people to get an education. That did it! "Deserving" cravers for education, young and old, descended upon him like the locusts did on Pharaoh! The poor man never appeared in public without being submerged in a swarm of mendicants and toadies.

He got to where he would slip out of town and take refuge on some friend's ranch, and I have some pleasant memories of his visits to the Sims' preemption. He and Mrs. Yates would drive down, send their chauffeur back to town and spend several serene and peaceful days just visiting. After supper, he, my father and I would repair to the long front porch, and how I enjoyed listening to those two old-timers reminisce. Those were times when I remained silent, believe it or not.

Old Iry had a good sense of humor and of the ridiculous and was a first-rate raconteur, so I got many a laugh out of his tales. One I especially relish was his bout with the Kansas City banker. This old cuss, president of a "cattle bank," was considered to be the crustiest, toughest old curmudgeon in the business and was the one who was riding Ira so hard just before the well came in. After things squared off, Mr. and Mrs. Yates slipped off to Kansas City to get away from it all and to pay old Scrooge off.

Mr. Yates got on a bus and rode out to the stockyards where the bank was located. As he walked in the front door, old toughie spied him and rushed up, all nods and becks and wreathed smiles. He might' nigh wrung "Colonel" Yates' hands off (heretofore, it had been "Yates" or "Ira"). He proudly introduced his "beloved" and "honored" friend to everybody in the bank, from the vice president to the janitor, and took the "Colonel" into the sanctum sanctorum. The "Great Experiment" was in full flower, and good likker was very hard to come by. But Shylock hauled out a jug of bottled-in-bond bourbon, called for ice and glasses, and proceeded to pour generous libations on the altar of friendship. He also hauled out a box of four-bit seegars (the kind reserved for big shots) about ten inches long, and pressed a pocketful on his guest. After a spell of sweet communion, Mr. Yates remarked that he had come to Kansas City to pay off his note, whereupon the dealer in sheckels airily tried to dismiss such a trivial matter, saying that the bank didn't care whether the Colonel ever paid it—they just wanted him on their books. After the account was paid, Mr. Yates rose to depart, and was asked how he was going back to town, and his "friend" was horrified that so prominent and distinguished a man of affairs would use a bus. He called his chauffeur and told him to keep himself and the car at Colonel Yates' disposal as long as he remained in the city. The banker draped his arm around the Colonel's shoulder and escorted him out to a Pierce Arrow about half a block long. Mr. Yates laughed aloud as he finished his story: "Mr. Sims, that old feller shore does love me."

The mendicants and schemers proved so trying to the kindly old ranchman that he gave up and turned his business over to a hard-headed businessman and his lawyers who had no scruples about sending these persistent pests on their way. All he had to do was to say, "See Mr. ———" and clam up. This did the job, but he never got entirely rid of hangers-on. I wonder if he would not have been happier as a struggling ranchman than an oil tycoon. I have observed many times that great wealth has its burdens, but most of us would be mighty willing to carry such an overload.

The oil business in West Texas has pretty well lost its aura of excitement and glamour, simmering down to the matter-of-fact status of any other well-run industry in the hands of experts who know their onions. That doesn't mean that they have stopped exploring. They still strike more dry holes than they do producers despite all the technological advances. These boys still have to gamble, but they know their odds about as well as the Las Vegas operators know theirs. West Texas is about as full of holes as Swiss cheese, and the daily oil pages are crowded with accounts of strikes and dusters, which excite little or no comment from us fellers who run and read. You bet, I'd comment if they brought in a well on me!

Now, be it known to all and sundry that I am not a geologist, although I did locate a show by means of a forked switch, witching for water. But a little rule of thumb geology has rubbed off on me through long association with friends, eminent in the profession.

The Yates structure was a well-defined anticline, and when they started to drill, it soon became evident that the hole was running "way high." As this layman understands it, oil in porous strata is forced upward by an ocean of water, practically always salt. When this oil field finds an upward porous slant (anticline) formed by folding of the underground formations by convulsions of the earth's crust, it accumulates on top of the structure.

We have had a lot of folding in West Texas, and geologists early spotted many surface structures, more than a few of them producing oil or gas. Two "deep" dry holes, one to the south and one to the north, drilled some miles away on other surface indications, served as markers for the scouts on the Yates test. Mr. Moore early discovered that the site was tremendously high, due to the erosion of some 2,000 feet off the top of the fold during the eons of geologic time. One of these friends once remarked to me: "What is a million years to a damned geologist?"

They struck the show and set pipe (casing) on the bottom of the hole around a thousand feet without cementing it in. Consequently, after the well really came in, the oil rose in the hole outside the casing and permeated the porous strata. Thus it is that most water wells in that area turn into oil wells. The well became a thousand-barreler and kept on getting bigger and bigger. I have been told that there were four four-inch lines carrying oil from this well alone. Other wells came in, and they soon had more oil than they could handle. The producers got together and formed, on their own hook, a plan for parceling out oil delivery to the pipelines by the various producers. This was the voluntary forerunner of the Texas proration of oil, one of the really wise and statesmanlike accomplishments of our legislature.

To my untutored layman's mind, the Yates complex is the miracle field, for it is still producing heavily despite the archaic methods of more than forty years ago. I consider it to be a perfect example of water-flooding, and it is produced by Mother Nature and copied by our production experts of today who have recovered millions of barrels of oil in other fields simply by pumping water down below the oil and forcing it up. There is a lot that we can still learn if we have sense enough to observe and apply the workings of the "Mother."

BANKS & BANKERS

IN RETROSPECT, I wonder where we ranchmen and farmers would be today had it not been for fortuitous happenstances and outside assistance. Despite abundant natural resources and occasional breaks (such as the rains that come just before we go to hell), oil discoveries and the like, together with all our own output of blood, sweat, tears and hard work, vagaries of weather, market fluctuations, overoptimism and abysmal ignorance of basic conservation practices, there were many times when we just had to have help. That succor came from the banker.

A good many people, then and now, picture the banker as an ogreish sort of an individual, cold-blooded as a bull snake, battening off us pore, misfortunate critters within his grasp, but never was there a greater canard. And, me, I ought to know, for I have been closely associated with him for some sixty years, both as client and colleague, and, brothers and sisters, I want to rise up on my hocks and testify that, with only a few, very few exceptions, I have found him to be honorable, ethical, understanding and truly concerned in his clients' welfare. As long as a man is honest and trying, I will stay right in there with him.

Banking is based on honor, and the very few crooks that occasionally muscle into the business usually don't last long. Their colleagues and the Feds soon spot them and give them a quick ride to the "big house." The *one* scamp I knew personally was a twenty-four–carat stinker. He was the only banker I ever dealt with who tried to throw me a curve. A good part of his business was with trusting, ignorant nesters who were easy pickings for a plausible rascal. I got involved with him through a deal with a renter on our place: when the paper came due, he tried to throw me a fast one. What I did to that jasper was a "God's plenty!" When my lawyers and his superior officers got through, he was reduced to a whining wreck who resigned and took off for far places. I think I got more kick out of that happening than any other of my business experience. Incidentally, that gent got into another bank on the West Coast, but he didn't last long. The last I heard of him he was making little rocks out of big ones.

I got into the banking business early, for shortly after I graduated from college, the local banker offered to sell me some stock and make me a director. This sounded like a good deal to me and I went to my dad for advice. But my canny parent refused to comment, save that I was now a "man growed, white and twenty-one" who should be learning to stand on his own two feet. After due deliberation, I decided to go into it, saying that while I didn't expect to make much money, I would gain a lot of experience. Boy, oh boy, never were truer words spoken, for after a few years, the dang thing busted right in my face. And thereby hangs a couple of tales.

Way back yonder, a bank in Brownwood got in bad shape, and the president went to Fort Worth, seeking assistance to tide them over the rough spot. The big banks were so tight run themselves that they could not help him. So there wasn't anything to do but to telegraph the boys at Brownwood to close the doors. Just before the message was delivered, an old colored man deposited his monthly salary check for $45. Shortly after he left the bank, he remembered a small bill he owed and went back to draw out $5. Just as he reached the teller's window, the shade was drawn down. He tapped on it and told the teller that he wanted to draw out $5. The perturbed young man bluntly told him that he could not be accommodated as the bank was busted. The bewildered old man just couldn't understand why he couldn't get his money, so the teller crossly said: "Uncle, can't you understand? I told you the bank was busted. Didn't you ever hear of a bank busting?" To which the old man replied: "Yas, suh, but this is the fust time I ever had one to bus' right in my face!"

Not long ago I told this yarn to a friend who happened to be in that bank at the time, and he told me another story. The Western Union messenger was a smart, red-headed kid who was studying telegraphy under his boss. He happened to be looking over the operator's shoulder as the message came in. He walked into the bank and drew out his balance before he delivered the telegram. I'll bet that smart cooky went places after he growed up.

For several years, as long as we kept our feet on the ground, we did pretty well, and they made me a vice president, purely an honorary title with little work and no responsibility attached to it—that's what I thought! No salary was attached, but it did bring plenty of dividends in souping up my ego when strutting around bankers' conventions and college class reunions.

We had a number of good crop years, and the railroad was building into Paint Rock. Newcomers were rolling in, and practically all of them needed "accommodations." Our board got the big eye, dreaming dreams and seeing visions. The caution of Scotch ancestry asserted itself in me, but my squawks got me nowhere. I was the kid of the bank and the lone pessimist, and the others rode me down.

A bad drought came on, our borrowers couldn't pay, another bank was organized and our deposits just withered on the vine. Our president had a nervous breakdown, and we became a bunch of badly bewildered and frightened amateur financiers. One day the "Executive Vice President" phoned me and told me to hitch up a buggy and come into town on the double. I thought the buggy business was kind of strange as I usually rode horseback as he well knew. However, I complied, and he was waiting at the bank door for me. He crawled into the buggy and told me to get out of town. We drove down into the flat, well away from "cowans and eavesdroppers," where he bluntly announced that the bank was a "gone fawn skin." Men and brethren, never did one small bud of a financier suffer such a blow. Like Chicken Little, the sky just fell in on him.

We called a board meeting for that night, and the other members, mostly ranchmen and nesters simply sow-pigged, threw up their hands and put the monkey on my back. Thus it was that during the next few weeks a thoroughly deflated financial genius learned the facts of banking life and accumulated a sizeable flock of prematurely gray hairs.

Through the wise counsel of my parent, the cooperation of a knowledgeable bank examiner and the assistance of other banks in the area, we worked out a deal whereby our depositors were paid off in full the same day we officially closed our doors, but we stockholders got it in the neck. After a long period of liquidation, I traded my equity for some town lots in Paint Rock, which I have never been able to sell. I lost some money, but I got what I set out to do: I got a lot of experience.

This experience so soured me on the banking business that I stayed out for some thirty years, during which time I had a number of opportunities to invest in what became banking bonanzas. When my father became incapacitated, I took over his stock in the First State Bank of Paint Rock, where I have served as director, vice president, president and finally as chairman of the board, which, confidentially, they needed about as much as I did a hole in my head.

Although I have had right smart experience inside the banking business, I have had a sight more on the outside. I have borrowed much more money than I ever lent, and I have had all kinds of contacts with individual bankers from the lowly teller in a two-bit country bank to the board chairman of a multimillion city bank, and I still stick to my earlier statement of respect for and gratitude to the banker.

The bank of my early days was about as much like a modern banking institution as a log cabin was to a present-day high-riser of forty stories, or as an ox wagon resembles a jet plane. All the work was done by hand. The clerks stood up at high desks where they could handle the ponderous, bound ledgers (no loose-leaves then). They made their entries in longhand, and a man couldn't hold a job unless he wrote a copperplate hand and was a good adder. It was a sight to watch an expert tot up a long page of figures: some could even do two columns at once. The poor cuss who was slow or inaccurate was in for it. I wonder how many times I have seen these birds poring over columns long after most people had gone to bed. They just had to balance, and that caused a lot of extra sweat.

Letters were written in longhand with a special kind of purple ink, and copies were made by means of a weird contrivance composed of pans of water, wet rags and a clothes wringer. One had to dry 'em off, especially the copies. The typewriter came in before the adding machine, but it was a ponderous affair that made about as much racket as a modern threshing machine. It was presided over by a prim spinster, dressed in black alpaca that went down to her heels, sporting white ruching around the neck. She also affected coiffeurs so tight that her lips had a primly permanent set, and the bun on the back of her head was always decorated with a bunch of varicolored pencils stuck into it. She also presided at the wringer where she turned out copies of the letters which she had typed with two fingers of each hand. The men worked in their shirt sleeves, decorated with ornate sleeve garters and their detachable cuffs protected by black poplin sleeve-protectors reaching from wrist to elbow. All men wore galluses and these clerks, in gesture to the amenities, wore vests. It was considered downright immodest for a banker to have his galluses showing. These boys were the aristocrats of the younger set and were veritable molds of fashion. A top hand could draw as much as $75 per month and was considered a great catch by willing maidens and their scheming mamas. Some of them even kept a horse and red-wheeled buggy in the livery stable and rated higher in the feminine regard than the mod of the present in his Alfa-Romeo sportster. High standing collars, huge colorful neckties, derby hats, high-buttoned shoes and waxed mustachios were strictly "de regle."

The officers, more conservatively dressed, also sported hirsute adornments from walrus mustachios to full beards— the muttonchop variety was favored as it was supposed to add dignity to the wearer's appearance. They wore coats, but they also had vests under them. Everyone wore a heavy watch chain embellished by an ornate charm draped across his vest. The heavy, gold hunting-case watch, which was always stashed in a vest pocket, closed shut with a loud snap, indicating to the client or visitors that the interview was over. He could make quite a production out of hauling out that big, old "turnip," snapping it open for a long gaze, and decidedly popping it shut, a most disconcerting procedure to a presumptuous borrower or a bore. It rarely failed to get rid of the pest. They always sat in a revolving chair at a huge roll-top desk, plentifully endowed with multitudinous pigeon-holes and many drawers in its pedestals. If everything else failed, he could stand up and haul down the roll-top with a bang—and that was all she wrote.

He was a courteous, understanding individual, who could take plenty of time with a worthy customer and might even administer the accolade when he reached down in his desk and hauled out a box of stogies and a box of long kitchen matches, even lighting the "rope" for an especially valued interviewer. He could fairly ooze friendship and brotherly love when he tilted back that chair and gazed expansively at his interviewer or he could freeze the pants off a brash pest! Every desk in the bank, except the small deal tables where the typists sat, was endowed, beautified and adorned by a huge, ornate, brightly polished brass spittoon that was highly useful as well as ornamental. Chawing was so universal that most males expectorated frequently through habit, whether they carried a cud in their jaws or not.

Credit was based on character and cosigners more than on collateral. Most bankers required at least one cosigner. So it was customary for a borrower to put the bee on a friend or two. Most men cosigned freely, and most of them lived to regret it. It was a rare individual who did not have to pay off a note made by a friend. Fortunately, most of such loans were for small amounts, but presumptuous characters could get mighty pestiferous. One banker caused my father much embarrassment when he sent many would-be borrowers to him. After Father had been burnt a few times, he would extemporize, saying that his signature would not be worth anything, only to have the favor-seeker say: "Oh, no, Mr. Dave said that he would let me have the money if you signed with me." This happened so often that Father jumped the banker out about it. That worthy reared back, chuckled and said: "D. E., don't you think that was a cute way of getting rid of those pests?" Father sourly replied that it would be a very cute way of getting rid of him also, because, "if one more man tells me that you sent him to me for my signature, I'll move my account to another bank." That did it.

I was with my dad one time when an undersized creep, bearing the somewhat descriptive sobriquet of "Yaller," came up to us and announced that he wanted to see Father privately on business and was told to state it right there. He importantly handed Father a good-sized note, saying, "I want you to sign this note with me." My papa turned on his bleak look and snorted: "Do you think I'm crazy or just a plain idiot?" Of course, I sniggered and Yaller left in high dudgeon. Somehow, I don't think that he liked either one of us much after that. But he soon wore himself out in the community which had so little regard for a "businessman."

In comparison with today's operation procedures, those old banks conducted their business in a pretty sloppy manner. In illustration, witness just one small item—checks. Most men simply didn't carry checkbooks around with them while on the works; consequently, checks might be made out on any kind of material at hand. A page out of a memorandum or tally book served very well, although the reverse side might be covered with writing, or a scrap torn from a paper bag from the church box. I even saw one written on a shingle. Wonder what one of these would do to a computer!

Just the other day, I received a notice from my bank that said, in part: "Federal Reserve Banks will no longer handle checks or drafts without the magnetic ink (MICR) transit number. The new electronic processing requires such magnetic encoding." What that would have done to us out in the boondocks!

The latest checks not only carry all sorts of numbers and symbols, but also the customer's individual account number. If this trend continues, people will carry long, hyphenated numbers instead of names. Just picture a swain of the 21st Century addressing his inamorata as "my sweet little 762–PDY–3201–OM–229." *Ay de mi, otra vez!*

Those old checks were invariably written with the stub of a soft lead pencil that required frequent licking when writing with them. Indelible pencils came along later, but they didn't take on too well: a man might carry a check around in his jeans pockets for some time before he could find the opportunity to cash it, and sweat could very well smudge the indelible markings beyond deciphering. But, you know, we had few forgeries and fewer check alterations. I guess that crooks are smarter now than they used to be. *En passant*, I never saw a fountain pen until I went away to college, but they were too frail to be carried around on the works. I finally made it when the ball point pen arrived. Incidentally, I bought the first one I ever saw, and it cost me five bucks. Now I could buy a half-gallon of them with five dollars at the supermarket. We just keep a-moving along!

There is about as much contrast between the leisurely, archaic day-to-day procedures of that early day and a modern set-up as there is in the other fields of science, technology and so on. Not long ago, I was in a large city bank that had just moved into its new forty-story building equipped with the latest of everything. One of the top dogs showed me the works. I think the department that intrigued me most was the mechanized division in a basement. A few pert young ladies, matter-of-factly playing tunes on the consoles of large, complicated machines, handled the veritable avalanche of paper that came pouring down from the banking floors above. Under the old dispensation, they couldn't have crowded enough clerks in the forty stories of that great building to have handled all that work done by those few young women.

My first experience with a city bank came when, as a callow youth, I went to Chicago for a somewhat extended stay. There were no travelers' checks then, and our San Angelo banker gave me a letter of credit addressed to their correspondent bank. This was an imposing looking document that authorized me to execute drafts aggregating one thousand dollars (a huge sum to my dazzled eyes). After I got settled in the city, I repaired to the bank to make my "important" transaction, but when I entered that vast cathedral-like banking room, aswarm with important looking people and a multitude of great mahogany desks, my self-importance oozed away. I just stood there like a lost sheel in Israel. Finally, a guard politely escorted me to the proper desk behind which sat a most imposing figure with the torso of a lumberjack, the head of a Roman senator, and the cool aloofness of Guatama Buddha.

I introduced myself, which seemed not to impress him at all, and announced that I wanted to open an account. He glanced at my precious document and coolly remarked that they did not handle accounts that small. I guess my bug-eyed amazement got to him, for he pleasantly said that he would cash my drafts as I needed the money. I went in there several times and finally "reached him." When I made my last withdrawal, he rose to his feet, shook my hand and wished me a pleasant trip home. My, what a let-down I experienced. That rooster was an undersized shrimp, no bigger than I was. But he was sure big behind that desk.

A number of years later I was in Los Angeles where I ran into an old friend from Texas who was bothered about toting some $500 around in his pocket. I asked him why he didn't take it to a bank, and he wryly related his experience. He had taken the money into one of the large banking houses and tried to open an account, only to be turned down by a snooty minor official who loftily remarked that they were not interested in small accounts. Sam replied: "Hell, man, if I went into my local bank and offered to deposit $500, everyone from the president to the janitor would kiss me." Old fish belly behind the desk coldly rejoined: "True, I dare say, but we are not operating an osculatory institution." Sam finally rented a safety box. One day I went with him to replenish his wallet. We got in a steel-barred elevator operated by a tough-looking guy who eyed us suspiciously down to the fourth sub-basement. Then, it was harder for Sam to get into the vault than into a Masonic Lodge. He not only had to sign his name three different times, but he also had two passwords which he gave in a whisper at the outer and inner gates.

However, this attitude has disappeared, for all banks are eager for business. They have come to the realization that "many a nickle makes a muckle." The new accounts department will gratefully accept a small deposit, while the small loans division will lend one a puny amount and let him pay it off in small monthly installments. Like the packers, they ultilize everything except the squeal.

I was reared in the Scotch atmosphere of pay as you go, so I have never thought much of installment buying. Among the other things so proudly shown me by my aforementioned guide in the city bank was an outside banking room crammed with more desks than I ever saw in one room before. Every desk was occupied by a banker, his secretary and a customer, all busy as one-arm crapshooters. My beaming guide said: "And this is our money making department—installment loans from $50 up." When we finished inspecting the great banking facility, our host insisted that we have lunch with him in the executives' dining room. He had a special table with a telephone instrument hard by. Directly, the phone rang. Old "big shot" listened a moment and offhandedly said: "Send 'em a million dollars." Whew!! It was all too much for a pop-eyed country banker. We small fry have gone into installment lending, but I still don't think much of it. Maybe, one reason that I don't stems from an experience I had during the great depression of the thirties. Mrs. Sims and I, like everyone else, were in right smart of a bind. Our young son needed a lot of corrective dental work. So, about all we could do was enter into an installment deal with the high-priced orthodontist. Every time I would think we were ahead in our bank balance, an installment would thin it down. Finally, after some two years of paying through the nose, I had to take the boy to the dentist. I handed the nurse the monthly check, and she smilingly announced that this was the next to the last payment we would have to make. When we returned home, I jubilantly yelled: "Mama, one more payment and the baby's ours." Never was a debtor so relieved, for I would awake shuddering at the thought that we would lose our baby if we failed to make the required payment. I don't ever want to get in that fix again, so if I can't pay for it, I don't buy it.

Although all bankers bear my respect, my preference is for my country cousin. This boy goes through practically all operations that his counterparts in the city do, though on a smaller scale: thus, he has to be conversant with every phase. There are not enough of him to specialize. The country banker is just as much of a general practitioner as old doctors were. Consequently, knowledgeable country bankers are sought after by the big fellers.

You, no doubt, gather that I lean towards the country banker, and I most certainly do, especially the old breed which I sadly realize is fast becoming extinct like the whooping crane and the old-time cowpoke. It was my great privilege to be closely associated for some fifty years with a specimen in the person of J. M. Patton. He was so typical of the breed that I think a short accounting of the man and his capers is a contribution to living history, now fast becoming legend.

Pat, as a few of us intimates were privileged to call him, was a nesterish sort of a young fellow who had attended a small business college and decided that banking was preferable to farming. He came to Paint Rock around 1912 to take the job as cashier of the First State Bank, later becoming president, and he ran that tight little institution for the more than fifty years allotted to him. I have known a lot of big people in my time, and I can truly say that he was tops among them. He early developed into one of the greatest country bankers in Texas, an opinion shared by his colleagues and the state banking department.

He was sparing of words, thinking much and saying little —my very antithesis, which probably accounts for our closeness under the doctrine that opposites attract. I was probably as close to him as any other person, and I know that of all the good friends I ever had, Pat was the closest. I know that his counsel, his loyalty and his assistance above and beyond the call of duty helped me over many a rough spot in the road.

His was one of the most incongruous personalities I have ever known. He hid a wryly humorous, kind, sympathetic, even sentimental disposition behind one of the gruffest, roughest, scuffiest, toughest facades imaginable. He especially delighted in infuriating me, only to turn around and do me a great service. How many times have I felt like wringing his neck, and how many times have I wanted to kiss his ugly old puss!! He might ride me unmercifully to hear me pop off, but woe betide anyone else who tried it in his presence. On more than one occasion he invited such a traducer to pull off his coat and go out in the alley behind the bank.

I believe that he was one of the soundest thinkers I have

ever known, but one had to dig it out of him. He had one of the most remarkable memories I have ever known. Many times have I asked him about a check that I had failed to stub, and he could give me the dope without ever referring to the canceled check. While I was prone to error, he rarely made one. How delighted he was to catch me in a mistake in figures, and how he would rib me! But I finally caught him in a $1500 error in my account (the only one, I think) and I crowed like ary rooster. It so humiliated him that he sneaked off to the dim recesses of his wool warehouse and there remained *incommunicado* for the rest of the afternoon.

He smoked smelly cigars, and what I mean, he really smoked 'em right down to the butt, which he carried around dead, slamped tightly in the corner of his mouth, so that he didn't look natural when he was in church or some other place where he had to get rid of his snipe. He was widely reputed to have a vocabulary of only two words during business hours—yes and no. When that boy said "no," *that's all she wrote.* He knew his people so well that he was always ready with the answer as soon as his customer stated his business. If the answer was "yes," the note and deposit slip were made out before one got through talking. If it was to the contrary, all one got was a blunt "no"—no apology, no promise for future consideration, and most of all, no remark that he would take it up with his board of directors. One sure got the message.

I must confess that I didn't have too high an opinion of him at first, that is, until I went hunting with him. If one wants to get the real, honest to God low-down on a man, he should just go hunting or fishing with him. If he has any dirty little quirks of character, they sure come out in hunting and fishing camp. After more than a generation of camping with him, Pat assayed 100%, 24-carat FINE with me. What more can be said about any man?

I dare say that every long-standing customer of his has many recollections of Pat's capers, idiosyncrasies, wry humor, and above all, his stark honor and loyalty. A few of mine presents a fair picture of one outstanding country banker.

My father kept his account in a larger bank in another town because the local bank was too small to handle his "line," or so he thought. We decided to buy a string of big steers, but times were so tough that our big town bank felt unable to handle the deal. I had been trying for years to move the account and suggested that we take the matter up with Mr. Patton, which we did. It didn't take long to make our pitch, and by the time we finished, Pat handed my bewildered father a checkbook and told him to hop to it and make the note when we had finished buying. As we walked out of the bank, Father gave forth with a soulful, "Well, I'll be damned!" We made some $20,000 on the deal, and my father was so intrigued with this country banker that he not only moved his account but bought stock in the bank and served on its board of directors for many years.

An example or two of Pat's whimsies: my young teen-age brother was starting out in the cow business and needed $600, so I took him into the bank and had him tell the banker just what his plans were. Parenthetically, so many customers fail to take their banker into full confidence, and they make a mistake in not so doing. Give him the whole picture and hold back nothing. He will respect your confidence and be better qualified to advise you. By the time the lad had finished talking, Mr. Patton had filled in the note and a long, involved mortgage, which, incidentally, he never recorded. We just wanted to give the boy a lesson in banking procedure, which we gummed up by our antics after the signing of the papers. The banker drew out a box of cigars and passed them to us. Little brother didn't smoke so I took two. I began to search for a match and was handed a box of big, old-fashioned kitchen matches. I grabbed out a handful, stashed all but one in my pocket, and looked around for a place to strike it. Pat handed me a silver dollar. I struck the match on the coin and pocketed the dollar. We arose, and I politely told the banker: "Thank you, dang you." To which he, just as courteously replied: "You're welcome . . . go to hell." After we reached the street, the bewildered youth asked if that was the way that banking business was transacted, and surely I did not intend to keep the dollar. He was solemnly assured that he was correct in both instances, with further abjuration to "keep everything a danged banker ever gives you." He went off down the street, shaking his head in bewilderment. I slipped back in the bank and returned the dollar, and we two pranksters had a big laugh.

One of our substantial ranchmen told me of a somewhat similar experience with Mr. Patton when he applied for his first sizeable loan. He was a young squirt just starting out, but he came from a good family and was a hard worker. He went to Mr. Patton's desk in fear and trembling and blurted out that he would like to borrow $3,000. Without a word, Pat filled out a note for the amount, said, "Sign here," and made out a deposit slip for the $3,000. The flabbergasted young man felt like he should say something and remarked that he was borrowing the money to buy a tractor. Pat was "juberous" of tractors and didn't like to loan money on them. He grabbed the deposit slip and tore it and the note into many pieces which he dumped into the wastebasket. The poor bewildered boy didn't know what to do or say and prepared to leave. Just before he reached the door, Pat called out: "Take a walk around the block. Then come back in here and ask for a $3,000 loan, and, Joe, dad-gum your time, don't tell me what you want with it."

Another banker friend, John Q. McAdams, president of a small town bank, told me this one. He was in a farming community with seasonal influx and outgo. The farmers were preparing for harvest, and nearly everyone needed a loan. One Saturday afternoon they swamped the bank. Every officer was busier than a cranberry merchant making loans. After a long, trying afternoon came to a close, they were busy totting up their loans, which they well knew were very heavy. A knock came on the door, and a young man was admitted. He went to Mr. Mac's desk and asked for a $400 loan. Mac was tired and somewhat tenderfooted about making more loans, and he fell back on the old-time country banking procedure. First he asked the customer what he wanted the money for, and then he went into the horse-trading technique of offering him half the amount. The customer said he wanted the money to fix up the "ladies' room" in his filling station and reluctantly had to accept the cut. The next day, the banker and his wife were going to a neighboring town and went by the station for gas. He told the young man to give him ten gallons. That worthy stood hesitating for quite an interval and said: "Mr. Mac, we have been having lots of calls for gasoline. Don't you think you could get along on five gallons?" The banker's wife was most indignant and suggested that they drive to another station. But John meekly accepted the cut. Then he burst into a hearty laugh and told the boy to come to the bank on the morrow for an increased loan.

There is an old story, probably 100 years old, about the country banker who had an artificial eye, and Pat pulled it on a crusty old farmer who asked for a loan of $300 and was refused, cold turkey. He needed the money badly and argued with Patton, who, by the way, was possessed of two perfectly good eyes. He told the man: "Let's make it a sporting proposition. I have one glass eye. If you can guess which one it is, I'll make you the loan. If you guess wrong, no soap." The farmer gazed long and earnestly and guessed the left eye. Pat professed amazement at the correct guess and proceeded to fix up the papers. After their completion, he asked the man how he happened to guess right. That worthy replied that, after looking at both eyes, he thought he detected a gleam of sympathy in the left one and just knowed it had to be glass.

Sometime ago, I was chewing the fat with Mr. Arch Adams, an executive in a city bank who knew Mr. Patton well, and I related this caper which evoked a bigger laugh than I thought the joke warranted. He told me of a related experience of his own. A good friend, head of a bank in a nearby small town, asked Mr. Adams to make the principal address at the annual dinner of his local chamber of commerce at which most of the neighboring ranchers and farmers were to be guests. Mr. Arch, well aware that it is strictly *en regle* to start off any dinner speech with a joke, cast about for one that was *appropos*, and he came up with the glass eye thing which he told on his banker friend. The joke was received in deadly silence, which lasted about a minute, until a loud-mouth let out with a great guffaw. That set the audience off, and they howled with laughter, which mystified the speaker more than ever. Before the evening was over, he learned that his banker friend really did have a glass eye.

Mr. Patton was a sound student of economics and a conservative thinker. When conditions appeared rosiest, he looked for "something dead up the creek." Consequently, when the '29 boom neared its peak, Pat was shortening sail and had his sound little institution all shipshape for the blow.

Banks were busting all around us, and when the largest one in our area and his principal correspondent folded, it looked like the bottom had dropped out of things. Although I was not a member of his banking family at the time, I daresay that he took me in to closer confidence than any other confidant during those troubling months, and I am still amazed at his stark courage and chuckle over his wry humor. It was business as usual in Paint Rock in spite of all the confusion and wild rumors. No bank can keep enough cash in its vaults to pay off all its depositors, hence a panicky fool or a crazy rumor may set off a run at any time. The least trivial incident may set off or forestall a run on a bank.

On the very day of the big failure, two such incidents occurred. A country school teacher had a sizeable account with the bank and became bumfuzzled over reports coming in over his radio. He hot-footed it to town to draw out his balance. He presented the check for the amount in fear and trembling. Pat matter-of-factly counted out the currency and passed it out without a word. The relieved customer carefully recounted the money and shame-facedly apologized, saying that it was all the money he had in the world and he just couldn't risk losing it. Pat bluntly said: "That's all right. It's your money, and you are certainly entitled to do what you want with it." After some hesitation, the man decided that he had better leave his money where it was and pushed it back through the teller's window. Quicker than a cat could bat an eye, Pat pushed it back and said: "Oh, no, you don't.

I won't have any man on my books who is the least bit juberous (one of his favorite expressions) about my bank's condition. Take your money and get th' hell out of here!!" It didn't
take but a few minutes for this to get out all over town, and
people started to laugh.

Within the hour, another fool thing happened that clinched
matters by furnishing more comic relief. One of his largest
depositors bought an automobile in a neighboring town and
gave his check in payment. The dealer was a smart cookie (in
his own conceit) and hot-footed it to Paint Rock and cashed
the check. He got back to his bank just before closing time
and deposited the money with relief. The next morning, his
bank failed to open, and the report of the transaction gained
immediate and wide circulation all over the area, creating a
lot of laughter. This did it: there were no more withdrawals,
and our deposits began to pick up. Nothing can so relieve
tension like a good belly laugh.

I was so impressed with Patton's handling of the bank that
I ditched my phobia about bank stock and bought into the
institution. I served as a board member and a vice president
for many years and had ample opportunity to savour this
man's wisdom and his saving humor. Directors' meetings also
furnish insight into a man's makeup, and my friend truly
measured up. I could go on and on, but I think I have given
you a pretty good picture of a real, honest-to-God country
banker and the kind of man he was. I know that I shall never
see his likes again.

LAWMEN

ANOTHER MAN, not too popular with a certain segment of our
citizenry, who played a most important role in the development of our area, was the lawman—call him by whatever
name you please, and they called him plenty.

When my father came to the Concho country there just
"warn't any such animile" around. It was a part of Bexar
County and so far from settlements that the law people just
didn't pay it any mind. There was a scattering of army posts

Members of Company B, Texas Rangers, in camp on the San Saba River, 1896

and a few peripatetic Texas Ranger Companies, mostly engaged in chasing Injuns. Consequently, Col. Sam Colt and Mr. Winchester had to take up the slack. A man simply had to enforce his *own law* "unilaterally" and ordinarily, and it got the job done. When cattle rustlers, horse thieves and the like got too promiscuous, a bunch of neighbors would band together and tend to matters. When offenders were caught, the posse acted as judge, attorneys and jurors. A short trial, devoid of technicalities, was held, a vote taken, and a verdict rendered in short order. If the verdict was "guilty," the prisoners were either told to "high-tail it out of the country" (and you bet they did) or "say your prayers." In the latter case, they usually took their punishment stoically, for they had known full well that they would stretch if they got caught. The felon's hands were tied behind him, a rope noosed around his neck and tossed over a limb of a convenient tree, the man was histed up on to his horse, and the horse popped on the rump with a doubled rope—no fooling and no appeal! The bodies might be left swinging for a spell as a warning to other evildoers. Usually only a few hangings would clear a neighborhood, and, believe it or not, very, very few innocents were ever executed. One old-timer grimly remarked: "There was just too many of us on the dodge. If we happened to be innocent of one charge, we more'n likely had it comin' to us anyways." My father and his close associates stoutly and tartuffishly refuted this statement (so I secretly thought).

There was a big old pecan tree on the Sims Ranch known as "the hangin' tree." It was some distance from the river, well apart from other trees and brush. It had a heavy horizontal limb some ten feet above ground, and it could have served as a made-to-order gibbet. According to "real old old-timers," this tree served that purpose several times and, in one instance, accommodated five hapless felons at the same time. My father scoffed at these legends, but more than one old-timer would grin and wink at me when he did so. Be that as it may, we younger fry devoutly believed it and gave the tree a wide berth even in daytime and a much wider one at night. I just wonder how many coon hunters have waded the icy, hock-deep waters of the Concho so that they could get runnin' water between them and the "hants" around the tree. It was stated by many "reliable observers" that five bodies could be seen hanging from that limb at midnight when the moon was in the last quarter. Now, me, I don't believe in ghosts—that is, not too much—but I never was about to hang around that tree at the witching hour, or any other time of night for that matter.

Along about 1879, Concho County was organized. Law and order took over, and it was all done legal (that is, might' nigh all). My father helped organize the county and, I daresay, served more times as foreman of the grand jury than any other man in Concho County. He was called up every six months, and the judge always appointed him foreman. If I do say it, he was such a tough exponent of law and order that he was considered as the man who broke up cow stealin' in Concho County. As soon as the jury was empaneled, he would send out a platoon of riding bailiffs to round up suspects and reluctant witnesses.

San Angelo's first jail

One old-timer amusedly told me about the time that D and O H's had just started working a large herd, and two strange horsemen appeared on the horizon. One cowpoke yelled "ridin' bailiffs, dam' old man Sims!" He took off for the bush. So many of his compeers followed suit that the herd had to be turned loose. That didn't mean that they were all offenders by any means, but they knew too much to stand up under the tough cross-examination they knew they would get in that grand jury room.

These stern law enforcers were not hampered with any silly notions about pampering the "poor down-trodden criminal," who practically always got a quick trial and a free trip to the pen. It was pretty tough on a good, honest cow thief, but it made a real believer out of him, for the prison board most unfairly and inhumanely put the convicts to raising cotton. Now if there was any form of endeavor that purely killed a cowpoke's soul, it was working in a cotton patch. If he were a confirmed criminal, he shorely left cow and horse stealin' alone after serving a term in the pen and went into train robbing and stagecoach hold-ups. He might get hanged if he got caught, but he didn't have to raise no blankety-blank cotton. Killings (especially those involving "crimes of passion") were not as likely to bring down condign punishment on the offender as stealin' a yearlin', for the "unwritten law" usually overrode the statutory variety. This kind of hangs on to this good day. Only a few weeks ago, a man stole a yearling heifer in these parts, and it was such an open and shut case that he pleaded guilty. The hard-nosed judge promptly gave him ten years, while, in a nearby county, a man convicted of killing his wife was given three years by a soft-headed jury.

The Mason County War was a real humdinger that resulted in so many killings and burnings that the whole countryside was virtually in a state of bushwhacking warfare. It took four Rangers to break it up in about two minutes. The Ranger Company, largely through shenanigans related in my *Gun Toters*, managed to gather enough evidence to have several ringleaders indicted, and trials were set for Brady. Threats and boasts were so prevalent that sober citizens, who were not called for jury duty, loaded their shotguns with buckshot and forted up in their homes.

Only four Rangers showed up for the trial, for they figgered that was all they needed to maintain law and order. My old friend, Allan Maddux, and his buddy were stationed at the southeast corner of the square and the other two at the northwest. Court was duly opened and the judge began to empanel a jury. The old "Bull of the Woods" (the leader of one faction) was free on bond and made repeated boasts and threats as to what they would do to the Rangers and the rest of the law. He burst out of the west door of the courthouse, mouthing invectives, and started towards the two men stationed at the corner. He reached for his gun, and a Ranger coolly shot him (like the insecticide ads on television, "killed him dead"). Friends and neighbors, that's all she wrote!

Trial began, and every loose warrior faded silently away. An old friend related to me that during the night a great procession of covered wagons, with a few hastily gathered livestock, headed for "Arizony" and old "Mayheeco."

These hombres were tough, gun-slinging warriors, but the prompt, matter-of-fact cutting down of a leader put the fear of God in their hearts. I have had considerable experience with the *genus criminalis*, and I know that the one thing that even the dumbest of the breed possess in common is *fear*. The sure knowledge that he risks a prompt going-over is a mighty deterrent to any hood. Don't tell me that a company of Rangers couldn't handle a gaggle of bottle-throwing punks more interested in looting liquor stores and T. V. shops than in real warfare. Also, I wonder how long the mob would last if a bunch of Rangers took on their leaders. You'd see another stampede towards Sicily and other foreign shores like unto that of the covered wagons aforesaid. Of course, a lot of fuzzy-minded "idealists" would begin to squawk "police brutality"; how's about "mob-brutality"?

I just flat cannot understand why the "poor, down-trodden" criminal should be given a break while the enforcement officers are shackled by dam' fool technicalities and weird court decisions. Even if I don't seem to like it, I have a great reverence and respect for the courts of our land. By the same token, my rather extensive vocabulary of invectives is unable to express the thoughts that arise in me when I consider our legislative bodies, and that includes the Congress. They are the boys who enact the laws so full of loopholes and double-talk that Solomon and a Philadelphia lawyer couldn't make heads or tails out of it all.

When I was in the "enforcement" business, both in the

field and on the bench, we were not handicapped by all this namby-pamby stuff. When a man broke the law, we went after him. We might have been a mite rough on him, but it sure got the job done.

I took over gavel-pounding right smack in the big middle of "The Great Experiment," when bootleggers and the scofflaws were riding tall in the saddle. However, I had a bunch of dedicated enforcement officers backed by a law-abiding and God-fearing citizenry, and we really went to town!

Shortly after I took over, the sheriff grabbed off a whole truck-load of wildcat booze, while its owner was making a night delivery to a certain "respectable" citizen. The poor, down-trodden entrepreneur of the "white mule" witnessed the seizure from the house where he was completing the transaction and left in a hurry via the back door. He got away, but he lost his truck and its expensive cargo to the brutal lawman. We took a fruit jar full of evidence out of each barrel and made quite a production out of pouring the rest into the gutter. We had quite an audience, sprinkled with a few thirsty throats who sadly watched all that nectar going to waste down the gutter. One of the bolder ones approached with a tin cup and craved a "sup." I gave him permission, and he hoggishly filled the cup to the brim. He was a case-hardened consumer of the brew and smacked anticipative lips as he raised his beaker. He took one big swaller, his eyes bugged out, and he retched and spat as he threw the rest away. As soon as he got his breath back, he said: "Judge, you did a danged good thing pouring that stuff out, and I hope you ketch the s.o.b. who was a-peddlin' of it. It's the worst stuff I ever tasted in all my life!"

Two of the "pure in heart" spectators, both of them deacons in the Baptist Church, were enjoying the proceedings. One of them, a great joker, noting that the juice was spreading over a bunch of Johnson grass at the end of the gutter, remarked: "Judge, you won't have to make the janitor dig out that grass, as us old Baptists will kill it by sucking on it all night." This got a big laugh from the crowd and a very dour look from his colleague. He turned out to be somewhat of a

Judge Sims pouring out bootleg whiskey during the "Great Experiment." Sheriff W. E. Warren is on the Judge's immediate right.

prophet all right as the grass was killed, not by sucking, but by the booze itself. If all our confiscated "White Lightning" had been poured on Johnson grass, we could have eradicated a lot of the pest.

Our enforcers in the field were tough, mean, and thorough, and they always had a good case when they brought a felon to trial. The offenders didn't get sympathy or breaks from the old gavel-wielder on the bench. It didn't take long for the word to get around in the underworld, and the scofflaws began to take roundance on our county. A friend told me about eavesdropping while having lunch in a small town restaurant in Central Texas. He was seated in a booth where he could overhear the conversation in the next one. Two traveling booze-peddlers were swapping notes. Concho County was mentioned, and my friend pricked up his ears. One fellow remarked that there was no "organization" in the county so it should furnish some good pickings. The other guy indulged in some fancy swearing and ended with the admonition: "You better stay out of that county, for them s.o.b.'s out there will throw the book at you." Sometimes it pays to have that kind of reputation. The leggers and their following of two-bit crooks practically quit bothering us.

I served quite a spell as a "deppity" and a sort of an unofficial Ranger's aid during my younger days. Then I learned something about what these boys were up against, even in a small and relatively law-abiding county. They are out in all kinds of weather, and much of their work is done while the rest of us are snug abed at home. They get shot at, actually and verbally, both by the underworld and in the print shops. It is a sad commentary on our times that so many of our respectable folk have a sneaking sympathy, even admiration, for the criminal—that is, so long as the punk don't bother them. One sure loses a lot of respect for these "respectables" when he is an enforcement officer. I have lived in a hotel for many years, and I am fully convinced that a large percentage of our citizenry is somewhat larcenous at heart. The petty thievery practiced by so many hotel guests is disgusting and truly amazing. I wonder how few homes do not boast a few "souvenirs"—salt shakers, ash trays, pens, wash-rags, towels, et cetera, et cetera. Recently, I made that re-mark about our larcenous proclivities to a high police official in one of our large cities, ending my commentary with the statement that I had about decided that 85 per cent of our population is slightly larcenous at heart. He grinningly said that I was 10 per cent too low.

Just a couple of true tales in illustration: A friend swore that he was at a party in one of our better homes, and went to the bathroom. Now, all you married gents know that the lady of the house always likes to show off her bathroom linens. In this particular room, the towels were not the fancy colored things bearing the embroidered inscriptions of "his" and "hers"—every one of them was a hotel towel bearing the name of some famous hostelry, indicating that they were more treasured than the usual "company" variety. On an-other occasion, the gals were having a hen party, and, as usual at such affairs, the conversation turned to kids, grand-kids and maids. One of the good housewives remarked that she had fired her maid. She was supposed to be a treasure, and every gal cocked an interested ear. On being asked how come, the housewife bitterly informed all and sundry that the maid was a "damned thief . . . she stole all my good hotel towels." *There you are!*

One sheriff was particularly successful in apprehending lawbreakers, and I asked him how he did it. He seriously replied, "The criminal has such twisted ideas that his think-ing is exactly opposite to that of yours or mine. So, when I am after a man, I sit down and reason out what I would do under similar circumstances, and then I do the opposite, and it works every time."

We had it all over the lawmen of today for we were not hog-tied by sneakily written laws and starry-eyed jurists so chock full of the milk of human kindness that their common sense is drowned out. We didn't pull any punches, but we were not accused of "police brutality" even by the felons themselves. They knew that they had it coming to them, and they took it without muling or whining, so different from the milksops of today. Those old guys were tough nuts and never sissies.

Not long ago, I was kidding a sheriff friend about the change, and he sourly remarked: "When I apprehend a criminal nowadays, I gently and courteously say: 'Sir, I am desolated at having to take you into custody, but I have a warrant issued by competent authority, which I now read to you. I want to remind you of your constitutional rights and warn you that any statement you make may be used against you in court. You are entitled to have an attorney present, and if you cannot afford one, the court will provide one." Of course, old lawbreaker clams up, and his lawyer does the rest. Some criminals are boastful windbags with a compulsion to talk about their exploits, well knowing that a confession will likely be thrown out of court and may even be grounds for an acquittal. I don't see how a prosecuting attorney can get a conviction even if the criminal is caught in *flagrante delicto*. If he does send the defendant over the road, the chances are that he will be sprung "before soon" so that he can continue to practice his nefarious trade and take advantage of the education acquired from fellow cons while in the big house.

No wonder criminality is proliferating so fast.

COURTS & LAWYERS

BEING AFFLICTED with an inquiring mentality and a flighty disposition, this rooster has messed with might nigh everything, more for the heck of it than anything else. When one experience was fully savored, another enticed. Hence, after some twenty years of local activities, the far places beckoned. So I decided to make a trip around the world "for to admire and for to see," planning to make it via automobile and tramp steamer with about as much forethought as an old cowpoke friend displayed. This feller also had a fiddle foot, and when the fall work was about over, he announced his intention of making a trip to Hawaii on horseback. Well, I got about as far as he did—Fort Davis, Texas—just another two-bit denouement attending my grandiose plans and stratagems. The country was so beautiful, the climate so wonderful, and the people so likeable and interesting that I just never got around to moving on.

But, after twelve months of happy pictographic discoveries and Injun hunting with archeologists, college personnel, artists, writers and old-time cowmen, the old foot began to itch again. There were two interesting experiences I had never explored: trotting in double harness and judging. A gorgeous red-head made the former most enticing, and the latter provided an opportunity to settle down. So I was a sitting duck when the county judgeship of Concho County was offered me. I had stars in my eyes about the double-harness thing, and I saw an opportunity to provide my county with a system of first-class roads and to do some writing. My friend, J. Frank Dobie, and I had played with the idea of collaborating on a couple of books, and I had never seen a county judge who appeared to be busy, while most married men that I knew never even had to chop wood for the kitchen fires or do other household chores. That's how much I knew!! We had to build a home, landscape a yard, and get ready for real living. The judge's office piled Pelion upon Ossa. I never had time to do a speck of writing, but I did put in a lot of rewarding time as a "house cat."

The county judge of those days, especially in the smaller counties, had to be sort of a jack-of-all-trades. As the head of the commissioners' court, he was the county business executive, purchasing agent, assistant janitor, yard man and general factotum. He also served as a tier of matrimonial knots, marriage counselor, umpire in disputes of every kind from PTA squabbles to family fusses. He was expected to be on call at any time that a speaker was needed for anything from preaching a sermon to delivering a commencement or a Fourth of July address on a few hours' notice, when some big gun had stood up the local committee. In addition to all this, he was judge of the criminal, civil and probate courts, as well as county school superintendent, a right smart passel of jobs, if you ask me.

I think my most frightening experience came when I had been in office only a short time and was called upon to tie the matrimonial knot. Being a "yeller dog" (synonym for "old bachelor"), I was totally unprepared when an old friend dropped into my office and casually requested me to solemnize the connubial bond for him. Playing for time, I stalled about getting an *important* letter in the mail. I scooted into the clerk's office and implored assistance and advice, but that hard-hearted worthy laughingly disavowed any knowledge of such proceedings. We got a form book, and I read over the statutory ceremony. I assembled the contracting couple and the necessary witnesses and, in a state of utter funk, proceeded to stutter out the required civil form. I never could have made it if I hadn't wedged myself between a handy filing cabinet and a good, solid wall. (Incidentally, I wasn't half so scared at my own wedding which occurred a few months later.) The knot held, and the contracting parties had a long and happy life together. They even named their first son for me (pore little feller).

It didn't take too long for me to acquire *sang froid*, and I became known as the "marrying judge." I even had the Episcopal marriage ceremony translated into Spanish and took most of the Mexican business away from my competitor, the local justice of the peace.

At first I was loath to accept a fee for such capers, but my competitor accused me of using unfair tactics, and so I began charging them anything the groom offered me. However, I had to charge a fee when I told a smiling groom to pay me what he thought it was worth, and he floored me with, "Heck, Judge, there ain't that much money in the world." I would say, "The statutory fee is $2." But that didn't always work either, for one old kid fished four bits out of the match pockets of his pants and said, "Well, with what the law allows you and this four bits, you ort to be pretty well paid, and besides that's all the money I've got." He also got off free. My most outstanding performance came when I tied the knot for two great-grandparents. He was eighty-five, and this was his fourth experience. The blushing bride was eighty-two, and it was her third. When the ceremony was completed, the groom pulled out a long, grimy and worn "poke" and tendered me the two bucks. I shook his hand warmly in congratulation, bussed the bride soundly and handed her the fee saying that if anyone paid, it should be me for such a privilege. That also proved a happy union. However, they were not always such: the prize went to the couple I married on a Wednesday who busted up on Friday. You just can't win 'em all.

Not being a licensed practitioner of the law, my appointment met with some disfavor with members of the local bar, who immediately dubbed me "Old Necessity" for, as is well known, "Necessity knows no law." What they didn't know was that I gained so much legal experience in public affairs and had been so tutored by eminent members of the legal profession that I was a tollable fair county lawyer on the county level.

Sensing this critical attitude, I took office in fear and trembling with a chip on my shoulder. Consequently, I had plenty of hassles with these wily critters. They rode me unmercifully, but "I know my rights," and I was fully aware of the power of the bench, and I never failed to use it. After a year or two of skirmishing, we achieved an *entente* and became friendlier than a cat and a dog. I cherish an abiding affection for those old practitioners, true friends out of court and chivalrous enemies within.

Speaking of practitioners calls to mind one of old George's capers. George was a cow-camp cook and a prankster of renown. Although a Negro, he was the friend and boon companion of every cowpoke in the area. We drew no color line then, just appraised the man underneath the skin. George was fond of "red eye" and held preemption rights upon the feller of the bar where he was always invited to bend an elbow. The shenanigans which that feller used to achieve those invitations are still celebrated in song and story by a few of us ancient compadres.

A young and uppity squirt had just received his license to practice law and hung out his shingle in Eden. He wanted to become acquainted and repaired to the saloon on Saturday afternoon where a large segment of the citizenry would be congregated, George among them at his usual spot. The young man came in and expansively invited all and sundry to belly up and partake of refreshment with him. Through accident or design, he failed to include George, who never was pushy or presumptuous. He hung back looking so sad and downcast that his friends sensed a prank. After they had taken their first swaller, one of them loudly inquired of George what was troubling him. He lugubriously replied that he was in sore trouble as he had "stole" a yearling and needed a lawyer to defend him. The man ceremoniously introduced George to the young stranger, saying, "This is Mr. ———— who is a practicing attorney." George critically surveyed the young fellow up and down and sadly said, "Naw, Suh, he won't do. I'm in bad trouble, and I don't want no feller a-practicing on me." A joyous yell went up from the assemblage, and George got his drink all right—a whole quart. The young man was a good sport.

I succeeded a kind and gentle man, who never made a false statement in his life, and couldn't feature anyone else doing so. This blind spot made him an easy mark for any crook or his finagling representative. It is axiomatic that time is the great defender, and any attorney worth his salt can think up more excuses for continuance than any hooky-playing kid can pull on parent or teacher.

In consequence, I inherited one of the largest criminal dockets ever known in a small county, and I made up my mind to clean house. I think every lawyer in the district who could spare the time assembled at the opening of my first court. They wanted to size "Old Necessity," and I knew it. Though frightened almost out of my wits by the horrendous array of legal talent present, I pretended *sang froid* and called them before the bar. I readily admitted my ignorance and my inexperience and solicited their forbearance until I could get my feet on the ground. I also stated that I had always considered that law was just the rule of common sense and would conduct my court accordingly. They made immediate and grave acceptance of both statements, a spokesman even complimenting me on my common-sense approach. But this interval of good feeling ended when I began to read the docket and forfeit the bond of every defendant who was not present. When I had finished forfeiting 122 bonds, I never heard such screams of anguish in all my days. Grinning on the inside, I listened coldly to their anguished pleas for an abatement of the order until the next term of court, arguing that they were acting on the custom of continuances in the county and had expected no change in it. With a great show of stern reluctance, I finally granted continuance. When court opened on the next term, that room was packed and jammed by what was, in all probability, the largest crowd ever in attendance on the County Court of Concho County. All but a dozen or so defendants were present, and a real docket cleaning took place. I gained stature and reputation through the sour remark of one critic: "That little old judge don't seem to give a damn whether he is re-elected or not."

I knew that the barristers were laying for me, and I spent considerable midnight oil boning up on procedures. But that didn't do too much good when I tried my first big case. Both the state and the defense were represented by some of the best and toughest lawyers in the area, and they really poured it on my sore back. I got so confused that I didn't know straight up from sideways. So I decided to turn those jokers wild-hog loose: few kangaroo courts ever provided more antics. Five or six might be making or arguing motions at the same time, and they gave little heed to my frantic gavelings. They pulled off their coats, unbuttoned their shirt collars and shed their neckties. They put their feet on counsel's table, ingested great chaws of tobacco, and disdained the spittoons. Everybody had a good time but me. I secretly enjoyed it, for I was laying diabolic plans for the future. The defendant was found guilty, and his attorneys vociferously demanded new trial, which I stubbornly refused to grant. Consequently, it was appealed, and I wonder if any appeals court ever reviewed a transcript so full of reversible errors. Of course, it was promptly reversed and remanded as soon as they got to it a year and a half after trial. By that time, the "Great Defender" had been at work as certain key witnesses had departed the scene, and the guilty defender came clear.

I boned up a lot more on procedure and gained experience and aplomb in the trials of lesser cases, so I was ready for the pranksters when the next big case was called. Before proceedings began, I again called the attorneys before the bar and proceeded to lay down the law to them. I had already instructed the janitor to remove all cuspidors, and I proceeded to lecture them on courtroom etiquette as it would prevail from then on. I also withdrew my previous statement as to law being a rule of common sense. If the antics of the clowns was my criterion, law was just the opposite of sense, common or otherwise.

Trial had just begun when one joker took a big chaw off a plug and cocked both feet on counsel's table. I jerked him before the bar and fined him one hundred bucks and lectured the hell out of him while he was just dying to spit. He couldn't even mumble an excuse. I had to call only one more bird down, and that's all it took. After that we had as decorously conducted a courtroom as any federal court. That is, might' nigh, for ever so often a strange attorney might pop off once, but only once (or there might be an occasional lapse by one of the old incorrigibles). On one occasion, "The Law West of the Pecos" took great umbrage at a ruling and transgressed the "field rules." He got the customary fine, which he refused to pay, saying that he would rot in jail before he'd pay a damn cent. So I accommodated him by ordering the sheriff to place him in jail and keep him there until he was ready to make public apology to the court. This he loudly and profanely declined to do as the sheriff dragged him out. After about twenty minutes a grinning sheriff escorted a subdued prisoner back into the courtroom. When asked to apologize, he made a sweeping salaam sort of a bow and launched into a most perfervid apology. He not only ate a great batch of crow, he also praised the judge for being an officer with backbone enough to uphold the majesty of the law. The oration was delivered and received in all due solemnity although there was a distinct touch of tongue-in-cheek atmosphere throughout the proceedings. His apology was accepted and fine remitted. The next time we met on the street, we both burst out laughing. We had no more trouble after that. The dark, bat-smelling jail was just too much for the offender when he became convinced that the sheriff was going to dump him in it.

Old "Pecos" might act meaner than hell, but he had such a saving sense of humor that I couldn't help loving him. On another occasion he was trying a civil case before me and made one of the most lengthy and involved motions that I ever heard in any court. We did not have a court reporter, and I asked "Judge," as we called him, to reduce the motion to writing during the noon recess.

Trial was resumed, and "Judge" made quite a production out of presenting two full pages of handwritten legal cap. He could not find a stenographer who could accommodate him, so he wrote it out himself in pencil. Most lawyers write as abominable a hand as doctors do, and Judge was no exception. I could only decipher the heading of the petition, so I handed it back for him to translate. He said: "Phew, Your Honor, it is as plain as the nose on a man's face." He read the heading through: "In the County Court of Concho County, Texas," and bogged down. He adjusted his specs and looked at it from several angles, finally bursting out: "Your Honor, it's got so cold that I don't know what in the hell it says." Needless to say, the motion was denied.

I dare say that every "Judge" from the lowly J.P. to the eminent Chief Justice of the Supreme Court recalls outstanding cases tried by him, and I here relate a couple of my prized ones from my own experience, one a civil case and the other criminal.

The civil case involved two bills of interest not only to members of the bar, but to another large segment of our citizenry who will quickly recognize a similar occurrence. A substantial landowner of the section divided his holdings among his surviving children, retaining his home place which he passed by will to an orphaned grandson. He executed a well-drawn holographic (handwritten) will which was duly admitted to probate after his death.

Some three years thereafter another will appeared that was dated after the first one, just a few weeks before the old man's death. It also was a well-drawn instrument, well-sprinkled with legal phrases, duly signed by two witnesses, but sloppily typed. Now, the testator had talked to me just a short time before his demise, and I knew that he wanted the boy to receive the property. I couldn't understand why he would cut him off and leave it to the married daughter who lived in California. However, everything appeared in order, and the case came to trial with each side well represented by outstanding members of the area bar.

The competent attorney for the proponents of the second will made a good presentation of his case, even to producing the surviving witness whose signature was on the will. This fellow was a jackleg house painter who was a well-known partaker of the brew. Opposing counsel backed him up in a corner and made him admit that he had been slightly spifflicated when he had signed some kind of document whose content he now couldn't recall. But it appeared to me that the proponents of the original will had not made a case.

However, when it came his turn, counsel arose, the perfect picture of the cat that swallowed the canary, and presented an imposing deposition from the general manager of the American Paper Company to the effect that paper bearing the watermark of the one on which the second will was typed had not been manufactured until two years after the old man's death. The opposing counsel demanded to see the document, but the court read it first with a great light breaking upon him. The attorney read it through carefully and then threw up his hands, admitting that he had been suckered into taking a case involving a palpable forgery, and requested the judge to instruct the jury to return a verdict in favor of the proponents of the original will. I heard a great clatter as two badly frightened litigants stampeded out of the courtroom. The sheriff wanted to know if I wanted them arrested, but I told him to let them go, as we would well be rid of unwanted rubbish. So far as I know, they have never been back to our county. They got the scare of their lives, and the county was not out a lot of expense and bother. Our gain was California's loss.

The other *cause celebre* was a criminal case that had about as bizarre an ending as the will case, and it also had an imposing array of counsel. The chief defense attorney was the "doyen" of criminal lawyers in the area, a veritable bull of the woods whom I consider one of the greatest criminal lawyers that I have ever known, fuller of plots and stratagems than a dog is of fleas and a master courtroom tactician. The charge was aggravated assault with a deadly weapon, and it had developed into a sticky neighborhood hassle that had serious implications. "Old Bull" was an expert at employing the "great defender" (time) and came up with more valid excuses than one could shake a stick at. So the case just dragged on and on until I finally lost patience and put all and sundry on notice that the case would go to trial regardless at the next term of court. Defense counsel appeared minus his chief witness, but accompanied by much medical testimony that the witness was in the hospital with a case of botulinus poisoning induced by eating some home-canned beans. After a learned and lengthy exposition of the bacillus botulinus by an imminent physician, both sides solemnly agreed to go to trial at the next term of court.

Sure enough, when that fatal day arrived, only one defense witness showed up—the defendant himself, and the old curmudgeon on the bench forced them into trial. The prosecution produced several witnesses who testified that they had been present when the defendant arrived at the neighbor's home and caught the plaintiff out in the horse lot. A cuss fight ensued, and the defendant pulled a pistol and chased the terrified man around the house until his wife let him in the front door and bolted it. The defendant did considerable prancing about, just double-dog daring the householder to come forth and meet him man to man. The bystanders finally persuaded the warrior to leave, and his adversary called the sheriff.

Things looked mighty bleak for the defendant as testimony mounted. Prosecution rested, and the defendant was put on the stand. He readily admitted that he had chased the other fellow, but he stoutly declared that he had not used a gun. When asked what weapon he had used, the defendant replied with a broad grin that it was a mesquite root whittled into the shape of a pistol and that his wife was so mad at him about his caper that she had "throwed it in the fireplace and burned it up." Of course, a grinning jury acquitted him, everybody had a big laugh, and a lasting peace was patched up.

While I still have serious doubt about that gun, I realize that it could be true for a similar thing happened to me. We had one of the last big Confederate reunions in Paint Rock, and several thousand of the unreconstructed were in attendance for the affair of three days and nights. Our county was dry, and the bootleggers did a thriving business, most of it transacted in a big mesquite thicket adjoining the camp grounds. The young squirts nearly ran the officers crazy with their capers, especially at night. I was in charge of the headquarters tent, and Sheriff Maddox deputized me so that I could have a gun handy in case of trouble. On the last night a bunch of pranksters, smelling of likker to high heaven, were skylarking around my "office," and as I shooed them off, I saw the bottom of a gun holster peeking out under Ollie Skipper's coattail. I got the sheriff and another deputy, and we started after them. They broke for the thicket, and the fun began. They had a fair head start on us, and it wasn't long before yells and guns began to sound all over the thicket. Ollie and a couple of his pals allowed us to capture them, and the sheriff went for that holster: the gun was a mesquite root whittled to resemble a pistol. The chagrinned sheriff disgustedly gave out with his most picturesque expletive: "Geronimo-popcorn!" We all indulged in even worse language when it developed that the jokers were shooting firecrackers instead of guns, and that the strong whiskey aroma came from a nearly empty bottle that a kid had swiped from his father and sprinkled its contents over their clothes. What are you going to do with such pranksters? We just turned 'em loose.

I learned to love and respect those old lawyers, even if they did run me ragged. What those roosters could do to a judge, especially in the lower courts, was a sight on earth. I finally learned to cope with them for I had the advantage, and I never failed to use it. When I caught one "where the wool was short," he could make the handsomest and most flowery apology, when all the time I knew that he was laughing up his sleeve. They were wicked infighters in the courtroom, but good friends on the outside. Many is the laugh that we have had together after I got out from under their didoes.

I think that I got more tired of "County Judging" than any other thing I ever did. People put upon their elective officers in so many ways that they wouldn't dare toward their "outside" acquaintances. One does have to play politics while in office, and one does have to have the soft answer ready.

At the end of my final term in office, I checked out our bond portfolio to the new court in a San Angelo bank and walked out of there once again a freeborn, common, everyday citizen, who could rare back on his hind legs and tell the cockeyed world to go jump in the creek. I approached the first man I saw on the street, a long, tall, squirrel-shooting type, about twice as big as I was, and greeted him with "You go to hell." The bewildered man looked me over but made no belligerent move. So I hastened to say, "Mister, there is nothing personal in this, but I have been hogtied in the county judge's office for seven long years, and this is my first opportunity to really speak up. You are the first man that I have run into since becoming a freeborn citizen and to show you what I mean, I'll either fight you or buy you a beer." That nice, understanding man laughed loudly and accepted the drink, and we became friendlier than a basket of chips over our drink. You know, two men can become friends over a bottle of beer as quickly as two women can over a small baby.

Anyway, be kind and considerate towards your county judge—the poor devil needs it.

POLITICS & POLITICOS

THERE MUST BE some mysterious element in the atmosphere of the North American Continent that produces addiction to politics. It is said that the Pilgrim Fathers no sooner landed on Plymouth Rock than they began politicking, even before they began erecting shelters against the beastly climate. I have it on the best authority that when Stephen F. Austin and his band had no more than reached Texas soil, politics began popping all over the place. 'Pears to me that men remain hooked on the habit to this good day, and it is doubtful that Boston or Texas will ever kick the habit.

According to pollsters and statisticians, all normal males become hooked within two weeks after moving into the state —the rate may be a little lower among females, but only a little. You know, I think it a good thing, for in my book no man can consider himself a true Texan until he has received the liberal education obtainable only by running for office at least one time, the irreducible minimum.

In the old days with their pitifully few forms of entertainment outside drinking, gambling, horse racing, and the like, politics, along with its handmaiden, practical joking, was about the only respectable form of divertisement left to the red-blooded male.

A lot of men, as they grew older, purely honed to become public officials (it still hangs over), and this is where the pranksters came in, especially when the lower offices were concerned. The offices of justice of the peace and constable didn't pay much, but one carried the title of "Judge" and the other carried the starred badge of the lawman. The usual jokester proceeding began with the selection of a victim, usually an older man who had more or less retired and moved to town. A "committee" would be formed, and elaborate plans made. The target was approached separately by the members who solicited him to run for office, promising all kinds of assistance and support. The flattered dupe took the matter under advisement and usually decided to give it a

JUDGE ORLAND L. SIMS

fling. He would be given all kinds of conflicting advice by his "supporters," but he did have to formulate a platform and do considerable handshaking and the like. When election day neared, he was assured of an overwhelming victory, and he complacently awaited his approach to fame. But the sky fell on him when he received only a half-dozen votes. His bewildered discomfiture furnished plenty of laughter and entertainment to the jokesters.

The practical joker is a peculiar kind of beast: he purely dotes on embarrassing and even hurting the object of his machinations, but it kills his everlasting soul to have a joke backfire or become the victim himself—something akin to losing face among the Orientals. Occasionally, a dupe was smart enough to turn the joke to the great enjoyment of most of the populace.

One old boy was cozened into running for justice of the peace in San Angelo and, of course, got a sound licking. He took it all in good part to the bewilderment of the jokers. He printed the customary note of thanks in the local paper which ran something like this: "I have always said that it is good for a man to find out what kind of folks live in his community, and I have shore found out that there are more damned liars in San Angelo than any other town in the United States."

My good friend, the late Dayton Moses, one of the greatest raconteurs I have ever known, related this prize: just such another old boy sold his farm and moved into Burnet. He had always led an active life, and he didn't know what to do with himself; he had the yen for public office. Consequently, he was a sitting duck for the local jokers. However, he didn't depend on his "supporters" to do it all: he had a bunch of cards printed and personally presented one to every voter in the precinct. People had become so tired of the antics of the pranksters that they elected the old man by a landslide. His only opposing votes were those of the jokers who did considerable tail-tucking, to the vast amusement of the community.

The old man took his job seriously and conducted his office in a very creditable manner. He didn't have much to do, but he was at his office every day and just loved taking acknowledgements. A justice of the peace is an ex officio notary public in his own county. They had an oil scare, and the judge, ever happy to oblige, accompanied the lease hounds as they interviewed landowners and took the acknowledgements. They inadvertently took one acknowledgement over in Travis County. The error was discovered when the attorneys examined the title. The pranksters learned of it and straightway laid plans to regain face. One by one, they went to their victim pretending deep concern and offering advice. It was not too difficult to convince him that he was in serious trouble and might have to spend the rest of his life behind bars. One rooster, who claimed to have a brother who was a famous lawyer, volunteered to write him for advice. He waited a few days and came up with the triumphant solution: all the judge needed to do was to resign his office, as the law couldn't touch a private citizen regarding taking acknowledgements. They had no difficulty in persuading their terrified prey to submit his formal written resignation, which he promptly proceeded to do, as follows:

"To the Honorable Commissioners Court of Burnet County, Texas; Gentlemen: I hereby and herewith tender my resignation as Ex-Officio Notary Public and Justice of the Peace of Precinct Number One of the County of Burnet and State of Texas, to take effect as of this date. I don't want no public office no more."

Out of a full heart was that pronouncement made, and don't I know it better than anyone else!

The political bug bit me when I was still a callow sophomore in the University of Texas, and I have never quite gotten over it. With the exception of the federal variety and women's clubs, I have contracted nearly every form of the malady: campus, church, P.T.A., service club, fraternal, school district, precinct, county, district, state—you name it. Believe me, they all follow a similar pattern. If you want to know how low-down and witless you are, just announce your candidacy for office, as Bud Houston's story witnesses about a friend of his over in Stephens County:

The old sheriff, who had held office for more than twenty years, announced that he was retiring, so a veritable spate of would-be successors announced for the office. A neighboring farmer, a good old man with no experience in politics, decided to enter the contest and sought Bud's advice. Now, Bud was too canny an individual to come right out and say that the old fellow had a poor chance, so he told him to go ahead and run, as that was the only way he could find out.

On one occasion, I failed to use that much gumption and, in consequence, got myself in mighty hot water. We had a perennial candidate who had run for every county office but one and had always failed to be elected. Before he announced for that last office, he came to me seeking advice. I didn't like him much, was out of humor about something else, and bluntly told him that he didn't have as much chance as a one-legged man would have at a tail-kicking. Right there I made an enemy who ever afterwards poured it on my sore back. So, when a man comes to you seeking your opinion as to a projected candidacy, always tell him what he wants to hear: "Hop to it, you have a chance."

Getting back to our story, the old gent had a slew of cards printed, put on his Sunday clothes, saddled up his horse, and took to the hustings. After a few weeks of campaigning, he came to Bud's house in great distress and announced that he was pulling out of the race. He said that he just couldn't take what people were saying about him. They were telling that he had stolen a sheep. Bud tried to soothe his wounded feelings with the observation that people would say anything about a man when he was running for office and that he should pay no attention to it because everyone knew that it was untrue. To this the poor man replied with a sob: "Yes, but my God, Bud, they are going to prove it on me." So, if you are planning on running for office, you had better lay off if you have ever stolen a sheep or committed any other indiscretion, even to a facetious remark made in jest. Talk about the elephant's memory! It's not a patching to a voter's. Also, you had better develop the epidermis of a rhinoceros to withstand the outrageous gossip that will be hurled at you.

The average voter is something of a sadist who delights in making a candidate squirm. He also considers himself to be something of a humorist and just purely loves to josh the supplicant for his vote and favor. You just gotta grin and take it, or you'll lose a vote. This cultivated faculty more than once served me well. Campaigning for state office, I was in a big country town on a Sattiday when all the countryside was in town. I approached a bunch of men, made my little pitch, and gave each one my card soliciting his vote and influence (don't ever forget to put in "influence," for it surely helps). They were most noncommittal, and I didn't hang around. The buildings were old style with deep doorways, so I hid in one nearby and eavesdropped. A fellow read the card and pitched it into the gutter, the rest following suit. I walked back and picked up every card, remarking that I was Scotch and hated to see anything wasted, that cards cost money, and that I would use them on somebody else. The whole bunch burst out in loud guffaws, and I knew I had it made. I hid again and heard one remark that he liked a fellow who could take a joke, and, by gum, he was going to vote for him, in which the rest concurred.

However, it didn't always turn out that way. People can ask the dangdest questions. One dassn't lie, and his truthful answer can kick him in the face. In that same campaign, I had two experiences that cost me votes. I was considered to be something of a "scientist" and was proudly shown a bunch of "petrified rattlesnake rattles" by an old lady who wanted my comment on them. I unguardedly told her that there was no such thing as a petrified snake rattle and that her treasures were fossilized shells of a small mollusk named *Turritella*. She was plumb put out with a feller who didn't have any more sense than that, and she didn't mind saying so.

On another occasion, I accosted a nice, motherly old lady who wanted to talk. She gazed speculatively at my card and asked, "Young man, are you a Christian?" That sort of flabbergasted me, and I replied that I wasn't a very good one. She wanted to know what church I belonged to and if I ever read the Bible. My reply was that I was an Episcopalian and that

I fancied myself as somewhat of a Bible student. She took another long look at me and sniffed: "So, you study the Bible, do you? Humph, I don't see how anyone with even half sense can read the Bible and not be a Baptist." Needless to say, I also lost that vote.

Another voter hazard is dogs. If you are afraid of dogs, you have no business running for office, especially in the rural districts. Now, me, I always got along with dogs, and I have gained many a vote by making friends with a bunch of the yapping, ravening critters. But I was bitten twice by sneaky little feists who slipped up behind me and nipped me on an ankle. I lost both of those votes: 1) because little Fido was a good judge of character, and 2) because I kicked the slats off the other pest, and anybody who would hurt a poor innocent little dog is unfit for my office. Well, you win a few, lose a few.

Nothing in politics succeeds like getting out among 'em, shaking hands, passing out cards, laughing at jibes, answering questions straightforwardly, and never running down an opponent. Don't ever (repeat: ever) pass out a card to the same person more than once. It is a cause for great offense if a candidate fails to remember a voter after he has made his pitch. One of the most valuable public servants I ever knew got the pants beat off him by a young, poker-playing squirt simply because he went to barbecues and gave about three cards to each voter there.

Running for office is an onerous and trying business, and older officeholders dread hard, brush-beating campaigns. I think that this accounts for so many inexperienced, smart-alecky, young squirts getting into office, especially in the lower house in our state legislature. It may also account for so many of the tomfool laws in our statute books. The youngster hasn't much of anything to do except to get out among them and shake every bush. The other fellow has been in office a good while, and folks are simply tired of looking at him. Besides, "He don't think enough of my vote to come around and ask for it."

I well know all about this, for I, myself, was once a

particeps criminis in such a caper. We had a good man who had represented us well in Austin for a number of years. Like any officeholder and most any preacher, such a man accumulates a string of critics, even enemies, during his years in service. People just get tired of looking at the same old face. This good man had such a crop, and some of them prevailed on me to make the race. I was a young smart alec with stars in my eyes and delusions of statesmanhood. So, without consulting the incumbent in office, I made a whirlwind trip over the district and brashly announced my candidacy. He had made a shotgun survey of the situation and found that he would have to make a hard campaign. He just flat didn't feel like making the effort. In my presumption, I supposed that he was afraid of me and dassn't run. I now know very well that he could have beaten me, but he would have had a horse race on his hands.

However, he got even with me, for another candidate also announced. This man, a Methodist preacher, was, by all odds, the best stump speaker I ever knew, and what he did to me at the speakin's was more than a plenty! Nearly every voting box in the district gave a barbecue, and we had to make a speech at every one. I attended ten of these festivities in eight days, and my opponent took the hide off me at every one of them. (Parenthetically, I loathe barbecue to this good day.)

Despite his flair for oratory, he didn't go over too well with the voters because he had a "forty acres and a mule" philosophy, and he just talked too much. Each candidate was allowed a certain time at each speakin'. It didn't take me too long to expose my ignorance, but he always got so wound up that he would have to be forcibly dragged off the platform before they could shut him up. So I beat him handily, but my ears still burn at times when I recall what a monkey he made of me on the stump. Did that victory pep up my ego, especially when I began to get letters addressed to "Honorable O. L. Sims." So I went to Austin with a whole constellation of stars in my eyes and the firm conviction that I was destined to be the savior of my country. However, it didn't take long for those old professionals down there to explode the stars and black out the visions. I was just another "Ned in the First Reader" come to town. Fortunately, I had several friends, experienced and influential members, who sort of took me under their wings and taught me the facts of legislative life. It didn't take me long to realize that a young, freshman representative was mighty small potatoes. Right there I learned a valuable lesson: when you don't know what the score is, it sure pays off for you to keep your mouth shut and your nose clean. By practicing those virtues and with fortuitous acquaintance with some of the leaders, I soon got my feet on the ground. I managed to acquire a few wonderful friends and a bumper crop of enemies. I worked hard, but I managed to have enough fun to spice life up a bit.

I was deeply suspicious and somewhat afraid of the lobbyists, but I found that they were not all as evil as the muckrakers of the time pictured them. There were a few skunks, who soon revealed themselves, and I had no truck with them. In the main, they were ethical and businesslike, and I'll say this: I had only one man try to get to me during my entire service as a lawmaker. I used my cow-camp English so thoroughly on him that he stayed away from me, and he evidently passed the word to his pals, for I was bothered very little after that.

I found most of the members to be dedicated gentlemen, actuated by a sincere desire to serve their constituents and their state to the best of their ability, something not always too evident. Of course, they all played politics on occasion, and there was right smart back scratching indulged in. I introduced very little legislation, but I sure helped assassinate a lot of fool stuff. I sometimes wonder if it would not be a fine thing if we had a congress or a state legislature that would pass the appropriation bills and then kill off all the rest. I think that I would support any candidate who would adopt that kind of a platform. Wouldn't he be a rare bird of a politician?

One thing that bothered me when I was a "gallery bird," prior to my incumbency, was the fact that so few members paid attention to the speeches. A member might be indulging in the most perfervid oratory while most of the others were reading newspapers, conflabbing with colleagues, writing letters, or dozing. I felt that they were displaying scant legislative courtesy to the speaker and making no effort to acquire pearls of wisdom and information from the carefully prepared address. It didn't take me long to realize that most of the time the speaker was just spouting off, fattening his ego, impressing his constituency, or seeking publicity. I have heard so many speeches in my life that I don't like to listen to my own.

I recall but two speeches in our legislative halls that really accomplished anything. One, delivered by a naturalized German, was the finest and most gripping piece of oratory that I ever heard, and the other was so short and so ridiculous that it was right down my alley. They both got the job done. The first began with, "Every other man in zis hall is an American citizen by accident of birth, but I am one by choice, for two score years ago I renounced my allegiance to the Imperial German Government and became an American citizen by choice, and I feel that I appreciate that precious boon more than any of you can." It accomplished the impeachment of a native-born citizen for subversive activities.

The other one "saved a hanging," and I repeat it in totum. We had a freshman representative from East Texas who had sense enough to keep his mouth shut—not like some of the rest of us. He was a tall, comical-looking cuss who bore a fancied resemblance to a comic strip character named Andy Gump, and he straightway received that moniker. This man had not introduced a single bill, and he never got on his feet. A bunch of promoters in his home bailiwick wrote a bill establishing an independent school district and persuaded Andy to introduce it. His seat-mate, long-time dean of the house, took over and had the measure passed without difficulty as it was strictly a local measure.

Some months later, the governor called us into special session, and Andy's friends prevailed on him to present for consideration a bill repealing the original measure. When it came up for the third reading and final passage, Andy was callously informed by his "seat-mate" that he had to make the speech himself. We were in night session, and it was one of those beastly hot muggy nights that only the Austin climate could produce before the days of air conditioning, and every member except the speaker had shed his coat.

When the reading clerk intoned the title of the bill, Andy, clad in an outrageous red and white striped shirt, sans necktie and further adorned by a broad pair of fire-engine red galluses, rose to his feet, absolutely petrified by stage fright, folded his brawny, hairy, bare arms across his chest, and began his deathless oration: "Mr. Speaker and Gentlemen of the House, you know very well that I only introduced one bill during the regular session. I was mighty proud of having that bill passed, and I just knowed that my constituents would meet me at the depot with a brass band. They met me all right, but hell, they carried a rope! So, if you want to keep them from using it, please, please pass this bill to repeal the other one." I doubt if the legislature of our sovereign state ever passed any measure with more enthusiasm. Every member rose to his feet and howled "Aye" so vociferously that it caused the blindfolded lady on top of the capitol dome to do a veritable shimmy.

We were kept in session so long that our pay had dwindled to five dollars per day, so we finally got busy, passed the redistricting act and went home broke flatter than a flitter. That, Friends and Feller Citizens, cured me of the yen for lawmaking. I learned a lot, and maybe I did a little something for my state, although that is subject for debate. I accumulated a good many friends in high places and a full crop of memories so large that it would take another book to recount only part of them, and I am getting danged tired of doing all this writing! But a few will give a fair picture of what went on in the halls of our lawmaking bodies.

From time immemorial, it has been the custom for the citizens of Austin to "put the big pot with the little one" when a governor is inaugurated. I had attended a few of these soirées which were strictly "soup and fish" (white ties, kid gloves, vests, tails and bee-gum hats). Of necessity, invitations were very limited and thus much sought after. On this occasion, the governor announced that every citizen of Texas was invited to his inaugural festivities and that they didn't have to wear a dress suit to get in.

My friend, John Quaid, representative from El Paso, and I were appointed to serve on the reception committee. So we repaired to the capitol early on the evening of the inauguration ball and reception, dressed out in full style, of course. Early as it was, we found the capitol a seething mass of humanity clad in the most amazing raiment imaginable. At that time, the hill country west of Austin was largely populated by a species of hillbilly locally dubbed "charcoal burners," and practically every one of them turned out to greet their "Guvner."

The prevailing style of male raiment was the "dashboard" overall, and the female style was "ginghams," so you can well picture how John and I stood out, especially our stovepipe hats. No two young molds of fashion ever got so much attention, most of it absolutely raucous, as we elbowed our way through the jam. When we finally reached the reception line, we found one of the good ladies in tears approaching hysteria. She was on the plumpish side, and her charms were enhanced by a beautiful gown with somewhat deep decolletage. The female of the species, whether she be "Judy O'Grady or the Colonel's Lady" purely delights in picking the feathers off a sister woman, especially when she is all dolled up. The poor lady was the center of a snickering jeering ring of disapproving "sisters under the skin." We got her the hell out of there as fast as we could work our way through the mass. We were a sadly rumpled trio when we finally got out of the building, but we did get out and that's what really counted. You bet, we let "His Excellency" greet his fellow Texans without our support in his receiving line.

That experience had such a traumatic effect on my subconscious that I still have nightmares wherein I am the center of a vast mob, laughing and peering at my attire, consisting of gaudy striped shorts, red sock-supporters, tails, boiled shirt, white vest and tie, white gloves and high hat.

As remarked before, my hitch was during Mr. Volstead's backfire, and real likker was more prized than rubies. I was juberous of the frequent offerings, but I did accept when a friend desired to celebrate the passing of a bill we had worked so hard on. He had secured some four ounces of bottled-in-bond bourbon from his doctor (strictly for medicinal purposes). We sneaked in the back door of the hotel and made our quick, self-conscious way through might' nigh everybody we knew in Austin, all aware of what we were up to and voicing loud hints for invitations. My friend was most embarrassed and kept apologizing to me that his little medicine bottle only contained two modest drinks. He locked and bolted the door and turned up his mattress for his hidden treasure. He held it up to the light, and never in all my days put together have I seen such a picture of utter dismay. The hotel maid had discovered the cache and had consumed it on the spot. I have long been a "connoisseurish" small-time tippler, but I enjoyed the drink I didn't get more than any vintage potion I ever sampled. I was literally rolling on the bed in laughter when there came a loud knock on the door and a whole bunch of South Texas cowmen came barging in demanding a drink. They also got a great laugh out of our friend's discomfiture, and every one of those whelps reached down in the bosom of his trousers and extracted a quart of the real stuff. It was all too much for me, and I slipped out at the first opportunity, but the report spread the next morning that high wassail had gone on for most of the night.

In those days, a legislator's pay was small, but he did have a few fringe benefits, chief among which was his annual railroad pass. You needn't make a snoot at such practice. It was all done fair, legal and aboveboard, but the kill-joys had to come along and break it up.

One of the most prized divertissements was the rail junket to inspect the Eleemosynary Institutions. The various chambers of commerce, the lobbyists, the railroads, and other civic-minded organizations would provide a solid train of Pullman cars and one baggage car well stocked with certain necessities. The procedure was pretty much the same wherever a state institution was located. The train would roar into town with the whistle tied down and the bell ringing like mad. The cotton gins, the ice plant, the waterworks and fire engines all joined in welcoming cacophony. A great crowd was gathered at the depot, the town's "Silver Cornet Band" would tootle, and the populace gave forth with mighty cheers. A pretty girl was assigned as hostess to each three members and a shiny automobile whisked us on inspection with all the interesting spots pointed out by the attractive hostess. Then dinner was served by the Methodist Ladies' Aid or some other organization possessing the best cooks in town: my, my, the viands that were set before us!! Seems like nearly every town had a specialty of some sort, and it was always served. One town that I recall was so famous for its sweet potato pie that its state institution always fared well with the appropriations committee.

Then the speakin' began. Oratory was a prized commodity, and these old silver tongues could really "make the welkin ring." This recalls the time that the train stopped in Weatherford. The "Doyen of the House" was a real orator in the style of Joseph Bailey and William Jennings Bryan, and he was always selected to reply to the addresses of welcome. His favorite phrase was "Imperial Texas," and he never failed to include it at least once in every speech he ever made. He was large, handsome and distinguished, and when he spread his arms, rising to his tiptoes and intoning "Imperial Texas" and dropping down kerplunk on his heels with a resounding thump for emphasis, it just flat did something to his hearers, no matter how many times they had heard it—all somewhat like being greeted nowadays by the "Eyes of Texas" on a foreign shore.

On this particular trip Weatherford was not a scheduled stop, but the chamber of commerce wired the trainmaster an invitation to stop for a watermelon feast. The distinguished visitors were escorted to the public square where a small mountain of luscious Parker County watermelons awaited. Our official "replier" had performed superbly earlier in the day and had partaken of some much needed refreshment. He had to be plentifully doused with ice water to get cranked up, but he responded nobly.

The band played the "Stars and Stripes Forever," a bevy of Parker County beauties (Boy, were they beauties! I ought to know for later on I grabbed one of 'em off for my own) sang "America" and "Hizzoner" gave a rousing speech of welcome. Our Paladin arose, somewhat shaky on his pins, but fiery-eyed and bushy-tailed, and gave out with this immortal introduction: "In all of Imperial Texas—(thump)—there is no county so well known and venerated as grand old Parker County, the home of the BIG women and BEAUTIFUL WA-TERMELONS!" It has been said that that *faux pas* cost our speaker the governorship of Texas, but that is a base canard —he just didn't want to be governor. However, one of his hearers still sniffs when the episode is mentioned to her.

Looking back over my experience in the legislature, I recall with special interest some of the contacts and acquaintances I made. Two cub reporters, just as squirty as I was, developed into publishers of two of our greatest metropolitan dailies, and many other acquaintances arose to high place in our state and nation. But the biggest one of them all had the most un-impressive and inauspicious beginning. One morning my friend and colleague, Representative Sam Johnson of Fred-ericksburg, came to my desk towing a tall, gawky, gangling, beanpole of a teen-ager whom he proudly introduced as his son. I must say that boy looked about as much like a president of these United States as I resembled the Queen of Sheba. It all goes to show that you never can tell!

In this year of our Lord, 1967, it appears to this dour ob-server that there is only one subject of common agreement in America today: we are in a heck of a mess! No two people, even husband and wife, seem able to achieve rapport on any-thing unless it is to give our public servants unshirted hell! Sure, lay the whole thing at their doorstep and smugly ab-solve yourself from further blame. Everybody has a different idea, and here's one old-timer's.

The onus of the whole boggle rests squarely on the reluc-tant shoulders of the great majority of *hoi polloi*—yours and mine, reminding me of the Negro's hound dog. An old friend, who was a bank examiner, told me this one which he swore was true. He was driving a livery rig to visit a bank in an interior hamlet in East Texas, and he got lost. He stopped at a cabin in the woods to get directions. The occupant of the little house was a wise and kindly colored man, who readily set the traveler straight. A dejected-looking old hound dog was sitting nearby, and every little bit would elevate his muzzle and give forth with a most dolorous howl. My friend inquired as to what was ailing the dog, and the old man replied with a chuckle: "They ain't nothin' th' matter with that dawg. He's jes' settin' on a mess of goatheads and is just plain too lazy and too sorry to move." To those of the uninitiated who never went barefoot in East Texas, the goathead is the wickedest, hurtingest form of sandburr there is. How's about you and me getting our hind sides off the goatheads of our discontent and doing something besides howling?

I can hear the querulous complaint: "I'm just a little feller. What kin I do?" Well, we can start by limbering up our razor strops and getting longer handled hairbrushes, giving our own noses a thorough wiping, getting good men to run for office and standing behind them, and doing a thorough cleanup job on the campuses of our colleges and universities. We can stop turning out so much intellectual riff-raff and so many kooks educated beyond their intellectuality. We can go to the polls beginning at the next school trustee election. We can forget the fetish of party and vote for intelligence and dedication. We could also sit on juries and throw the book at the punks, whether they be from the stately halls of learning or from the so-called ghetto. That's what we could do, but I'll bet we don't do it. Consequently, when the commies or some other cult, just as silly, take over, we have no complaint coming, even if we dared voice it.

I make you this challenge: The next time you feel like pointing your muzzle skyward, get out and run for office yourself. I double-dog dare you to! Win, lose or draw, I'll guarantee that you'll come out of it a somewhat chastened, but vastly wiser, individual.

MEDICOS & MEDICAMENTS

WHILE ALL the foregoing categories had their large share in the taming and development of a raw land, the persons who were mainly responsible for the presence today of so many of us second and third generation West Texans were the doctors, male and female. Without them, many of the progenitors of our "F.F.W.T.'s" would have never survived the broken bones, gunshot and knife wounds, pneumony, smallpox, typhoid, etc., incident to the times.

Of course, the first doctor in these parts was the Injun medicine man, and you needn't turn up your nose at him. I knew several of the old, original frontiersmen who implictly believed in him and were positive that they owed their lives to the ministrations of an old "Shaman." In addition to being a master psychologist with a good concept of psychosomatic medicine, he was a first-rate surgeon and bonesetter. He was also a knowledgeable herbalist holding the conviction that "The Great Spirit" has provided an herb or natural cure for each of man's ailments.

Wherever a few families assembled on the western frontier, whether with wagon train bound for the Promised Land or in a scattering settlement of isolated cabins, two ministering angels always showed up to minister to the physical and spiritual: the doctor and the preacher—rarely, if ever, licensed by competent authority. However, they got the job done, strengthening the fainthearted, comforting the sorrowful, tending the sick and burying the dead.

In the beginning, most of these medics were granny doctors—wise old women who had raised a passel of young-uns fur away from ary doctor or drugstore. They just flat had to larn healin' whether they were turned that way or not. They used a lot of roots, "yarbs" and barks, out of which they concocted remarkable and unpalatable potions: "The wuss it tasted, the better it did the job."

The granny doctor specialized in obstetrics and pediatrics. She not only delivered the babies in good order, under conditions that would cause one of our young specialists of today to faint dead away, but she also pulled them through the ills of childhood (and they had a plenty) in good style. I can just picture the bewilderment of a modern pediatrician viewing one of those old girls pacifying a squalling baby with a "sugar tit" (a bit of rag dipped in sweetened water) or anointing his chest with goose grease and mutton taller to cure the croup. They always laid out the female corpses and took charge of the disorganized home. I wonder why some historian-anthropologist has not come up with a definitive study of this valiant, wise, and knowledgeable healer whose contributions to humanity of her day has been so largely overlooked in history as well as song and story. Everybody knows who Billy the Kid was, but whoever heard of Aunt Mandy Johnson who ministered so well and so tirelessly to all the folks in the Possum Trot community without money and without price.

Granny's male counterpart, most likely, was not the product of any medical schooling except the experience gained from helping a doctor back in the older states. Many of such early physicians had a helper, a sort of apprentice, whom he took along on his calls, especially those involving distance and bad weather. This young man tended the office, often sleeping there, where he read his patron's books and generally soaked up medical lore by watching and assisting the doctor in his work.

When he decided that he had learned enough, he bought himself a horse and saddle sporting tremendous saddlebags, a book on materia medica and one on anatomy, a few makeshift instruments, a plug hat, and a long-tailed coat, and sallied forth to heal the ailing on the frontier. He carried his own drugs, largely on the cathartic side, along with him (Epsom salts and mercury compounds, principally calomel which was especially favored). These early practitioners devoutly believed in strong purgation, and they sure obtained it with a good "thorough" of calomel, being careful of the dosage lest they salivate the patient. Most internal ailments, especially those involving cramps and nausea, usually came under the generic term of "cholery morbus" which included everything from green-apple bellyache to appendicitis, gall bladder, and so forth. This treatment usually killed or fattened.

The germ theory had not yet been hatched, and they took very sketchy precautions in the treatment of wounds. They did like to have plenty of hot water, and most of them washed their hands—even with soap—before doing surgery. I might remark in passing that the lye soap of the day was strong enough to kill any kind of germ, though it was mighty hard on human hide. A favored procedure for cleaning bullet wounds was to run a black, silk handkerchief through the hole, especially if the bullet had passed on through. I know of my own knowledge that some of those old-timey doctors did carry a silk handkerchief in their black bag of surgical tools, and they did wash it out when they got back to hot water.

They just flat had to get out a lodged bullet, whether by gentle probing or by "main strength and awkwardness." After the bullet was extracted and the wound cleansed, a favored dressing was a wad of half-masticated chewing tobacco bound to each opening. I can personally testify as to the efficacy of this poultice, as my father devoutly believed in the healing power of partially-chewed tobacco. He applied his remedy several times to injuries we kids sustained, to the great disgust of my mother who hated the nasty stuff. But even she had to admit that it did the work.

They had no anaesthetics, and when surgery was called for, the patient was copiously dosed with whiskey, if it was available, and enough of it could pretty well knock a patient out. In any event, three or four stout fellows were enlisted as helpers to hold the patient down. If he was not too drunk, he was given a lead bullet to chew on. As a case in point: my father once had a man working for him who had participated in the Dove Creek Battle. A bunch of peaceable Kickapoo Indians were emigrating from the Indian Territory to Old Mexico, where they had arranged for homes. They were moving under a permit issued by the Bureau of Indian Affairs and the U. S. Army and even carried a large U. S. flag. However, these didn't protect them from the Glory Hunters. Excitable fools discovered the band and reported it to the settlements. There was always a "glory hunter" in the settlements who purely ached to achieve fame by doing in a batch of Injuns no matter if they were friendly and had their women and children along. Killing any kind of an Indian, whether an old squaw or a little kid, was a mark of valor, achievement and fame. Such a criminal assembled a sizeable, though motley, army and took after the raidin' Injuns. They caught up with them on Dove Creek, west of where San Angelo now stands, and the Indians gave them a thorough licking. My father's hired hand was a big old kid at the time and was detailed to hold the horses along with a bunch of other buttons. They had an old jackleg doctor along as their surgeon. When a man was wounded, he was taken to the rear where Doc and the horse-handlers were. If the casualty had an arrow sticking in him, the surgeon would order four or five kids to hold him down on the ground while he planted his foot on the patient and yanked the arrow out, to the piteous squalls of the sufferer. Of course, more than a few points remained in the victims to plague them the rest of their lives. The dead were hastily buried, and the rest beat a precipitous retreat taking their wounded along. Those unable to sit on a horse were carried on makeshift stretchers made from a blanket and a couple of poles attached travois fashion to a gentle horse. Strange to say, most of the wounded survived.

Doctors also doubled in brass as dentists, and there was only one procedure—yanking out the offending tooth. Consequently, nearly everybody was snaggle-toothed by the time they were forty years old. And the tools they used!! In a museum in Tombstone, Arizona I saw a collection of dental instruments purported to have been used by the illustrious Doc Holliday, who was really a graduate of a reputable dental college and practiced his profession between gunfights. The weird extractors were fashioned like miniature stevedore or cotton hooks, with very sharp curved hooks, and straight shanks with wooden cross handles. After locating the offending molar, the dentist simply socked the sharp point of the hook into the gum under the tooth and yanked. No wonder the mutilated victim always howled piteously even if he were tanked to the gills with redeye. On more than one occasion in cow camp, I saw a jumping tooth extracted by being knocked out with a twenty-penny nail and claw hammer. The patients always reported that it sure felt good after it quit hurting. I guess the patients were just a lot tougher then than they are now.

The surgeons with the troops stationed on the frontier supplanted the Shaman, and they did a lot of patching and doctoring on the frontiersmen in addition to the soldiers. Some of these men were "contract surgeons" with little training and small ability. The old plainsmen had a saying: "Doc's pills will do one of two things—they'll either kill or fatten." Several chroniclers of the time commented that their surgery was limited to extracting bullets, setting bones and doing amputations. I'll say this: there were many more amputees when I was a boy than there are now, even with all our population explosion. One old peg leg solemnly assured me that a surgeon cut off his leg to cure him of chills and fever. But, strange to say, I have heard very few of these men ever complain of pain in their stump. More than one amputee attributed this to the postoperative procedure of applying boiling pitch to the stump, heroic, though standard procedure to stop bleeding and prevent gangrene. One man assured me that he had more trouble with itching toes on his amputated foot than pain in the healed surface of the stump.

My father's first experience with such a doctor came when he had newly settled on the Concho River. He had picked up a hired hand from East Texas who took sick and just got worse despite frequent dosages of sulphur and molasses, Epsom salts, and external applications of turpentine and camphor. As a last resort Father went to Fort Concho to consult the post surgeon, the only doctor in the entire section. After listening to the somewhat sketchy description of the illness, the surgeon diagnosed it as chills and fever (malaria) and gave Father three enormous pills (about the size of the end of a man's thumb) of "Blue Mass," a vile concoction composed of a mercurial compound and something resembling axle grease. The doctor cautioned Father that the medicine was very powerful and was only to be given the patient at eighteen-hour intervals. The Mexican camp-tender was given the job of nurse and instructed over and over as to how to administer the pills. An emergency arose at another camp, and Father did not get back to headquarters for two or three days where he found the patient apparently *in extremis*. He questioned the "nuhse" closely and was told that he had administered all three pills at one time so he wouldn't forget about them. Besides, if one was good, three should be better. After some twenty-four hours of intense suffering and teetering on the brink, the patient fell into a deep sleep. He was clear of fever and hungry when he awoke. He was up and about in a few days, due no doubt to the wonder-pills and the expert nursing.

Some of these old surgeons were cultivated men, well educated, learned and dedicated. A number of them remained in the area after their hitch had expired, and they contributed much to the health, culture and progress of their communities. Doctor S. L. S. Smith of San Angelo was such a man, and his imprint endures to this day. He was not only a good physician, but he was a master psychologist. He was wise and distinguished looking, the very picture of self-confidence, which naturally rubbed off on his patients who just knowed he hung the moon. In addition, he had the best bedside manner of any doctor I have ever known, kind, soothing, understanding, sympathetic and inspiring. He could give one a *placebo* (a bread pill coated with sugar and bitter aloes) and cure him of might' nigh anything that was not fatal. He was also a tower of strength when sorrow did come, and I recall with deepest gratitude his kindly and strengthening ministrations when tragedy struck in our own family. In earnest of the respect and affection in which we held him, I do not recall ever hearing him addressed in any other manner than "Doctor Smith," although it was universally customary to address every doctor as "Doc." He also knew how to get along with kids, and he possessed the sense of cute humor that every urchin loves. Among his pranks was his wooden leg. He had a peculiar gait, and he let the word get around that he had a wooden leg but that he was so sensitive about it that he would never tell which one it was. The only way to tell was to slip up behind him and stick a pin in a leg. If he didn't jump, that was the wooden leg. Somehow, the pin never found the right one, and the curious small squirt got a quick kick on the shin. This was part of the initiation every kid underwent. The doctor always carried a supply of small peppermint candy pills in a coat pocket and soothed the victim of this and other pranks by gravely dosing him with a few pills. We old-timers still cherish his memory.

As the Army posts in West Texas were de-activated, due to a shortage of customers incident to the reservationizing of the Injuns, immigrants really began to pour into the area. Towns sprang up everywhere, railroads proliferated ever westward, and in the forefront came the doctor as I first knew him. He was a more finished product than the old originals for he was a graduate of a medical college as evidenced by an imposing diploma. Some of these schools turned out an M.D. in two years, and their sheepskins were the most ornate of all. But even the four-year institutions pitchforked their graduates out into practice without benefit of internships or residencies. But they were well trained according to the standards of the times. Each one took the Hippocratic oath, and, by doggies, he lived up to it, in spirit as well as in letter.

Boy, what would I, an avid snooper, give for a recording of some of the conversations between doctor and patients when gunshot wounds were being treated. Many a frustrated grand jury tried in vain to make stubborn old "Doc" talk. Sure, he believed in law enforcement, but he just flat wouldn't give away his patients' secrets.

The new M.D. acquired an office, usually behind the prescription partition of the drugstore, hung out his shingle and went to work. His office consultation, examination and operating room was furnished with a barbershop sort of chair which served as examination-operating table and dentist's chair. A deal table served as desk, and bookshelf accommo-

dating his library of maybe a half-dozen ponderous, impos-
ing-looking doctor books. The rest of his furnishings included
a few surgical instruments, a lot of odds and ends, two cow-
hide-bottomed chairs, a wood-burning heating stove (always
topped with a tin bucket full of water), a wash pan and a slop
jar. The office was embellished and adorned with his ornately
framed diploma, usually written in Latin. Latin was a great
stand-by for a doctor, and he never used the English name
of an ailment if he knew the Latin one. He could make an
impressive production out of a simple bellyache.

The drugstore location was preferred, as few druggists had
pharmaceutical training, and the doctor came in mighty
handy as a prescription filler. He usually got his office rent
free together with a small salary and his drugs at wholesale
cost. The office served more as a loafing place and dental
chamber of horrors than a medical center, as most of his practice was connected with house calls. At first, he usually made
his calls a-horseback, carrying much of his equipment and
books in large saddlebags. As he prospered, a horse and buggy—even a double team for longer calls—provided transportation. You bet, he answered every call no matter the time,
the weather or the distance. There was no more welcome
sound to a distraught household with an ill member than the
klop, klop of Doc's old nag's hoofbeats.

Doc, dressed as if he were going to church, came in toting
his small black bag and fairly oozing confidence, most re-
assuring to the frightened family grouped around the sick
bed. He would ask a few questions, place his hand on the patient's forehead, have him stick out his tongue (which was
long and carefully scrutinized), ask for a teaspoon which
doubled as a tongue depressor, haul out his old big turnip
of a watch, and make a real production out of pulse-taking.
If conditions warranted, he would thump the patient's chest
and tummy, stick his ear down and listen intently—he didn't
have a stethoscope. He could get more sounds out of an ailing
torso than a canny thief could produce by thumping a big
watermelon to test its ripeness. He would gaze long and fixed-
ly at the patient, while humming or softly whistling a tune-

less air. He would then decisively come up with his diagnosis, and you know, it was surprising how many times he was right. He would open up his little black bag and take out a probe or other instrument and a wad of cotton if lancing, swabbing or other surgical procedures were indicated. If he was careful and a believer in germs, he might call for some hot water and slosh his tools around in it.

If medication was indicated (and it always was, regardless), he would spread his little black bag wide open exposing an imposing array of drugs all in small glass bottles about the shape and size of a ten-gauge shotgun shell and stuck in webbing loops something like a cartridge belt fastened to hinged boards. He would arrange ten or twelve slips of white paper, some three inches square, on a chair or table, take out his pocketknife, open a small blade and dip it into various drug containers. It was remarkable how uniform the amounts were. When he had put in a number of drugs, he would fold the papers into the neatest little packets. He would write down explicit directions as to when a powder was to be administered. He would gravely and confidently assure the worried family that everything was going to be all right and leave them "hoped up" a lot. If it was a simple surgery or a bonesetting job, he usually ran the squeamish ones off, keeping a couple of stout, tough men to hold the patient down, and paid no attention to the patient's hollering.

When it was a confinement case, a rider was sent posthaste for Doc, and the grapevine alerted two or three officious neighbor women who came bustling in to provide plenty of hot water, fresh sheets and clean rags, and usually to make a general nuisance of themselves. The kids were packed off to a neighbor, and the menfolks were banished to the barn where some forethoughted soul had usually stashed a jug which "beat all holler" the present-day practice of smoking endless packs of cigarettes as a tranquilizer for the expectant father. Doc pulled off his coat, rolled up his shirtsleeves, doused his hands in a basin of hot water and set to work.

Directly, a squall would come from the house, and another young citizen would be protesting his entry into a cold and cruel world. The sheepish daddy would be called in and given the latest young'un to "nuss" amid congratulatory sniffs from the women and jibes and innuendos from the men. Poor mama would be given a cup of tea and told to go to sleep. Right here might be a good place for a really primitive *accouchment*. One night Juan De Anda, our Mexican sheep boss, waked me up with the announcement, "Ol' Lady Cruz —she pretty seek." Cruz, a small, meeky Moses sort of a man, had a large and portly señora who presented him with a new heir every twelve months. They lived in a tent and were the dirtiest, happiest and healthiest family I ever saw. I phoned the doctor and went back to sleep. The next morning I was in town and saw the doctor who reported that Mrs. Cruz' "seekness" was childbirth. I got out my checkbook to pay the doctor, who said that he would only charge me for a house call because Juan had already delivered the baby by the time he arrived. When I asked Juan, "How come," he replied with a grin: "I help dem ole sheeps many times."

From the foregoing, it is fully evident that Doc really was a specialist: he just flat specialized in every branch of medicine and surgery. You know, he did a very good job of it!

In illustration of my statements as to the cavalier attitude of some of these old-timers regarding germs, witness this one: A man on the ranch suffered a bad scalp wound in an accident. He bled like a stuck pig, and it looked pretty serious. I rushed him into town and to the doctor's office. This practitioner was a real old-timer of the old school. His office, in the back of the drugstore, looked like it hadn't been swept out or dusted for weeks: it was the very antithesis of the shining, sterile emergency room of today. Doc sat the man down in the shabby old barber chair and proceeded to probe the wound with his bare hands which he hadn't even rinsed off. He reached down into his black bag, fished out some rusty instruments and started to use them. I protested that his hands and instruments were not sterilized, and he got madder than a wet hen because a young whippersnapper like me was trying to tell *him* how to run his job. It took a regular cuss fight and threats to tell on him to the other doctors to get him to boil his instruments and waller his hands in a weak solution of carbolic acid, but the old pup just flat wouldn't clean his fingernails. Well, anyhow, he sewed the patient up, and the man was back at work in a couple of hours. Sure enough, he suffered no post-surgery complications whatever.

The old-timer had no office hours, as he was literally on call twenty-four hours a day, and he unhesitatingly bucked any distance in any weather at any hour when his services were called for. He jolly well knew that he would be lucky if he got paid for 50 per cent of his calls, even in beef, eggs, poultry and garden "sass." I once saw an old doctor drive up to his house and extract a protesting old goose, all done up in a towsack, from the back of his buggy—his fee for spending most of a night bringing another wuthless young-un into the world. Doc was tired, sleepy and just plain out of sorts; besides, he never liked a dam' goose, nohow. He was a champion griper, crusty of exterior and tender and sympathetic as a good woman on the inside.

The Madison Avenue bunch say that one picture is worth a thousand words: in earnest, I refer you to Melvin Stone's portrayal of Doc Adams in "Gunsmoke." I knew one old-time doctor in the area who was the livin', spittin' image of Doc Adams, looks, mannerisms and all.

Along about the turn of the century, a new breed of doctors from the school of Lister, Pasteur and Company began to show up in our country, and they changed the whole concept of surgery and internal medicine. With chloroform, germicides, a practical idea of prophylaxis, and advanced techniques, these newcomers literally performed miracles, making do with sketchy tools under primitive conditions unimaginable to the slick practitioners of today with their paraphernalia and sterile surroundings.

The experiences of one man, whom I knew so intimately, were so typical of "The New Day," that a few are here recorded as living history. Dr. A. J. Marbury, graduate of a four-year medical school, served as "riding intern" under a wise old country doctor back East. He was in the vanguard of the new professionals of our area. He had one of the best minds I have ever known, a student who never quit studying and a thinker some forty years ahead of his time. Many of his forecasts are coming true only today. We thought that he was hipped on vitamins (known then as "vitameens") and snickered behind his back at the idea of anybody needing any other diet than frijoles, sow bosom, cornbread and molasses. Many mothers just flat balked at the idea of giving their young-uns that nasty, smelly cod-liver oil. He was the first man I ever knew who mixed psychoanalysis with medical practice as laid down by Freud and Company. He specialized in just about everything: surgery, internal medicine, heart, stomach, etc., on through obstetrics and pediatrics. Surgical instruments were somewhat on the primitive side, and when he needed a special tool, he worked out the design with Choctaw George, mechanic and blacksmith extraordinary.

He was credited with performing the first operation of appendicitis (called "appendeseetus") in West Texas and told me about it one time when I caught him in an expansive mood. A cowpoke on a ranch some forty miles from San Angelo came down with such a bad case of "cholery morbus" that a rider was sent for a doctor. He went to see the new doctor and described the symptoms so accurately that Dr. Marbury suspected that it was appendicitis. Although he had never performed the operation, he grabbed a can of chloroform and his kit of tools, rented a buggy and team from the livery stable and lit out for the ranch. When he got there about dark, he found a mighty sick cowpoke with the classical symptoms of appendicitis. There was nothing to do but to operate right then and there. A whole bunch of punchers was on the scene, so he had plenty of help. He had them build a fire under the big black washpot out in the yard so they would have plenty of hot water, put a crew to scrubbing out the kitchen with hot water and lye soap, found some sheets and put them in the stove's oven to bake. He had them shine up the globes of the two kerosene lanterns, appointed two men to help him, making them scrub up, rolled up his sleeves, and went to work. He knocked the patient out with raw chloroform and had one helper grab a hold on the patient's tongue to keep him from swallering it. Two men held the lanterns for light, and one handed Doc the instruments. Sure enough, a very bad appendix was removed and the wound sewed up. Doctor stayed around until the patient came to, told the punchers how to take care of him, and set out for San Angelo as soon as daylight appeared. A week or two later, he made a trip to see his patient who was settin' up and hollerin' for some steak and frijoles, as he was about starved on the soup and sweet milk he'd been getting.

This successful operation was a nine-day wonder, and I dare say that it was discussed in every cow camp in West Texas. It just beat tarnation what the world was coming to when a sawbones could cut a man's belly open, take out part of his innards, sew him back up like sewing a towsack full of oats and have him get well. I am sure that Dr. Marbury performed about as many operations under makeshift conditions as he ever did in the operating room of a hospital. I helped him in one major operation which was performed in his office. He and his one nurse prepared the patient, one of our ranch hands, and the other doctor who was scheduled to administer the anesthetic failed to show up. So I scrubbed up, got into a surgical gown, and went to work. My principal duties were to watch the patient's breathing and keep him from swallering his tongue. Sure enough, right spang in the middle of the operation, the patient stopped breathing. The nurse began slapping his face and chest while Doctor grabbed the tongue with a pair of forceps and pulled it way out, sternly admonishing me to keep it that way. I had no idea a man had such a long tongue. Why, that puncher's tongue was as long as any yearling steer's! The patient recovered nicely, but he never paid me for my part in the operation that saved his life, nor did he reimburse me for what I paid the doctor for operating on him. The doctor didn't want to take the money, and I had to make him accept it.

Doctor was a great scientist, healer and thinker, but I think he was by all odds the world's worst collector. It actually embarrassed him to send a patient a bill, which his long-suffering wife and business manager had to force him into doing now and then when well-fixed patients failed to pay his ridiculously low charges. Why, if that man had charged his patients 10 per cent of what they tax us nowadays, and if he had collected only one-half, he would have been the richest man in Tom Green County.

Incidentally, I never knew but two old-timey doctors who accumulated more than a bare living, and they made their money in business separate and apart from their medical practice. Dr. Marbury's life story is by no means *sui generis*; in fact, most every other sizeable community had a dedicated disciple of Aesculapius with an almost identical career.

We of the second and third generations of these parts owe a lot to all the pioneers who developed our good land, but I often wonder if we don't owe more to our old mothers in Israel, our old-timey doctors and preachers who gave us something more than material blessings.

Anyway, *Laus Deo*, Doc, it was my privilege to have known you.

THE PREACHER

ANOTHER UBIQUITOUS CHARACTER on the frontier was the holy man, the preacher. Like the first healer, he also was an Injun who quadrupled in brass as healer, magician, priest and teacher of the holy doctrine. Our earliest mountain men and plainsmen got along well with the Indians, even marrying or being adopted into the tribes. During the long winters, more than a few of them sat at the feet of the medicine man and absorbed, and even practiced, some of his mystique. He frequently referred to the "Great Spirit" and to the "Above People" and apologized to the spirits of the man and some animals he had killed. It is well authenticated that some of them intoned their death chants when they realized that they were dying. I have been assured by two or three of the men who came on the scene as late as the buffalo kills that the Injun had a good religion.

The first real preacher in our section was the Catholic priest who always accompanied the explorers who fanned out of Mexico. These men were dedicated, even fanatical missioners passionately intent on bringing the Christian religion to the Indian and riding herd on the members of their expeditions. They established missions in Western Texas, which became outposts of civilization, ministering chiefly to the Indians and Mexicans rather than to the white American frontiersmen who had largely Protestant backgrounds.

The Army supplied the first Protestant preachers in the persons of the chaplains who ministered to the spiritual needs of the troops and the few settlers around the Army posts. One of these men at Fort Concho was the Reverend Norman Badger, an Episcopalian who was stationed there in the early seventies. He was a man of many parts who left a lasting imprint on our area.

Along with the emigrant trains and in the scattered settlements, there were always preachers of sorts, lay or professional, who ministered to the spiritual needs of their flocks as their conferees, the doctors, did the physical. They were even more underpaid than the doctors. More than a few of them were unlettered and unlearned, seldom coming from a theological seminary or ordained by competent authority. But they knew their Bibles almost by heart and they knew their people. They just "got the call" and went about the Master's business. They were products of a tough environment, guntoters all, who more than likely had been cowpokes, wagon train guides, Injun fighters, lawmen, even gamblers, rustlers, or just plain hell-raisers in general. But when they became converted, they stayed converted. They had all the experience and the skills of the frontiersmen (they just had to, in order to survive), as they were largely itinerants who roamed the country o'er, dodging the Indians and enduring all the perils of weather and a lonely, hostile land, to bring spiritual consolation to all (especially to the womenfolks who sorely needed it) and comfort and consolation to the sorrowing. They married the lovelorn (largely without benefit of legal license), buried the dead, acted as unofficial mail carrier, and served as news media, carrying news from settlement to camp to settlement. Consequently, they were welcome wherever they went, which was mighty handy for them, as they didn't pay much heed as to wherewithal they would be clothed or fed.

They were rugged old saints, and I use the word "saints" advisedly, as a man had to have the guts of Saint Peter, the dedication of Saint Paul and the vision of Saint John in order to function under the almost unbelievably primitive conditions of the frontier. He rode a horse, usually kind of bony and underfed, and he carried his worldly possessions, including his entire wardrobe, his Bible and hymn books in a pair of enormous saddlebags. He dressed, frontier style, in boots, linsey shirt, jeans britches, and big hat, but he most always sported a long-tailed coat under which was his trusted forty-five, cap and ball revolver. He might have a long, heavy Army overcoat and even a blanket or two. He carried a stake rope and a canvas grub bag swung on the horn of his saddle containing a few cold biscuits, a piece of fat, homecured bacon, a few handsful of ground coffee and a tin can. So, it didn't bother him much if he got caught out for nights "on the ballies," even though he had to keep his eyes peeled for Injuns. He was too good a plainsman to be caught napping by hostiles whether they be men, weather, varmints, prairie fires or a breakaway horse. If the weather permitted, a convenient creek provided bathing facilities and a washtub for his laundrying.

He held services wherever and whenever he could assemble worshippers: out in the open, in a one-room log cabin, under a brush arbor, or in a church of sorts. There is a faithful restoration of such a meetin' house near Palestine, Texas. It is a small log structure that might accommodate some forty worshippers, with a dirt floor, a flimsy box of a pulpit, two windows with heavy slab swinging shutters (no glass) and a heavy door made of hand-hewn timber. Its seats were low benches made from split logs, flat sides up, with short legs stuck in holes bored in the logs' round sides. A puncheon floor of hand-hewn planks later superseded the dirt floor. There was enough room in the back for the worshipers' rifles, and the staunch little house could double in brass (as it did on more than one occasion) as a snug and effective fort against Indian attack. These old boys had what it took and our country owes them a lot.

The Sims home at Paint Rock was a haven for all preachers, of whatever flavor, and I had early exposure to all the different kinds. By the time I was old enough to know what the score was, our visitors were principally circuit riders and practically all Protestants, principally Methodist, Baptist and Presbyterian (in that order), with a small sprinkling of Campbellites. I only recall two or three Catholic priests, as our section was so predominantly Protestant. The Protestants might differ in various ways, but they held one thing in common—they purely distrusted, even disliked Catholics. However, one branch of our forebears was Irish Catholic, so the Simses, although devotedly Protestant, were tolerant towards the Catholics, to the annoyance and criticism of our neigbors.

The routine of the circuit rider's visits pretty much followed the same pattern in all homes. Along in the shank of the afternoon, a worn and weary traveler, diked out in a long-tailed coat and astride a gaunt and bony horse, would ride up to the front gate and holler, "Hello." A welcoming committee of a woman and a passel of small fry would greet him cordially and invite him to light and rest his saddle. After introducing himself as Brother (practically all preachers were called "brother" in them days), he would diffidently inquire if it would put out the family for him to spend the night with them. You can just bet that he was welcome, for his visit was an event bringing much needed spiritual refreshment to the mother and the news of the country to the mister.

The visitor removed his saddlebags, draped them over his shoulder and toted them into the house, while the oldest boy took his horse to the lot to unsaddle, water and feed it. This kid also alerted the head of the household that the preacher had come.

The kids were set to catching frying-size chickens, or sent to a neighbor's to borry a few if the supply was short, for it was, and still is for that matter, proverbial that every preacher, no matter what his flavor, purely loved fried chicken. The honored guest was ushered into the living room, given the latest copy of the *Christian Advocate* and told to make himself to home, which he proceeded to do in spite of his audience of bug-eyed, finger-in-mouth smaller fry. Through the operation of the grapevine, a neighbor woman or two showed up, and things really began to "June" throughout the menage.

The good man of the house would come in about dark, and although he might not be too enthusiastic about having a preacher around underfoot, you bet he jolly well kept his fat mouth shut. Mama might be meek and long-suffering about most things, but she could really get on the peck, and how!, if the preacher was the least bit slighted. So Papa would wash up, slick back his hair, put on a clean shirt and proceed to make himself agreeable.

After much scurrying around, the womenfolks would round up a good supper, and man, oh man, it was good. The whole family, including the hired hands and the stranger within the gates, would decorously seat themselves around the board which groaned under the weight of great platters of real, honest-to-God country fried chicken, bowls of white gravy, garden "sass" in season, mashed pertaters done up in rich cream and country butter, big hot biscuits, chow-chow, sweet pickles, preserves, jelly and knick-knacks of all kinds.

Every head was reverently bowed while the guest of honor asked the blessing, eloquent but overly long to a bunch of hungry kids savoring the enticing aroma of the fried chicken. You can also just bet that the heads remained bowed until the lusty "Aman." Although Mama's head was bowed as low as the others, that didn't prevent her from keeping a roving, vigilant eye on the lookout for violaters of the proprieties. Woe be unto an offender who might try to sneak a look around!

Most mothers wore a thimble during the waking hours, for they had a lot of on-the-spot mending to do and that old thimble also doubled as an instrument of correction. Boy, what a resounding thwack it could make on the pate of an offending urchin!

Father sat at the head of the table with the chicken platter immediately in front of him, while Mother sat at the foot, flanked by a large black coffeepot and a pitcher of buttermilk, which was another favorite of the preacher, especially if he was well bewhiskered. I still recall the fascination of watching such a guest get rid (without benefit of napkin) of the buttermilk remaining on his whiskers after a copious draft.

Platters of hot biscuits were passed around before the actual serving began so that they could be buttered while they were hot. Generous dishes of butter were circulated into which the guest dipped his knife for a generous blob, and this continued throughout the meal as the biscuits made their rapid disappearance. One's knife was supposed to be clean when he dipped it into the butter not by licking, but by carefully wiping it on his biscuit.

Papa helped the plates, and the honored guest got the pick of the choicest chicken pieces, tapering off to the littlest kid who got the leavings, usually the necks and the feet. Yes sir, the feet, which didn't provide much nourishment, but they were mighty flavorful sucking. Many an old-timer would solemnly swear that he was a growed man before he knew that a chicken had any other parts than necks and feet. Incidentally, I knew one old lady who was so tight that she fed threshing crews mostly on chicken wings and feet. It was a wry joke among the crews that Mrs. Blank's chickens only grew feet and wings.

After supper, the men retired to the sittin' room, or the front gallery if the weather permitted, where they put the finishing touch to a good meal, a copious chaw of terbacker. Pipes were tolerated, but cigarettes were banished to the backyard. Once settled, much man-talk ensued: range news, weather, politics, killin's and the like. Meanwhile, the womenfolks redded up the kitchen, stacking the clean dishes and surplus food of the keepin' kind in the kitchen safe which was a tall, wardrobe-like piece of furniture with many shelves and two full-length doors with tin panels full of small holes

punched in intricate designs and curlecues, providing ornamentation as well as ventilation for the contents. I was a
man growed before I ever saw a kitchen cabinet. A modern
housewife would be hard put to make do with one of those
primitive old kitchens.

By that time, the men, who had pretty well finished their
chaws, would dump their spent cuds, the kids would be
rounded up, and all would gather in the sittin' room for the
high point of the parson's visit. After everyone was decorously seated, the honored guest would haul out his Bible and
read several chapters that seemed appropriate to the occasion.
Then he would say, "Let us pray." Everybody, and I mean
everybody—preacher, Mama, Papa, guests, hired hands and
kids—would get down on their knees. The men might comply awkwardly and somewhat sheepishly, but down they got
for vigilant Mama saw to it that everybody really got down
on his marrow bones—no squatting! The preacher would
pray long, fervently and eloquently for the spiritual health
and welfare of the family, and everyone went to bed feeling
kind of clean spiritually.

I have no thought of trying to be cute or facetious: I simply
describe a rich spiritual experience as I witnessed it many
times. Such sessions were not exceptional even between visits
of the preacher. Folks just took their religion more seriously
and more openly than they do now. I am sure that it has been
at least fifty years since I have witnessed family prayer, and
I deplore its going out of fashion.

These old preachers held services wherever and whenever
they could assemble a gathering. Hymn books might be so
scarce and some worshipers so illiterate that the preacher
would line out a couple of lines and lead the congregation in
singing them. He would offer a lengthy prayer that covered
might' nigh everything, read a number of chapters from the
Bible, announce his text and then swing into his sermon. Let
me tell you, these sermons were no sweet, fifteen minute lit-
erary gems read from a carefully prepared manuscript. They
were pure old hell, fire and brimstone peremaids that poured
forth off the cuff in a solid stream.

The sermons were really productions, especially if delivered during a "meeting" or at night. When the preacher "got in a weavin' way" he would stomp and prance, wave his arms, pound the pulpit and slap the open book which he usually carried in his hands. These Bibles were nearly always bound in limp leather that bore up under manhandling better than boards. Even at that, he wore out many during his career. He knew his Bible, and he believed every word of it from cover to cover. Every few minutes during his sermon, he would refer to it and always slap the opened pages resoundingly for emphasis. I knew one of these men who would read a passage, close the book, slap it and say with utter finality, "And that's all they are of it."

Such sermons usually lasted an hour and a half and were delivered at top voice regardless of the size of the meeting place. Every long sentence usually ended with a drawn-out sing-song, half melodious "Ah-h-h- . . . And I tell all you sinners, you are going straighter to Hell than a crow can fly if you don't repent and mend your ways . . . Ah-h-h." Also, he would holler his head off and stomp his foot to emphasize a point. He was all in a lather and plumb wore out by the time he finished. He would then somewhat calmly and soberly invite sinners to come to the mourners' bench. If there were a choir leader who could carry on a hymn, the preacher would plead for mourners all through it. If the response were heavy and the message powerful enough, "amens" would resound, and somebody might get religion and go to shouting.

As a small urchin I had the pants scared off me one night by this shouting—the first I ever heard. My mother took me to church with her that night (there weren't any baby-sitters then). I fell asleep and was awakened by an eldritch shriek right close to me. A terrified kid took off for the far places only to be stopped by his mama who caught his jacket tail in the nick o' time. When she got me quieted down, I asked what the matter was with the poor lady who was doing all that squalling. I was mystified by the reply that she was doing the shouting because she was so happy.

In earnest of the statement as to the hell-fire ingredients

of those sermons, I well recall another scare I got when I was a good-sized urchin about a coming seven-year-old. Mother took me to church with her that night, and, of course, I fell asleep. During the preacher's lurid description of Satan, I heard enough between noddings for my subconscious to sop up a good picture of the old boy himself. It was a hot night, and the doors and windows of the church were wide open to catch the breeze which was strong enough to put out most of the kerosene wall lamps. Reaching the climax of his description, the preacher let out with a horrendous shriek and slammed the pulpit for emphasis, jerking me terrifiedly awake—and there, right in front of me in the deep gloom, stood the Devil. He was a tallish gent, some seven feet high and broad in proportion, with the most evil, malevolent leering countenance imaginable, topped off by a pair of ten-inch horns growing out of his temples. His skin was a fire engine red, and he had a cloven hoof and a long, restless tail ending in a sort of blunt spearhead. It made such a dent in my subconscious that I can still see him leering at me when I close my eyes after doing something mean or acting hypocritical.

By the same token, that same old preacher could paint an equally moving and gripping picture of Heaven and its joys beyond compare. I also have a good picture of it with its green pastures and still waters.

I dare say that all this seems mighty primitive and emotional to all you comfortable, conformative, conventional church-goers of today, and it was. But remember, those were rude, primitive times with primitive needs and raw emotions which those old-timey preachers filled in a way that their pleasant, cultured, intellectual, somewhat sissified like of today could never have met. Those old zealots fitted their times.

The old circuit rider and I appeared on the scene about the same time, when permanent settlements and towns were being established. It was my privilege to be exposed to those old saints, three of whom stand out in my memory: Parson Potter, Brother Bloys and Brother Millican. These were really ordained ministers with solid church connections who had more or less well-defined circuits which they traveled.

One of the most picturesque individuals of the time was the redoubtable Parson Andrew Jackson Potter, about whom more legends have sprouted than any other character in our section. Every one of them could very well be based on fact, as Parson was a man of many facets. He was a long, tall, gangling man with rugged features that were enhanced rather than ambushed by a luxuriant spade beard, a most impressive individual. He was reputed always to have a big forty-five stashed beneath his long-tailed coat and to know how to use it. He stayed at our house several times, and I remember him well. He baptized me, and it stood up well enough to get me into the Episcopal Church many years later, although the way my bishop and my rector sometimes look at me, he might have sort of botched the job.

Parson had plenty of intestinal fortitude, and he stood up to the tough characters of the times. One well-authenticated story about Parson told of the time he preached his first sermon in San Angelo. There were a lot of tough characters hanging around in the early days, and they delighted in harassing and even assaulting innocent and timid folks. Preachers could be a special target for their pranks. Parson had secured an empty saloon building and equipped it with pews, made of two-by-twelve planks supported by empty beer kegs, a few kerosene lamps and a big "goods box" for a pulpit. Word got around that the toughs were going to break up the meeting that night, so Parson appeared with a Winchester and leaned it up against his pulpit. He also pulled out his old forty-five "pet maker" and laid it beside the Bible on the pulpit. He grimly announced to the congregation that "according to rumor, some unregenerative sinners have bragged around town that they are going to break up this meeting. Maybe they will, but I'll guarantee one thing: they will be a bunch of mighty sick roosters before they get it done." Needless to say, he was not disturbed in any way by an attentive and decorous congregation.

After sizing up the situation, Parson decided that it was about time that St. Angela (San Angelo) had a church house. There wasn't much loose money around in those days, and a canvass of the faithful failed to provide sufficient funds to build the small, modest frame house he envisioned. Incidentally, as I write this, I can gaze down from my ninth-story window upon a great, beautiful, cathedral-like First Methodist Church building located on the spot where Parson, building better than he knew, erected the first place of Protestant worship in San Angelo. I can also see three other churches just as imposing and just as grand. Parson and his ilk did a good job, but we have sort of let them down in spite of all our vaunted scientific, technological and cultural progress.

Anyway, Parson just flat needed more money, and there was no place left to go except to the publicans and the sinners. So, along in the shank of the evening, he hied himself to the Blue Goose, a flourishing saloon with a gambling room upstairs. Parson strode into the barroom, drew his old forty-five, pounded the bar with its butt to gain attention, and roared, "Now, see here fellers, what this town needs is a church house, and each one of you sinners is a going to chip in and help build it." Then, gun in hand, he passed around his hat for contributions from each sheepish barfly. The proprietor of the joint happened to come downstairs while this was going on, and he was so intrigued that he invited Parson upstairs and ordered every gamester to chip in, enforcing the order with his own gun supporting the Parson's.

Parson had a robust sense of humor and, like all true humorists, loved to tell jokes on himself. One of his prized ones was about his first trip to San Angelo. As he crossed the North Concho River, he stopped to "howdy" with a couple of urchins who were fishing. He had a letter that he had written the night before and inquired the way to the post office. The kids did a pretty sketchy job of directing him, and he had to ask them to repeat and enlarge on their directions. He thanked the boys and invited them to come to preaching that night when he would tell them how to go to Heaven. One kid snickered to the other: "How kin he tell us how to go to Heaven when he don't even know how to get to the post office?"

Parson continued to serve the smaller, outlying communities for many years, literally "dying in the harness": he dropped dead in the middle of a sermon across the pulpit of a small church in Coleman County.

Brother Bloys, a Presbyterian, also another frequent visitor in our home, was the very antithesis of Parson Potter. He was a small, quiet, inoffensive man, and I doubt if he ever toted a gun in all his life. Consequently, he left few, if any, rip-snorting legends. But, like the Parson, he was filled with a burning zeal to serve humanity and his Lord, which he did so well and so long. He wound up in Fort Davis where he served as pastor of the Presbyterian Church for the rest of his life. He founded the Bloys Cowboy Camp Meeting which he located at Skillman Grove, one of the beauty spots of the Davis Mountains. Starting with a few ranch families, interdenominational services were held under a brush arbor. Each ranch brought its chuck wagon and several beeves which were penned nearby and slaughtered as needed. The womenfolks were housed in tents, and the men slept on their bedrolls out under the stars. Under the guidance of its saintly founder, the camp meeting has grown every year until it has become a big operation owning a section of land and operating waterworks, an electric light plant and a great tabernacle which seats more than 1500.

The ranch families have built comfortable cottages and large dining halls. The visitor is made welcome without money and without price. It is supported by the people of the area and operates on a cash basis in the black. It runs for an entire week each August, and ranch business practically ceases in the Davis Mountain area during that time. Those old cowpokes really attend the services, and they have three or four a day. I think the most unique religious service I have ever attended is the daily men's prayer meeting, held under the "Prayer Oak" which is off limits for the womenfolks. Along in the shank of the afternoon small groups of punchers will casually saunter over to the old tree and seat themselves flat on the ground, cross-legged, cowboy fashion. Each one pulls out his pocketknife and begins to whittle a stick (an ancient ceremonial when momentous matters are up for discussion, something like the ceremonial council smoke of the Indians). Outside of a few city slickers, the men are dressed in ranch clothes including their boots and big hats. It is a sort of a Quaker session with men speaking as the spirit moves them. They may have a lay leader, but preachers are conspicuous by their absence. It's purely a meeting of men who do Man Worship, simply, matter-of-factly and reverently. Maybe a cowpoke will testify or maybe one will hesitantly and awkwardly offer a short but earnest prayer. One sure feels like he is being "led through the Green Pastures." I guarantee that it gets under one's hide, no matter how thick or how scabrous it may be. And one goes away from that old tree feeling like he has had a spiritual bath.

These wonderful people, friendly, kindly, unassuming and hospitable make one feel so at home that he is attuned to the Sunday service. The tabernacle will be jam-packed to capacity with more folks sitting around in cars on the outside. An eminent preacher (any preacher in Texas would be happy to be invited to serve on the preaching staff) delivers the sermon of the day. Then the organ booms as the large, well-trained choir bursts into the "Hallelujah Chorus." And if one doesn't get a spiritual kick out of it, well, he's just flat past redemption. The "Light upon these Mountains" just seems to bring out the best that is in a man.

These folks take their religion seriously, and they practice what they preach, as evidenced by the fact that practically all law violations in the mountains are committed by flatlanders.

Practically every poke in the mountains looks forward to camp meeting week and attends, unless absolutely tied down, leaving the chores to any boomer who might be drifting through. And this reminds me of another one. Some years ago, a couple of drifting punchers, sort of on the saddle-tramp order, took jobs on a ranch just under the Rim Rock below Valentine. The family and other hands were making great preparations for their annual trip to the camp meeting. The newcomers didn't take much truck in camp meetings and volunteered to hold down the ranch. The next morning, after the folks had left for the meeting, the new hands rose early: one rustled the horses while the other cooked breakfast. Just about daybreak, the Valentine earthquake hit. The earth bucked and sun-fished, while great rocks "bigger'n ary house" rolled down the thousand-foot cliffs, roaring, crunching, colliding, exploding and kicking up a fog of dust. Fortunately, no damage was done, nor any man or horse injured, but a couple of shook up cowpokes some how lost their appetite for breakfast. Tremors continued while they gulped their coffee and smoked their cigarettes. After a bit, one of them remarked, "You know, I've been thinking that I might just enjoy the camp meeting after all." The other chimed in, "That's funny, I've been thinking the same thing myself; what you say we go?"

Brother Millican, a Baptist and the third member of my triumvirate of circuit riders, like Brother Bloys, was a small, quiet, unassuming man, but like Parson Potter, he packed a gun, and he jolly well knew how to use it, for a lot of his circuit included "Injun kentry." I have no recollection of ever meeting up with him until long after the Injuns had departed the scene. During my Sabbatical year in Fort Davis I had many visits with Brother Millican. I believe that he was about as well-beloved and respected as any man I ever knew, so it was hard to visualize him as a gun-toter. He was so modest about his exploits that one literally had to pry them out of him. One day I caught him in an expansive mood, and he broke down and told me about the brush he had had with an Apache war party nearing Skilman Grove, the present site of the Bloys Camp Meeting. He was jogging along one day on the trail betweeen Barrel Springs and Skilman, studying over the sermon he was to deliver on the morrow in Fort Davis, when, all of a sudden, his horse threw up its head and snorted. Old plainsman Millican well knew that a white man's horse could smell Injuns a long way off if the wind was right. So he was off and running, and dragging out his iron quicker'n a cat can wink its eye. The Indians were almost within bowshot, and a real hoss race ensued. Brother Millican was a busy little man, what with quirting his horse to get a little more speed out of him, and tossing an occasional shot back at the warriors to make them keep their distance. He really began to sweat when his horse commenced to tire and his supply of ammunition to run short. Then he met a bunch of cowpokes coming down the trail, and the red "sons of Belial" lit out for the Mount Livermore country a-yelpin' and a-screechin'.

I asked him if he was "skeered," and he replied: "Of course, I was. Anybody with half-sense and one eye would have been skeered half to death if he had been in my boots." He also 'lowed as how that bunch of dirty, unkempt, unshaven cowpokes was about the finest lookin' body of fellers he ever laid eyes on.

Now, maybe you know why I categorize the old circuit riders with Saint Peter and Company.

Although written largely in the vernacular for the sake of atmosphere and, in my mind, to give a clearer picture of the mores and the times, let me assure you, again and again, that it is in no way intended as tongue-in-cheek. I have the deepest love, admiration and respect for these old saints and, by the same token, for their flocks of which my mother was an ardent and prominent member.

What they had was the "old-time religion." It was good for Paul and Silas, and it's good enough for me: it's just what our confused, unhappy and upset world needs today.

"And that's all they are of it."

GLOSSARY

WHILE I in no wise consider myself a lexicographer or an etymologist, I feel impelled to append this short Glossary to *Cowpokes* for the edification and enlightenment of the younger fry whose abysmal ignorance of words and phrases of yesteryear, even spilling over into the present idiom of our Southwest, amazes and appalls me. I love these coloquillismas and slanguages as they add color and flavor, and I hope this will help preserve a few of them. Just recently, a brilliant young woman, a graduate of one of our great universities, asked what the word *awl* means. Also, a sophisticated and knowledgeable businessman was unfamiliar with the word *pee.* Evidently such folks never watched a bootmaker at work or field-weighed a sack of picked cotton on steelyards. *Ay de mi*! Here follow just a few words:

AWL—A tool used for punching holes in leather and heavy fabrics.

AY DE MI (Sp.)—Alas, shucks, well I'll be dogged.

BANTER—To challenge.

BROOM TAIL—A poor or sorry horse, usually applied to mares.

COOSIE (Sp. *Cusinero*)—A cook.

DANG—An epithet-sissified form of damn.

DOODLEBUG—A device for locating oil—similar to the switch used by a 'water witch.'

ET—Ate.

ECK—A smart aleck.

FITTEN—Fit for.

FOX TROT—A horse's gait.

GALL—Presumptuous arrogancy.

GOTCH—Deformed, mangled, missing, *i.e.* a gotch-eared horse.

HANKER—Yearn, hone.

HIGH POCKETS—A tall, long-legged feller.

INNARDS—Insides, interior organs.

JUBEROUS—Suspicious, afraid.

LICK—Syrup, molasses.

KAPOODLE—All, every bit.

MEDDLESOME MATTY—A meddlesome person.

NESTER—A farmer.

OILERS—Nesterese for oilmen.

PEN—The penitentiary.

PEE—A scale weight.

QUICKER'N SCAT—Fast, quick.

RED-UP—Clean up, usually applied to house-work.

RUNNING WALK—A horse's gait.

SLAP DAB—Right there, in the middle.

SUT—Soot.

TOOL PUSHER—Superintendent on oil rigs.

TOTE—To carry, have on one's person.

USE—To range, to occupy, *i.e.* "A big uses over thar."

VITTLES—Food.

WART—To bother or worry.

WASP-NEST—WEDGEASS—Poor or soggy bread—usually applied to baker's bread, which Cowpokes purely disliked.

I don't remember any Z's.